THE SOCIOLOGY OF NEWS

Second Edition

RECENT SOCIOLOGY TITLES FROM W. W. NORTON

Code of the Streets by Elijah Anderson

The Cosmopolitan Canopy by Elijah Anderson

Social Problems by Joel Best

The Real World: An Introduction to Sociology, 3rd Edition by
Kerry Ferris and Jill Stein

Introduction to Sociology, 8th Edition by Anthony Giddens, Mitchell Duneier,
Richard P. Appelbaum, and Deborah Carr

Essentials of Sociology, 3rd Edition by Anthony Giddens, Mitchell Duneier,
Richard P. Appelbaum, and Deborah Carr

The Contexts Reader, 2nd Edition edited by Doug Hartmann and Chris Uggen

Mix it Up: Popular Culture, Mass Media, and Society by David Grazian

When Sex Goes to School by Kristin Luker

Inequality and Society by Jeff Manza and Michael Sauder

Readings for Sociology, 7th Edition edited by Garth Massey

Families as They Really Are, edited by Barbara J. Risman

Sociology of Globalization by Saskia Sassen

The Social Construction of Sexuality, 2nd Edition by Steven Seidman

The Corrosion of Character by Richard Sennett

Biography and the Sociological Imagination by Michael J. Shanahan and
Ross Macmillan

A Primer on Social Movements by David Snow and Sarah Soule

Six Degrees by Duncan J. Watts

More than Just Race by William Julius Wilson

American Society: How it Really Works by Erik Olin Wright and Joel Rogers

**For more information on our publications in sociology, please visit
wwnorton.com/soc**

THE SOCIOLOGY OF NEWS

Second Edition

MICHAEL SCHUDSON
COLUMBIA UNIVERSITY

W. W. Norton & Company
New York • London

W. W. Norton & Company has been independent since its founding in 1923, when William Warder Norton and Mary D. Herter Norton first published lectures delivered at the People's Institute, the adult education division of New York City's Cooper Union. The firm soon expanded its program beyond the Institute, publishing books by celebrated academics from America and abroad. By midcentury, the two major pillars of Norton's publishing program—trade books and college texts—were firmly established. In the 1950s, the Norton family transferred control of the company to its employees, and today—with a staff of four hundred and a comparable number of trade, college, and professional titles published each year—W. W. Norton & Company stands as the largest and oldest publishing house owned wholly by its employees.

Project Editor: Diane Cipollone
Production Manager: Ben Reynolds
Series design by BTD / Beth Tondreau Design, Inc.
Manufacturing by Courier—Westford, MA
Composition by TexTech / Jouve—Brattleboro, VT

Library of Congress Cataloging-in-Publication Data
Schudson, Michael.
    The sociology of news / Michael Schudson. — 2nd ed.
        p. cm. — (Contemporary societies)
    Includes bibliographical references and index.
    ISBN 978-0-393-91287-6 (pbk.)
    1. Journalism—Social aspects.   I. Title.
    PN4749.S38 2012
    302.23—dc22

                                            2011012044

W. W. Norton & Company, Inc., 500 Fifth Avenue, New York, N.Y. 10110
wwnorton.com
W. W. Norton & Company Ltd., Castle House, 75/76 Wells Street, London
W1T 3QT

1 2 3 4 5 6 7 8 9 0

Contents

Preface to the 2011 Edition

In 2002, WHEN I finished writing the first edition of this book, it was a different world for journalism. The *New York Times* had just begun to update its online edition round-the-clock in 2000. Wikipedia launched in 2000 and most college professors (including me) instructed students that they would not be permitted to cite Wikipedia as an authoritative source in their research papers. Today I find Wikipedia indispensable for my own work, as do my students for theirs. Only in 2000 did Craigslist become a site for placing ads beyond San Francisco and thereby begin to be a serious threat to newspaper advertising revenue. Bloggers were establishing a public presence but their first political splash came only in 2002 when several bloggers' efforts ultimately forced Mississippi Republican Senator Trent Lott to resign as the majority leader in the U.S. Senate.

Even Google was new. Google incorporated at the end of 1998; it was just beginning to be everybody's best research assistant. Jon Stewart's *The Daily Show* had begun in 1999 and built an audience during the 2000 election campaign, but it would grow much more in the years to come and would spin off a second "fake-news" show in *The Colbert Report* in 2005. Smart phones were just coming onto the market (the BlackBerry first appeared in 2002). Social networking was in its infancy (Friendster was the first in 2002, MySpace would come the next year, and Facebook a year after that). YouTube did not yet exist.

Online-only news organizations did not yet exist. One of the first was VoiceofSanDiego (2005); there are scores more today. One of the largest and best funded, ProPublica, began in 2008 and won its first Pulitzer Prize for reporting in 2010.

Not even on the horizon in 2002 was the sharp contraction of the news business since 2007 in the United States and to a lesser degree elsewhere—for reasons the final chapter of this new edition will explore.

For a book that tries to review and synthesize not only what is happening to journalism but what is happening to scholarly understanding of journalism, changes in the study of journalism in the past decade have also been significant. "Journalism Studies" is more organized—a journalism studies "interest group" of the International Communication Association began in 2004 (with 50 members) and by 2008 had over 500 members. New journals dedicated to the scholarly study of journalism have appeared, including *Journalism Studies* (affiliated with the European Journalism Training Association and the ICA's Journalism Studies Interest Group) in 2000; *Journalism: Theory, Practice and Criticism* also started in 2000; and *Journalism Practice* in 2007.

These journals publish in English and, although they have international editorial boards and make efforts to cover journalism around the world, they have a predominantly Anglo-American orientation. Even so, the study of journalism has become conceptually more global than ever before. The most important single study in the globalization of the study of journalism is Daniel Hallin and Paolo Mancini's *Comparing Media Systems* (2004), a work that compares and categorizes the news media systems of eighteen European and North American democracies. This book has been internationally influential

Acknowledgments

THIS SECOND EDITION is a tale of two cities. I remain grateful to students and colleagues at my former academic home, the University of California, San Diego, who made the original edition possible. Rosie Hoa and Carrie Sloan contributed as research assistants. Barbara Osborn provided a wonderfully careful and critical reading of the whole manuscript. A book like this, intended to help with teaching, stems from teaching. I am grateful to the many college students whose interest in news pressed me to refine my thinking about it. I am indebted to Ph.D. students whose own work on the news media taught me so much, especially Elliot King, Barbara Osborn, America Rodriguez, David Ryfe, and Silvio Waisbord. Colleagues who have influenced my thinking about the news media are visible throughout the book by way of the footnotes, but I wish to single out for special thanks the late Jim Carey, Herb Gans, Todd Gitlin, Dan Hallin, Rob Manoff, and Barbie Zelizer.

For this revised edition, let me add thanks to my colleagues and students at the Graduate School of Journalism at Columbia University. Changes here reflect not only the transformation of journalism in the past decade and the growth of journalism studies but also my new vantage as a scholar of news working in a professional school. I owe a particular debt to Dean Nicholas Lemann and to students and colleagues in Columbia's interdisciplinary Ph.D. program in Communication for enhancing my understanding of journalism and journalisms, both in the United States and elsewhere around the world.

At W. W. Norton, the production of this book has been carefully attended to by editor Karl Bakeman, editorial assistant Rebecca Charney, and the expert copy editing of Jude Grant.

Introduction
MAKING NEWS

IN NEW YORK CITY in the 1890s, a young, ambitious Californian named Lincoln Steffens was making a career for himself in journalism. By that time, journalism had become a world of its own—that is, an occupational setting distinctive enough to be a way of life, thick with people, habits, traditions, revelry, and rivalry. At least in big cities, journalism was large enough and rich enough that its denizens could easily believe that the boundaries of journalism marked the borders of life.

Steffens was a part of this world, as he recalled some decades later in his best-selling autobiography. For journalists, the most famous chapter of that charming memoir is titled "I Make a Crime Wave." In it, Steffens described how by simply hanging out with police officers lounging around headquarters, he learned of crimes that other reporters did not know about. As policemen one day began talking about a particularly intriguing crime that involved a prominent citizen, a story that they did not want reported, Steffens feigned sleep. Later, he wrote it up for the paper. The city editor of a rival paper then berated his police reporter, Jacob Riis, for failing to pick up the same juicy tidbit. Riis, who was not only a rival of Steffens's but also a friend, did a little snooping around to discover some crimes Steffens had not gotten wind of. It was then Steffens's turn to be called on the carpet by *his* editor. Then the race was on: which would never get the publicity he had hoped for. Why? Because a mentally unstable pilot had just crashed his Cessna aircraft into the backyard of the White House precisely where the ceremony was to be staged. The news media predictably swooned over this bizarre and unprecedented event and could scarcely be bothered about the launching of AmeriCorps—an occasion no doubt more important than the plane crash but infinitely more routine.[6]

Social scientists typically insist that most news is produced by people like Eli Segal, not deranged pilots. Quantitatively, they are right: the vast majority of daily news on television or in newspapers comes from planned events, press releases, press conferences, and scheduled interviews.[7] Even so, journalists find their joy and their identity in the adrenaline rush that comes from unhinged pilots; hurricanes; upset victories in baseball or politics; triumphs against all odds; nobility in the face of suffering; tragedy or scandal in the lap of luxury; and other unplanned and unanticipated scandals, accidents, mishaps, gaffes, embarrassments, horrors, and wonders. The sociologists delight in revealing how much of news is produced by the best-laid plans of government officials and other parajournalists who maneuver to shape news to their own purposes; the journalists enjoy pointing out that the best-laid plans often go astray.

Both the scholars and the journalists are right. The news media cover both events that strike everyone as original, like a plane crashing onto the White House lawn, and happenings that are routine and anticipated yet can be framed in a way to qualify as news. News is what is publicly notable (within a framework of shared understanding that judges it to be both public and notable). It is also a machinery of notation, a social institution working within technological, economic, political, and even literary constraints for recording and interpreting various features of contemporary life.

None of this would be of great interest if the news did not build a world that people took seriously or if the news did not affect how people act. The conviction that news influences human action undergirds nearly all studies of news. Just how or to what extent news affects us, however, is a matter of controversy and uncertainty. This book will begin with the question of the effects of news and work backward to a view of the news as manufactured. It will also discuss the social and historical conditions that have made news making a manufacturing process with certain predictable and describable features. Some dimensions of news making are vital to democratic government and to a sense of community in the modern world; other features of news making, however, are deeply troubling and may even work at cross-purposes with democracy or community. It is not my task in this book to defend or attack the news business as we know it today. Instead, I propose a framework in which both the criticisms and defenses are informed by historical and comparative understandings of news that are alert to current research and attuned to arguments from different sides of the key questions.

I focus on U.S. journalism. Even so, more than a few remarks will be made about news making in the United Kingdom, France, Germany, Sweden, Norway, Japan, China, Mexico, and elsewhere. Comparative research on the news media has begun to develop seriously only in the past decade or so and may be the most important new domain of academic research on the news. I draw on it while still keeping American news media at the center.

Very often I do not distinguish between television and print news (newspapers and newsmagazines). In some contexts, TV and print journalism operate quite differently, but in many contexts both print and television journalists understand their jobs and understand news in very much the same terms. In fact, most TV news, including almost all local TV news, begins with what TV journalists read in their morning newspapers. "Welcome to Plagiarism News!" a TV reporter cheerily greeted one researcher.[8] In this sense, citizens who say they get most of their news from television are nonetheless getting most of their news indirectly from newspapers. Online news journalists are developing criteria for news judgment, styles of news presentation, and work rhythms of their own, but most fundamentals of reporting and writing online, as on television, derive from the traditional newspapers that in 2011 remain, along with the wire services that date to the nineteenth century, the primary engines of news on which the entire news system feeds. The continuity between conventional newspapers and online journalism can be seen inside the newsrooms of major newspapers. Although the websites of newspapers were once separate operations—the *Washington Post*'s website operated out of a building on the other side of the Potomac River from the paper's central Washington location—now the *Post*, like the *New York Times*, the *Wall Street Journal*, the *Guardian* (London), and others, has a so-called universal news desk where journalists writing for the print and the online editions work alongside one another.

No one needs to have worked in a newsroom or taken a course in journalism or sociology to understand this book. This is meant to be an introduction to the study of news. But for students who are already well versed in aspects of journalism and even for scholars who have themselves contributed to the literature about news, there are ideas presented here that have not appeared elsewhere, and I have simplified and organized a complex field in ways that a wide audience of readers may find useful.

When on September 13, 1994, the *New York Times'* lead story, and two related stories, covered the plane crash at the White House in which the pilot, a Maryland trucker with a history of substance abuse, died, other news vanished or was relegated to inside pages. On page 17, there was a story on the AmeriCorps swearing in, but even there it seemed to be folded into the big story of the day. The third paragraph read, "Some 850 were inducted as more than 2,000 dignitaries and supporters took part in the ceremony on the North Lawn of the White House. They were kept sweltering there for more than two hours, and an elaborately synchronized satellite television transmission was thrown awry, because of the crash of a light plane early this morning on the South Lawn where the event was supposed to have taken place."

How are we to understand why the plane crash, without a single living source or a single dollar spent on public relations, claimed attention while the launching of a major new federal program backed by the weight of government publicity was subordinated to it? How are we to understand why, on ordinary days without disasters, the news-making machinery feeds stories to the media with reasonable efficiency and success? This book attempts to answer questions of this kind by taking a sociological approach to journalism, one that encompasses the blend of chance and intention, normality and catastrophe, instrument and accident, expectation and surprise, narrative and interjection—all of which make up the news.

PART I

JOURNALISM NOW

through shared symbols and meanings. To say that journalism is a mode of communication, however, says nothing about how journalistic communication differs from poetry, encyclopedias, how-to manuals, pornography, the *Boy Scout Handbook*, and the *Star Wars* or *Harry Potter* films. Nor does it tell us about the social and historical conditions that gave rise to the longstanding social organizations of journalism. Journalism shares with many institutions, including school systems, legislative bodies, hospitals, and scientific organizations, a key attribute of modernity: that it has existed for only two hundred to three hundred years. Schools socialize the young, legislatures govern, hospitals care for the sick. For those studying these institutions the key question is *how* schools socialize, how legislatures govern, how hospitals treat the sick, how the operation of these institutions varies over time and from place to place and how their valuable social functions could be better executed. The same is true for the study of journalism: how does journalism communicate about contemporary public matters of interest and importance, and how could it do this better?

News is the product of journalistic activity. We can speculate, without much in the way of proof, that news builds expectations of a common, shared world; promotes an emphasis on and a positive valuation of the new; endorses a historical mentality (note how much less "dated" is a myth, novel, academic paper, or sermon than a news report); and encourages a progressive rather than cyclical or recursive sense of time. The novel, as literary scholar Ian Watt pointed out,[1] has a very similar resonance, and it is significant that it emerged as a prominent element in the cultural landscape of Europe and colonial North America at the same time that the newspaper did—in the eighteenth century.

Media scholar John Hartley referred to news as "the sense-making practice of modernity" and, as such, "the most important textual system in the world."[2] This is too ambitious a characterization of news. Could one not claim that science is the sense-making practice of modernity and the most important textual system in the world? Or constitutionalism and law? Or price and the marketplace? Still, despite the general neglect of news by most prestigious academic disciplines, it has become—where it was not three or even two centuries ago—a dominant force in the public construction of common experience and a popular sense of what is real and important.

Think of how odd this is. Why should news, a textual form that, as we shall see, operates within a set of narrow and peculiar constraints, be of such general import? The orientation of news is sometimes gloriously off-kilter. Consider the 1974 newspaper obituary of Fred Snodgrass. This wire service story (dateline Ventura, California) began: "Fred Carlisle Snodgrass, who muffed an easy fly ball and cost the New York Giants the 1912 World Series, died Friday at age 86." The next sentence tells the reader that Snodgrass played nine years in the major leagues and later became a banker and rancher in California as well as the mayor of the city he lived in. Then a full paragraph details the easy pop fly he dropped.[3] Is this a reasonable portrait of a life? What kind of discourse finds his dropped pop fly of enduring interest and the rest of Snodgrass's life scarcely worth mentioning?

Note Hartley's emphasis that news is to be understood as a "textual system." This is one approach to defining news—to emphasize its textuality, to take it as a rhetorical form or set of rhetorical forms, a discursive structure, or a cultural genre within a larger literary and representational culture. Alternatively, one can stress that news is a manufactured good, the product of a set of social, economic, and political institutions and practices. The typical sociological impulse is to trust in what is empirically observable and to recognize in every cultural product its immediate origin in human action and human purposes. Since news—until recently—was invariably produced by a set of identifiable organizations that we call the press or the news media, and since their personnel are responsible for the decisions that give us the news every day, sociological analysis of news takes this empirical approach. This is strategically sensible. It zeros in on those individuals and organizations that are held accountable (and hold themselves accountable) for the production of news. But this is not the whole story. To hold news organizations accountable for news is something like holding parents accountable for the actions of their children—it is convenient to locate responsibility somewhere, and it reminds news organizations (or parents) that they have a serious job to do for which they will be judged. Still, they sometimes have to work with unyielding materials.

There is a creeping desire to define journalism normatively, as a field with a public mission. "The core purpose of journalism is and should be about producing and distributing serious information and debate on central social, political, and cultural matters," asserted Norwegian media scholar Jostein Gripsrud. "Journalists regulate much of what the public gets to know about the world they inhabit, and this activity is vital to a functioning democracy."[4] I am reluctant to smuggle "democracy" into the very definition of journalism. But this is a matter of honest contention among journalism scholars, if not among sociologists, and I take it up in a later discussion of democracy (see chapter 11).

It is only fair to acknowledge some smuggling of my own. I have defined journalism as "information and commentary on contemporary affairs taken to be publicly important." However, in any day's newspaper or news website or radio or television news broadcast, there is a great deal of material that is interesting but not important. Restaurant reviewers assess the consistency of the béchamel; humor columnists poke fun at their mothers-in-law; sports columnists predict the outcome of next week's game; and reporters delve into every available detail of a celebrity's divorce, debauch, or lawsuit. And then, of course, there are the newspapers' comics, advice columns, crossword puzzles, bridge instruction, and horoscopes. It would be hard to dignify any of this as "publicly important"—except that, by attracting readers, these popular features help subsidize the costly, and less popular, investigations of government malfeasance and the essential but mundane coverage of school board meetings and federal agency policy changes. The focus of this book is news that touches directly on political affairs, for this is the part of journalism that makes the strongest claim to public importance. But which news is that? What counts as publicly important has changed, sometimes very dramatically, in our own time; and what is shifting now, more rapidly than analysts can keep up with, is what is public or what publics are. Suddenly, in the Internet era, the study of journalism has become the study of society itself and of human consciousness, attention, memory, and imagination.

Chapter Two
DOES NEWS MATTER? (MEDIA EFFECTS, PART 1)

PEOPLE HAVE LONG COMPLAINED about the power of the press. George Washington viewed the unfettered press as outrageous, strident, and irresponsible. The American novelist James Fenimore Cooper observed in the 1830s that "the press tyrannizes over publick men, letters, the arts, the stage, and even over private life." "The government of such a democracy as ours is practically a government by newspapers," wrote the publisher Edward Scripps early in the twentieth century.[1] Media power today is likewise widely attacked. Left-wing observers say the mass media support corporate power, the military-industrial complex, and the interests of the wealthiest slice of the population. Right-wing critics insist that the media make our culture unduly liberal, promoting a pro-choice agenda, costly environmental regulations, and acceptance of same-sex marriage across the country. Leaders from various sectors of society who disagree on almost everything else agree that journalists are the most powerful, dangerous, and irresponsible group in the country. Observers note that control of broadcasting studios has been crucial to political revolutions in the late twentieth and early twenty-first centuries; this was a strategic objective of insurgents in the Philippines in 1986 and in Eastern Europe a few years later. Ayatollah Ruhollah Khomeini's 1979 revolution in Iran was promoted by the circulation of his speeches on audiocassettes; Chinese students used fax machines to bring their Tiananmen Square rebellion before the eyes of the world in 1989; dissidents in Iran kept alive their protests over election irregularities in 2009 using Twitter accounts; and the popular overthrow of dictators in Tunisia and Egypt in 2011 was aided by a wide variety of new media. The news media, established or insurgent, seem enormously potent.

Political insiders are especially impressed with media power. A *New York Times* reporter suggested that people drinking up the dominant culture of Washington, D.C., "believe in polls. They believe in television. . . . They believe that nothing a politician does in public can be taken at face value, but that everything he does is a metaphor for something he is hiding. . . . Above all, they believe in the power of what they have created, in the subjectivity of reality and the reality of perceptions, in image."[2] This outlook points to an unsettling view that the world we once knew has been turned upside down and inside out by the presence of the media. "It is a striking yet banal fact," wrote British critic Geoff Mulgan, "that we now live in a world in which fantasy and reality are impossible to distinguish."[3] This point has been made over and over again in the past several decades, generally in the form of apocalyptic warnings or in tracts of deep cultural despair.[4] The same point was classically stated, without accompanying hysteria, by journalist Walter Lippmann in his 1922 book *Public Opinion*. Like the crime wave "created" by Lincoln Steffens, noted in the introduction, the media seem to have the terrifying power to create the world we live in.

Examples are not hard to come by. A particularly illustrative one was identified by communication scholar Joshua Meyrowitz during the 1992 Democratic Party primary elections. Larry Agran, the mayor of Irvine, California, threw his hat in the ring and campaigned for the presidency during the New Hampshire primary. The news media immediately discounted him: what chance was there for Agran's bid when he had previously held only local office? The chairperson of New Hampshire's Democratic Party barred Agran from participating in a televised forum on health care. Despite the effort by New Hampshire's Democratic officials and the national news reporters to peg Agran as a fringe candidate from the outset, Agran tied California governor Jerry Brown and Iowa senator Tom Harkin in a major poll at the end of January. A later poll showed Agran ahead of Brown. But the news media systematically ignored these facts. In reporting the poll, ABC News simply skipped over Agran and moved from mention of Harkin (in third-to-last place) to Brown (last place). *Washington Post* columnist Colman McCarthy observed, "A major abuse in the media is not that we slant the news but that we can arbitrarily choose the news. The Agran blackout exemplifies that this is a journalistic crime easily gotten away with. Who is going to report it? Not the criminals, for sure."[5]

There is no question, then, that members of the media have some autonomy and authority to depict the world according to their own ideas. They do not simply transcribe a set of transparent events. This was made clear in a *New York Times* story on U.S.-Japanese trade talks, which began, "What is striking about the summit meeting this week between President Clinton and Prime Minister Ryutaro Hashimoto is what is not being heard or seen."[6] The story then focused on what was not happening—that there were no demonstrations or protests, no evidence of mutual recriminations as had been common in years past. The power of the media to analyze and construct reality is certainly clear when stories directly assert that the most important thing to examine is that which is not in any way visible.[7]

AN ILLUSION OF POWER

But for all the media's capacity to shape news according to their own biases, leading news organizations today try to describe, from empirical observation, a world that exists. This was forcefully and disparagingly acknowledged by a top White House official (presumed to be Karl Rove) who told a *New York Times* reporter in 2004 that journalists are part of "what we call the reality-based community," people who "believe that solutions emerge from (your) judicious study of discernible reality." But the official continued, "That's not the way the world really works anymore. We're an empire now, and when we act, we create our own reality."[8] As chilling an assertion of political power as this is, it confirms that journalists seek to portray the world as it is. What it—this pronouncement of a Goliath sneering at David—fails to acknowledge is that a slingshot can fell a giant, and what we call reality, for lack of a better term, can sometimes exact revenge on the supposed power of images.

One reason that people tend to overestimate the power of the media is that the media are the visible tip of the iceberg of social influences on human behavior. We see them, we hear them, they are readily available—in fact, nearly unavoidable. They are the squeaky wheels of social life: loud, garish, and insistent. Many important nonmedia factors are simply harder to see, from demographic shifts to business cycles, from changes in the tax code that prompt behavioral changes when they take effect years later to droughts or floods that make agricultural produce scarce and expensive months after the fact. Journalists around the world know that in 1972 and 1973 *Washington Post* reporters Bob Woodward and Carl Bernstein bravely persevered in reporting on the Watergate scandal and, as young slingshot wielders themselves, helped force President Richard Nixon to resign. What is more rarely recalled is that their efforts were made possible by government officials who leaked information to them, by federal judge John Sirica's iron will and high-handed courtroom tactics that pressured the Watergate burglars to spill the beans, by the Senate Watergate committee that unearthed the White House tape-recording system, and by the pressure of subpoena power that the attorney general–appointed special prosecutors kept aimed at the White House. Most of these other significant forces did not get even cameo roles in the book or movie versions of the Watergate story.[9]

Would President Nixon have been forced from office without the *Washington Post*'s reporting? No. But nor would the newspaper have had a trail to follow if not for Frank Will, the Watergate's night watchman; the District of Columbia police officers who responded to his call; and later, the guidance provided to Bob Woodward by Mark Felt, a high-level FBI official who leaked information to him—not to mention a partisan Democratic Party majority in the U.S. Senate eagerly keeping the investigation alive and the presidential hubris that led Nixon to secretly tape-record conversations in his office.

Many instances of presumed media effects fade or disappear on close examination. In the late 1960s and early 1970s, no one seemed to doubt that television coverage of the horrors of the Vietnam War turned the American people against the war, strengthened the antiwar movement, impressed on Washington that this was an unpopular war, and so forced the United States out of Vietnam. This role of the news media was proclaimed everywhere—but there was no evidence to support it. Television news coverage was overwhelmingly favorable toward the U.S. war effort up until 1968. Far from demonstrating the horrors of war, television sanitized the conflict, and the networks were particularly loath to show American soldiers killed or wounded.[10]

Yet well before 1968, there was substantial public dissatisfaction with the war effort. A 1967 poll found that 50 percent of Americans believed involvement in Vietnam was a mistake. When television and other news outlets grew more critical of the war, polls actually found a temporary increase in support of the war as people rallied around the flag, which they tend to do during times of national trouble. When on February 27, 1968, CBS News anchor Walter Cronkite declared on air that the war was a stalemate, he was only coming around to a view many ordinary Americans had already embraced. It is hard to disagree with historian George Moss who wrote that public opinion influenced television coverage of the war more than television influenced public opinion. Moss concluded that the role of the media in determining the outcome of the war was "peripheral, minor, trivial, in fact, so inconsequential it is unmeasurable."[11]

A second reason people tend to exaggerate media power is that they do not distinguish the media's power from the power of the people and the events the media cover. That is, it is often not clear whether the media exercise much choice, freedom, or autonomy in producing news or simply relay to the general public what truly powerful forces tell them. At least since

Franklin D. Roosevelt, and in some respects since Theodore Roosevelt, presidents have given a great deal of time and thought to how their actions will play in the newspapers. In the decades since the Vietnam War, presidents have kept media consultants and pollsters at their elbows to shape and "spin" presidential actions and reports of actions and to anticipate press response. These consultants, who plan for the reactions of the journalists around them, are our premier parajournalists.

Suppose you announce a garage sale by placing an ad in the newspaper or on Craigslist. Dozens of people turn up outside your door an hour before the announced opening of the sale. Surely this is a powerful "media effect" (leaving aside the important fact that 999 out of 1,000 of the people who picked up the newspaper that carried your ad or consulted Craigslist that day did not come to your sale). But in this case the newspaper served merely as a conduit for your message. You were the parajournalist. The news site did not craft the message at all. If the mayor makes a speech urging citizens to honor veterans by wearing red, white, and blue ribbons for a day, and television and newspapers report the speech, and thousands of people adorn themselves with ribbons, is this a media effect or a mayoral effect?

An entire domain of media research on "agenda setting" founders on precisely this point: this research demonstrates that people at large will name as important subjects on the national agenda those items they find frequently in the news. But how did those items get in the news in the first place? In 1992, TV coverage of children starving in Somalia was widely credited as the key factor in moving the United States to intervene with humanitarian aid. Closer analysis subsequently found that there was negligible TV coverage of starvation in Somalia until several leading senators, both Republican and Democrat, publicly supported active U.S. intervention. News coverage mirrored elite Washington opinion in the 1990s and beyond, just as it had during the Vietnam War.[12]

It is possible to be a member in good standing of the media research world and claim that the media are all-powerful and that everything else in social life flows from them—this is the hypothesis that made Marshall McLuhan both a household name and a joke. One might just as easily claim that the media do not matter at all, that they are at most the registry of other social forces, and that to blame them for social ills is to "blame the messenger." Consider the effort to impeach President Bill Clinton over his affair with intern Monica Lewinsky. On the one hand, as political scientist John Zaller observed, public opinion was entirely unaffected by the scandalous news from the White House. Public approval of Clinton's job performance did not decline at all; in fact, it increased a bit. On the other hand, critics objected to the media's headlong pursuit of a story that could only reduce political discourse to the level of whispered gossip. I will return later to the question of why, and to what effect, news increasingly presents details of the private lives of public figures. The Monica Lewinsky reportage is just one more vivid reminder that at the heart of media studies there remains the embarrassing question of whether the media are worth studying at all. If the Monica Lewinsky coverage did not reduce the public's faith in Bill Clinton at all, what, if anything, did it do?

This kind of question is certainly not confined to the United States. In Argentina, President Juan Perón is reported to have said that "with all the media in our hands we were thrown out in 1955, and with all the media against us we came back in 1973."[13]

One reason it is difficult to establish media effects is that we operate with oversimplified models of how the media affect society. We ask simplistic questions. We fail to separate out the different questions that address media effects. Many people view the model of media influence as a model of propaganda in which a dictator or a Machiavellian publisher or an elite of self-serving journalists campaign for an idea or program, insinuate it between the lines, and repeat it ad nauseam until at last it sinks in, and then the public follows along despite its own best instincts. According to this model, the media are a weapon of psychological warfare. They may not always be the best weapon, any more than a tank is always the best weapon for the military, but under the right circumstances (whatever they are) media propaganda will do the job.

In this "hypodermic" model, the media inject ideas into a passive and defenseless public. The problem with the model is not that it posits media power but that it takes the mechanism of power to be indoctrination. Models of indoctrination in main-stream communication research have grown more subtle through the years but have not fundamentally changed. Notions of media influence that have been popular among scholars through the years, such as "agenda setting," "hegemony," and "priming," all refine but do not discard the concept of indoctrination.

But the media do not indoctrinate nearly as much as media culture, social science, popular reflexes, or the media suggest.[14] How is it that half the American public believes in devils when there's not a trace of the devil to be found in the relentlessly secular mainstream media?[15] In fact, books about religion are selling like hotcakes—but people still regularly seek out these works online or in religious bookstores or other nonmainstream outlets. This is a good indication that the mainstream media are no more influential than churches on the fabric of society. It also suggests that other institutions such as the family, schools, the criminal justice system, or—to choose two institutions that are not cultural objects in popular or media culture at all—state governments and federal regulatory agencies may retain great influence over society.

The news media's primary, day-to-day contribution to the wider society is that of cultural actors, that is, as producers and messengers of meanings, symbols, and messages. They offer neither paychecks nor cudgels to their audience, neither praise nor criticism, neither license nor confinement. Most of all, they do not offer direct address to an individual the way a teacher, parent, friend, lover, child, colleague, or even supermarket clerk does. If you are feeling faint, or think you are having a heart attack, would your television notice? No, but the checkout clerk might. The media offer only words and images, not love or hate, nothing but symbols, not aid, not notice, not attention, not sentience. They are a part of culture, and culture, as anthropologist Clifford Geertz observed, is not itself "a power, something to which social events, behaviors, institutions, or processes can be causally attributed" but rather "a context, something within which they can be intelligibly . . . described."[16]

That is exactly what must be understood. A school is a social institution in which authorities come face-to-face with ordinary people. A television news show or a newspaper is a cultural institution that purveys information, ideas, and attitudes without ever being in a position to reward people for taking up those ideas or to punish them for failing to take them up. A television set can never punish a child, but a teacher can, a parent can, a police officer can, a peer group can. Media power is power of a special sort, and this is what makes figuring out the effects of news so difficult.[17]

Culture is the language in which action is constituted rather than the cause that generates action. How does culture influence action? Media scholars are all over the map on this. There is talk of how "discursive structures" constitute self and society, of how the "hegemony" of the dominant ideology expressed through advertisements, news stories, or popular song lyrics ideologically reproduces subtle racist or sexist or liberal or conservative biases. But there is no agreement. In fact, a whole wave of scholarship in the 1980s and 1990s pointed to the extraordinary capacity of individuals to reinterpret, resist, or subvert media messages, no matter how ideologically nasty or subtly encoded they may be. Studies abounded on how children subvert their own favorite cartoon characters or pop culture idols by singing parodies, how women find grounds for independence in the very process of gobbling up romance novels that portray females as subordinate, or how prejudiced people read racially loaded sit-com humor one way and tolerant people take the same jokes to have the opposite meaning.[18]

It is difficult to let go of the old-fashioned language of causation and the model of indoctrination. Does television lead to a more violent or a more fearful society? Did yellow journalism push the United States into the Spanish-American War? Did bloody scenes of battle on television turn Americans against the Vietnam War? Did the media build public support for the first Gulf War by submitting to the military's effort to sanitize bombing raids in Iraq? Or for the second by deferring to White House assertions that Saddam Hussein threatened his neighbors and even the United States with weapons of mass destruction? These questions are recurrent and unavoidable. They even become questions of public policy. Should advertisements on children's television programs be banned? Should pornography be outlawed? Do sex education classes initiate young people in sexual practices or help young people who will engage in sex anyway do it more safely? Do warning labels on cigarette packages make a difference?

These questions are necessary if we are to determine whether our public policies—say, requiring health warnings on cigarette packages—matter. Still, they presume an indoctrinational model of media influence. If they were to move toward a cultural model of media influence, they would have to consider two broad ways in which the news influences its audiences: First, it helps to construct a community of sentiment. Second, it helps to construct a public conversation. In neither respect do the mass media implant a belief or behavior in individuals; instead, they establish a web of meanings, and therefore a web of presuppositions or background assumptions within which people develop beliefs and viewpoints and in relation to which people live their lives. Can we say more than this? Yes, but it takes some effort to disabuse ourselves of the indoctrination model.

News is not so much a "cause" as it is a common locus for three distinct facets of a cultural message, each of which may have some causal force. The first is information itself, which when distributed to a large audience, may be a causal factor in human affairs. The second component of a cultural message is simply that its dissemination in general public media afford it an aura of legitimacy. The third facet is the slant, frame, or bias with which the information is presented.

Almost all discussion of the power of the press centers on this third point, which, under ordinary circumstances, may be the least important of the three. But because thinking about the media, both among scholars and among journalists themselves, centers so heavily on the question of bias, I consider only the first two facets of news influence in the remainder of this chapter. In the following chapter, I take up bias in or framing of the news.

INFORMATION AS CAUSE

First, then, what is the causal force of raw information itself? Distributing information has visible and measurable consequences. Copycat crimes would not be committed without the media having reported on the original criminal act. Alleged criminals are apprehended because citizens recognize them from the television show *America's Most Wanted*.[19] Cancer screenings rise by the millions after news that a president has had an operation to remove a cancerous growth.[20] Businesses advertise their liquidation sales in the local paper, and customers descend on them. People read the business page and call their brokers to buy or sell. News of hurricanes in Florida causes tourists to change their travel plans. Transmitting information has real consequences. The value added by the way the media inflect information is often just a fractional increase of the sheer force of mass distribution of information. No one remembers just how the news stories of the Cessna crashing onto the White House lawn were played. What endures is the fact that the plane crashed.

Sociologist Herbert Gans has argued that news media "remain primarily messengers. . . . If they report news about rising unemployment, for example, the effects they produce stem from the unemployment, not from their reporting it."[21] They are messengers of their major sources more than they are autonomous setters of the political agenda.

Experimental research by Donald Kinder and Shanto Iyengar in the late 1980s showed how people in laboratory settings respond to information. As the number of stories about unemployment on television increases, viewers judge unemployment to be an increasingly pressing national problem. Kinder and Iyengar found statistically significant and relatively persistent traces of television's influence on attitudes, based on small increases in the number of stories on a given subject.[22]

This finding is neither surprising nor distressing. It is perfectly reasonable for people to take cues like this from TV news. News reporting about the partial meltdown of the Three Mile Island nuclear power plant galvanized the American antinuclear movement in 1979. But was this a media effect or a Three Mile Island effect? Iyengar and Kinder's work documented that people learn from television and appropriately take intensity of coverage to reflect what national elites judge to be intensity of importance.

News as Amplifier

In a much more complicated and much less understood way, the media do add something to every story they run. When the media offer the public an item of news, they confer on it public legitimacy. They bring it into a common public forum where it can be known to and discussed by a general audience. They not only distribute the report of an event or announcement to a large group, but they amplify it as well. This stimulates social interaction about "newsworthy" topics. In the early nineteenth century, amplification through the media brought rural Americans in contact with their local communities and a wider world as little else in their lives could.

Public amplification grows with each new medium and with each change in a medium that enables it to reach a larger audience. Tom Paine's pamphleteering reached beyond the traditional audience for political pamphlets in the 1770s because he eschewed the Greek and Latin references of standard political writing of the day and wrote in plain language. The mass-oriented popular press in the nineteenth century created more of a common language and view of the world than did the small-circulation elite press it challenged. The pictorial newspapers of the 1920s gained an audience beyond that of traditional newspapers; radio and later television encompassed audiences that print media barely touched.

What is amplified in popular media is, first of all, subject matter. In the United Kingdom, for instance, the state-run BBC forbade discussion of birth control in the 1930s and 1940s. In the face of competition from a commercial network in the 1950s, and amid a changing social climate, birth control, divorce, and other controversial topics became subjects for the BBC. Competition, as historian Paddy Scannell put it, "gave the BBC something other than its political masters to worry about."[23] This was a matter not only of substance but also of style, conveyed by a certain tone, attitude, and irreverence toward constituted authority as broadcasters began to speak on behalf of the general public or the public's "right to know."

Public amplification provides a certification of importance. High school athletes grow in stature in the eyes of their friends and family when the daily metropolitan paper, and not just the school paper, reports on high school games. To take a more significant example, writer Alice Walker recalls growing up in the South during the civil rights movement: "The face of Dr. Martin Luther King, Jr., was the first black face I saw on our television screen. . . . I saw in him the hero for whom I had waited so long." It was, for her, like "being born again."[24]

This is amplification but something more: the news has been infused with a moral dimension. News on television, radio, or in print produced by journalists differs from messages a government official or corporate executive might deliver straight to the public on the Internet or by a direct-mail circular. Not only does the journalist have the opportunity—indeed, the professional obligation—to frame the message, but in addition, the newspaper story or television broadcast transforms an event or statement into the cultural form called news. A news story is an announcement of a special kind. It is not like an advertisement, the self-interested purpose of which one can presume. It is not like a public relations event, which is suspect on its face. It is a declaration by a familiar commercial or state agency, staffed by news professionals, that an event is noteworthy. It announces to audiences that a topic deserves public attention. Placement on the page or in the broadcast and frequency of mention indicate how noteworthy, and readers and viewers understand (with different degrees of sophistication) this calibration of importance.

Attention is the scarce good that all aspects of culture vigorously struggle to capture. In this struggle, news has special advantages. It is the language in which most other claims to attention circulate. In this regard, John Hartley's assertion (cited in chapter 1) that news is the dominant textual system of modernity makes sense. News controls the hold of the various other claimants on public attention through its editorial presentation. In the relative emphasis it gives to different topics, it creates a hierarchy of moral salience. It is no wonder that the center of the working day at a newspaper is the "story conference," at which it is decided what stories will make the front page and where on the page they will go.

There is a corollary: the media organize not just information but audiences, too. They legitimize not just events and the sources that report them but also readers and viewers. They have a capacity to publicly include. That you and I read the same front page or see the same television news as do the president of the United States and the chairperson of IBM is empowering; the impression it promotes of equality and commonality, illusion though it is, sustains a hope of democratic life.[25] Moreover, visibility—public visibility—is of enormous importance even if few people bother to read or watch the news. As long as information is publicly available, political actors have to behave as if someone in the public is paying attention. If the news media are the messenger services for political elites, they are not private messenger services, and this is an essential element of news as a social activity.[26] Contemporary journalism presumes that the public is eavesdropping; even if the public is absent, the assumption of the public presence makes all the difference.

In the next chapter, I discuss the media effect that comes from the bias or framing of a news presentation—not the information itself and not the public aura around it but the particular shape that the media have given the information. As mentioned earlier, almost all studies on the media focus on this effect, and not without reason. Decisions about framing that journalists inside news organizations make are moral, ethical, and political judgments, whether conscious or unconscious. Moreover, these judgments are ones about which news institutions, professional journalists, and various traditions and conceptions of journalism differ. So there is much at stake here. Framing most strenuously calls journalists to account and raises questions about their moral and political judgment. Although media bias requires a chapter in itself, in the end, the power of framing can be understood only in relation to the two other media effects just discussed—the force of information itself and the power of the public aura of news.

Chapter Three
MEDIA BIAS (MEDIA EFFECTS, PART 2)

NEWS IS NOT a mirror of reality. It is a representation of the world, and all representations are selective. This means that some human beings must do the selecting; certain people make decisions about what to present as news and how to present it. *Washington Post* columnist David Broder wrote that "the process of selecting what the reader reads involves not just objective facts but subjective judgments, personal values and, yes, prejudices. Instead of promising 'All the News That's Fit to Print,' I would like to see us say—over and over, until the point has been made—that the newspaper that drops on your doorstep is a partial, hasty, incomplete, inevitably somewhat flawed and inaccurate rendering of some of the things we have heard about in the past 24 hours—distorted, despite our best efforts to eliminate gross bias, by the very process of compression that makes it possible for you to lift it from the doorstep and read it in about an hour."[1]

Broder rightly emphasizes selection but misleadingly implies that the primary factors in distortion are personal. They are not. Rather, they are socially organized distortions built into the structures and routines of news gathering. Broder seems to suggest that if only journalists had a little more time they would be able to iron out most of the flaws in their work, but it is not so simple. Most of the subjectivity in news is not idiosyncratic and personal but patterned and predictable. Journalists do not make their decisions at random. Precisely because they are under pressure to churn out a product every twenty-four hours or online repeatedly during the course of a day, they depend on reliable shorthand; conventions; routines; habits; and assumptions about how, why, and where to gather the news.

Many critics of the media assume that there is a perfectly objective or fair way to represent each event in the world (leaving aside the fundamental question of what constitutes an event and why events rather than, say, underlying processes should be the subject matter of news). They further assume that any deviation from fair representation can be accounted for by media bias. "Bias" in this context means that the reporter, editor, or news institution owner knows what the real event looks like but will color it to advance a political, economic, or ideological aim.

Intentional political bias certainly exists in the news media. In fact, it is well institutionalized—the very purpose of the opinion columnist or the editorial page is to interpret, analyze, and persuade. More generally, publishers, editors, and news directors set policies with strong political, though not necessarily partisan, implications. Executives choose, for instance, whether to publish a letter or tract from a terrorist, such as the Unabomber, or to air a videotape from Osama bin Laden. They choose whether to reveal or conceal information that might bear on national security, especially during wartime. They may decide to play down a murder or a suicide because they fear it could inspire copycats; they may choose to limit coverage of a riot for fear of inciting a riot elsewhere. All of these are decisions a news executive makes out of a set of wider social and political allegiances, not out of insular news professionalism. And there are times when judgments go further still. The executive producer of the *ABC Evening News* in the spring of 1969 asked his correspondents to shift their coverage of the Vietnam War from combat to interpretive reports focused on "the eventual pull-out of the American forces."[2] In short, he insisted on changing the framework for reporting the war; he imposed a particular view of how the chaos of war was to be sorted out in news reports.

All this acknowledged, it is still true that intentional, ideologically driven or politically motivated bias does not dominate most U.S. news institutions. A quest for fairness, balance, nonpartisanship, and moderation does. The most prominent exceptions are on cable television, where FOX News has an insistently conservative cast, especially in its line-up of aggressively conservative news commentators with their own shows, and where MSNBC, some years later, began to offer for liberals what FOX provided for conservatives. Elsewhere, however, the attempt to be evenhanded still dominates. As a result, in the social sciences, the idea of bias has largely been replaced by that of framing. Frames in the media are "principles of selection, emphasis, and presentation composed of little tacit theories about what exists, what happens, and what matters." One can offer fancier definitions than this, say, "persistent patterns of cognition, interpretation, and presentation, of selection, emphasis, and exclusion, by which symbol-handlers organize discourse, whether verbal or visual."[3] I am partial to the first definition because of the nice phrase "little tacit theories," which seems to me to sum up what actually *goes on* in journalism better than more ponderous definitions.

Framing is as central a concept as there is in the study of news. It moves the analysis of news away from the idea of intentional bias. That is, to acknowledge that news stories frame reality is also to acknowledge that it would be humanly impossible to avoid framing. Every narrative account of reality necessarily presents some things and not others; consciously or unconsciously, every narrative makes assumptions about how the world works, what is important, what makes sense, and what should be.

Media scholars Robert Entman and Andrew Rojecki offered a useful example in their 2000 study of images of African Americans in the U.S. news media.[4] They reviewed studies that found, for instance, that local television news shows a higher percentage of blacks as perpetrators of crimes (and a lower percentage of blacks as victims of crimes) than police statistics reveal. Does this mean that TV news is biased and should work harder to reproduce police statistics more accurately? Should blacks accused of crimes be portrayed on TV news in proportion to their percentage of all accused perpetrators? That might be a poor choice because it would reproduce a bias against blacks in arrest rates—police arrests overrepresent blacks. Should television transmit to the public without comment the bias built into police routines and police statistics? Perhaps what would be more important is to be sure that the percentage of blacks portrayed on TV news as criminals is the same as the percentage of people in the black population who are criminals. That is, if, say, 5 percent of blacks have criminal records, then should TV news show nineteen law-abiding black citizens every time it shows one black lawbreaker? But are blacks in general the right comparison group? What if 10 percent of black men between the ages of eighteen and thirty have criminal records—should TV news feel obliged to show nine young black men without criminal records studying, working, or playing every time it shows one who has committed a crime? Should the comparison statistics the TV news use to make such judgments be from national or local data? On what basis should local TV news executives make these decisions?

It should be apparent that there is no agreement about what feature of reality would be the "right" one for TV news to seek to mirror. It should also be apparent that the more one seeks some model of reality that describes the whole social scene, the less likely it is that standard news practices will lend themselves to its representation. The news picks up the exceptions more often than the rules, the events and actions that take place at the borders and the margins of the norm. If the weather report paid as much attention to sunny, mild days as it did to hurricanes, floods, heat waves, and cold spells, it might be a more accurate representation of the weather, but it would no longer be news.

It is worth noting that the weather and the stock market are reported daily; they are simply not emphasized daily. The same cannot be said of the black community or any other demographic group in the population except, perhaps, high-ranking government officials, especially the president. If the president takes a vacation, goes to a concert, or catches a cold, this is reported as news. It is not news if any of the rest of us go to Hawaii or have a sniffle.

To consider framing rather than bias, then, opens the discussion to examining unintentional (and even unconscious) as well as intentional selective presentation. It diminishes the extent to which evidence of selection can be automatically read as evidence of deceit, dissembling, or prejudice of individual journalists; it also draws attention to ways journalists select certain traditions and routines of the culture at large and the news business specifically. By discussing framing instead of bias, we accept the possibility that news might speak in more than one voice, even in the same news institution at the same time. "Is it possible," asked John Hartley, "to tell a society by how it edits? Is redaction a symptom of the social?"[5] The editing or framing of news brings matters of human interest into a certain form in a particular cultural apparatus, the news.

Some scholars persist in emphasizing the media's uniformity, which derives from its role as a necessary component of advancing the interests of corporate capitalism. Popular in some quarters of the left, this approach sees capitalist self-interest at every turn, as each cover of *Time*, each episode of *60 Minutes*, and every *New York Times* front page shores up a capitalist system. To these critics, every apparent sign of debate or controversy merely covers up a deeper uniformity of views.

For media scholars Noam Chomsky and Edward Herman, the whole matter is just that simple: the *New York Times* is no better than *Pravda*, the propagandist official newspaper of the Soviet Union. The state is apparently little more than a front for the ruling class.[6] This is a misleading and mischievous stance, for four reasons. First, the *New York Times* has never intended to be anything like the late, unlamented *Pravda*. Pravda journalists understood that their primary aim was to support the socialist agenda as interpreted by the Communist Party of the Soviet Union. *New York Times* journalists may, indeed, be American patriots, but if they are, it is of their own initiative and not because their employer requires it, and their loyalty is to a national idea and not a particular incumbent administration. They see their day-to-day task as reporting the news, not elucidating a party line. They believe in fair and objective reporting, and it is unusual for a reporter to use a strong political framework to interpret events of the day. They almost always embrace professional ethics. Media owners, obedient to market demands or at least to their sense of what the market demands, limit news coverage, notably by setting budgets. But they rarely seek to use the news as a soapbox for their own political views or the views of whatever political orthodoxy they subscribe to, if they subscribe to any. (FOX News, MSNBC, opinion magazines, many political blogs, and the editorial pages of most newspapers are a different matter.)

Second, there is a vital arena of legitimate controversy in the United States. Neither Republicans nor Democrats question capitalism; neither questions economic growth as a paramount national objective. Yet differences between the parties are real and consequential. The contemporary news media seek to represent both sides fairly. Consider, just in the past ten years, the different consequences of Republican and Democratic policies for gays in the military, women seeking abortions, men and women needing welfare, poor people needing medical care, business owners soliciting tax breaks, manufacturers feeling burdened by environmental regulation. These differences are prominently reported. Are they trivial in comparison to the fact that both parties accept private ownership of the means of production? Perhaps. But try maintaining that view as you look in the eyes of the young gay man or lesbian building a military career, the woman seeking a safe and legal abortion, the people whose "preexisting conditions" keep them from obtaining health insurance. Can you tell them that their concerns are insignificant?

Third, there are multiple voices in the American news media. True, the American media do not have a wide-screen view of the range of possible political positions. Compared to the press in most liberal democracies, they foreshorten the representation of views on the left, as does the American political system generally. But these tendencies stop far short of uniformity. If competition often pushes the media toward the least common denominator of news reporting, other competitive pressures push news institutions not to miss a hot story—at least, not when it has reached a certain level of notoriety. And a hot story is not necessarily one that pleases the powers that be. It may turn out to be the My Lai massacre; Watergate; Iran-contra; the photos of prisoner abuse at Abu Ghraib; the failures of local, state, and national governments in Hurricane Katrina; or the BP oil spill in the Gulf of Mexico. The American press is unusually aggressive among Western news institutions in pursuing scandal.[7]

Finally, the media are obligated not only to make profits but to maintain their credibility in the eyes of readers. "The most valuable asset a paper has is its credibility," a *Baltimore Sun* editor has observed. "If people think we don't cover stories because they involve us, people will start wondering what else we don't cover."[8] The media must retain credibility not only with the population at large but also with expert and often critical subgroups in the population, particularly in Washington, D.C. As long as there is heterogeneity among those subgroups, there will be pressure for fairness in the press.

Although the *New York Times* is not *Pravda*, some of the more carefully directed darts of leftist critics hit home. Certainly the

media are generally statist and deeply nationalist.[9] Chomsky
and Herman's extremely critical view of the U.S. press is based
on analysis of foreign reporting during the cold war, and there
is no doubt that the press's objectivity weakens in the case of
foreign reporting. Indeed, it weakened during the cold war in
just the direction Chomsky and Herman suggested—toward
hypercritical reporting of communist regimes and overly
generous reporting of noncommunist authoritarian governments.[10] It is also true that journalists take pleasure in and
garner rewards for being insiders; the corporate media do not
make life comfortable for the likes of bold, challenging journalists like Edward R. Murrow, Daniel Schorr, Bill Moyers, Syd-
ney Schanberg, or William Greider. Certainly the press more
often follows than leads and reinforces conventional wisdom
more often than it challenges it.[11] Views at the margins get
little coverage not because they lack validity or interest, but
because they lack official sponsorship. If the corporate structure
of the media does not in itself determine news content, it still
tends to marginalize some news and some ways of telling the
news. It still tends to subordinate news values to commercial
values. Critics from various political persuasions rightly worry
over what CBS news anchor Dan Rather termed the "showbiz-
ification" of news.[12] But this should not lead us to conclude that
"in all press systems, the news media are agents of those who
exercise political and economic power" and that "the content of
the news media always reflects the interests of those who finance
the press," as one journalism scholar does.[13] This view overrides
every important distinction, every precious way in which the
press in liberal societies differs from the press in state-run, one-
party systems.

Of course, the press has prominent critics on the right as well as the left. Critics from the right cannot point to media structures as biased against their views; critics from the left win hands down on this point. In the United States, almost all influential media institutions are owned and operated by large profit-making corporations, and every one of them depends on government officials and representatives of other powerful, established social institutions as news sources. There is no getting around this. Critics on the right, however, present an argument that bears serious consideration. They argue that reporters and editors at leading national news institutions have a predominantly liberal outlook. News has a liberal bias because writers and editors of news are recruited from left-liberal circles. If corporate organization tilts unmistakably rightward, patterns of occupational recruitment veer just as sharply the other way.

President Richard Nixon, his spokesperson Patrick Buchanan, and Vice President Spiro Agnew made this case in 1969. They had a point: in surveys conducted by Robert and Linda Lichter and Stanley Rothman, 54 percent of journalists at the prestigious national news outlets identified themselves as liberals, 17 percent as conservatives, and the remainder as "middle of the road." The survey's methodology has been sharply called into question, but its results are consistent with the more casual observations of many other people.[14]

The political views of American journalists as a whole, in contrast to the Washington- and New York–based news elite, are closer to the views of Americans in general.[15] Even with national journalists, however, Lichter, Lichter, and Rothman found a very thin liberalism. The journalists turned out to be liberal socially (53 percent thought adultery is not wrong) but plain vanilla on economic issues (only 13 percent thought government should own big corporations). Even the bare majority (54 percent) of journalists who declared themselves liberal, in other words, fully accepted the framework of capitalism, although they wished it wore a more human face.

The right-wing critics, moreover, never satisfactorily deal with the question of whether journalists are effective at putting professional norms of objectivity ahead of their personal views. Liberal leaning though a majority of the surveyed national journalists may be, close observers find them not highly political or politicized. Journalists see themselves as professionals rather than partisans, and they normally act accordingly.[16] It does not surprise observant readers, then, that the same *New York Times* that repeatedly endorsed Eliot Spitzer's bids for office in New York (including governor in 2006) in 2008 broke the sex scandal that led to Spitzer's resignation as governor. Nor is it a shock that the *Times* broke the story that Connecticut's Democratic candidate for the U.S. Senate in 2010, Richard Blumenthal, had repeatedly made public statements implying falsely that he had served in the military in Vietnam. (Despite the ensuing scandal that damaged the Blumenthal campaign, the *Times* endorsed him and he was elected.)[17]

Professionalism accounts for much of this, but a field that puts a premium on detachment probably also attracts a certain kind of person. *Washington Post* reporter turned media reformer Paul Taylor has written eloquently about his own attraction to journalism. Investigative reporters, he observed, become indignant quickly. They readily see "high conspiracies and base motivations."[18] But most reporters have a very different frame of mind. Taylor continued, "I rarely see anything but nuance, and my first instinct runs toward benefit of the doubt. I find it painful to render harsh judgments about anyone in print. I find it equally difficult to praise anyone, however. I suffer from 'fear of flacking,' a common occupational disorder."

Do Taylor's attitudes make him unfit for hard-driving daily journalism? Or, as he suggests, do they give him the perfect temperament for the professionalism of modern journalism? "By aiming for the golden mean, I probably land near the best approximation of truth more often than if I were guided by any other set of compasses—partisan, ideological, psychological, whatever. I'm still wrong much of the time, and I don't kid myself about where I'm headed. Yes, I'm seeking truth. But I'm also seeking refuge. I'm taking a pass on the toughest calls I face—which may explain why I chose to be a watcher, not a doer, in the first place." [19]

Where reporters make tough calls, personal political bias rarely seems the best explanation. Political analysts Michael Robinson and Margaret Sheehan's careful study of television and print coverage of the 1980 presidential campaign found, for instance, that the media were strictly neutral in the overwhelming majority of cases. When the media made judgments, those judgments were more often negative than positive, but the negative evaluations landed evenly on both Republicans and Democrats. Being a member of a particular party did not make one more likely to receive negative coverage. What invited criticism was being a front-runner in the primary election contests, regardless of party or ideology. [20]

Implicit in the critique from the right is that market competition in the news media drives journalists toward scandal and sleaze. Reporters will improve their careers more quickly by uncovering scandal than by recording achievement; they will burnish their reputations more by writing with an edge or an attitude than by writing with cool and scientific detachment. Thus, they contribute to the downgrading of established authority, their reporting diminishes trust in our leading institutions, and their liberal ideologies weaken American values. This is a risky argument for conservatives to make, of course, because it calls attention to the anarchic tendencies of a marketplace left to its own devices. Conservatives generally embrace this very marketplace.

In any event, critics on the right have called attention to both who writes and who owns the news. And journalists' personal characteristics do make a difference, if not always in the direction the right-leaning critics presume. Indeed, increasing affluence may influence national journalists much more than do their professed political views. In this case, the left has more cause for complaint than the right. Journalist William Greider lamented that working-class, street-schooled reporters have been replaced by the "well-educated."[21] Concern about this surfaces in acerbic newsroom humor. As Merrill Goozner, former chief economics correspondent for the *Chicago Tribune* put it, "News is anything that happens within 100 feet of an editor's house." An even more cynical wisecrack that also circulated in the *Tribune* newsroom is "News is anything that an editor sees while driving into work from the suburbs."[22] How can such journalists cover poverty or other problems of the inner city? *Washington Post* media critic Howard Kurtz wrote, "The plain fact is that newspapers reflect the mood and values of white, middle-class society, and that society, by the early '90s, had simply grown tired of the intractable problems of the urban underclass."[23]

But it is more than a matter of boredom or weariness. Journalists, like other human beings, more readily recognize and more eagerly pursue problems and issues that concern people like themselves rather than those beyond their social circle. Two examples may illustrate the point. When the "Zoe Baird problem" arose in the 1992 controversy over President Bill Clinton's nomination of Baird as attorney general, media coverage was uniform in a way that escaped notice. Baird and her husband had hired two people to care for their children in their home. Like many Americans in the same situation, they failed to pay Social Security taxes, as required by law, for the domestic employees; the revelation of this fact doomed Baird's appointment as chief law enforcement officer. News coverage in almost all cases examined the legal, moral, and political issues raised by this incident—from the viewpoint of Baird or other people in similar circumstances, not from the viewpoint of the child-care workers.

One exception was coverage on Univision, the Spanish-language television network, which profiled the domestics Baird had hired and did an extended story on child care from the viewpoint of underpaid and overworked immigrant care providers.[24] Journalists at Univision, just as committed to professional norms as other journalists, educated in the same schools, participating in the same broader journalistic culture, nevertheless could identify not only with Baird, an attorney, but with the Latino domestic workers she hired. The consensus in the mainstream press arose not from journalistic routines or from patterns of media ownership but rather from the broad class and racial bias in American society and in mainstream journalism.

Or take the remark of the late Randy Shilts, the *San Francisco Chronicle* reporter who covered AIDS full-time for his paper.

When his book on AIDS, *And the Band Played On*, was published in 1987, he said in an interview, "Any good reporter could have done this story, but I think the reason I did it, and no one else did, is because I am gay. It was happening to people I cared about and loved."[25] Shilts's remark is simple and obvious yet generally neglected in most analysis of journalism. A female reporter is more likely than a male reporter, other things being equal, to see rape as a newsworthy issue. An African American reporter is more likely than a white reporter, other things being equal, to find issues in the African American community newsworthy.

Empathy, fortunately for us all, is not beyond human capacity, and good journalism may both stem from empathy and evoke it. Still, the person who writes the story matters. When minorities and women and people who have known poverty or misfortune firsthand are both authors of news and its readers, the social world represented in the news expands and changes.

AN EMPHASIS ON FRAMING instead of bias calls attention to how decisions in the manufacture of news have more to do with the marketplace, the nature of organizations, and the assumptions of news professionals than with individual bias. Critics of political bias ordinarily presume that the journalist should be a professional who tells the truth and that it is possible to do this without prejudice. For those who emphasize framing, professionalism is as likely to be the disease as the cure.

Whether part of the problem or part of the solution, professionalism is a hallmark of the contemporary American press. This is not to say that journalists encompass all the features of a "classic" profession like medicine or law—they are not licensed, they are not required to have any particular formal education, they do not need to pass exams to practice, they do not master a body of theoretical or abstract knowledge, they do not police the ethics of their own professional practice as fully as doctors and lawyers do, and they have little control over the conditions of their own employment. All that acknowledged, in historical perspective, as chapter 4 shows, there is nothing more striking than the transformation of journalism from nineteenth-century partisanship to twentieth-century commercial-professionalism. A comparison of any leading metropolitan paper of 1995 with one of 1895 demonstrates instantly that today's news is shaped much more by a professional ethic and reflects fewer partisan hopes or fears than a truly political press. Reporters no longer march in step behind their publisher as they once did. The antipolitical, antipartisan perspective of professionalism is an essential feature of the contemporary press. What follows from recognizing the press as "professional"?

Beginning in the early 1970s, sociologists and political scientists conducted studies, usually based on ethnographic observation of newsroom practices, which showed that media bias derives not from intentional ideological perversion but instead from professional achievement under the constraints of organizational routines and pressures; news organizations and routines produce bias regardless of media ownership or the outlook of individual reporters. The quest for objectivity itself, in this view, is a source of distortion.[26] Five kinds of distortion are frequently cited, which I will discuss in turn: news is said to be typically (1) event-centered, action-centered, and person-centered; (2) negative; (3) detached; (4) technical; and (5) official.

First, news tends to be event-centered, action-centered, and person-centered. News focuses on visible events, often involving conflict or violent conflict.[27] As Bill Frenzel, a Republican member of Congress from Minnesota, complained, "The press thinks it can only report events. Congress is not an event, it is a process. Either the press doesn't understand that, or it assumes the public doesn't understand it."[28] News tends to simplify complex social processes in ways that emphasize melodrama, turning a complex set of phenomena into a morality tale of battle between antagonists, often between good guys and bad guys. Generally, clearly identified individuals personify or stand in for larger, more difficult-to-grasp social forces. One reason, among several, that the news media were slow to cover the AIDS epidemic is simply that AIDS was "a slow-moving disaster," not a dramatic event of flood, fire, or earthquake suddenness.[29]

The eventfulness of news is not something we are obliged to see as a failure—that is, a failure to dig deeply into social forces and processes. It can be taken as an achievement, a social accomplishment in its own right and one that we take so much for granted today that it has become invisible. Provincial Britons noticed it in the 1920s, when radio brought distant public life to their villages. "I live in a dull, drab colliery village as far removed from real country as from real city life," one villager wrote in 1923, "a bus ride from third rate entertainments and a considerable journey from any educational, musical or social advantages of a first class sort. In such an atmosphere, life becomes rusty and apathetic. Into this monotony comes a good radio set and my little world is transformed."[30] Into this world, the radio brought events. As British media scholar Paddy Scannell observed, "Whereas the public world beforehand was over the hills and far away, now it is close at hand and graspable. Its eventfulness enters into uneventful lives giving them new texture and substance."[31] Whether liberating or stultifying, the emphasis on event is a characteristic feature of news.

Second, there is a tendency for journalists to focus on bad news. President Lyndon B. Johnson once complained about this to Henry Luce, publisher and editor of *Time* magazine. He waved the current copy of *Time* at Luce and exclaimed, "This week 200,000 blacks registered in the South, thanks to the Voting Rights Act. Three hundred thousand elderly people are going to be covered by Medicare. We have a hundred thousand young unemployed kids working in neighborhoods. Is any of that in there? No. What's in here?" (His next remarks, according to the aide who reported the conversation, were not fit for delicate ears.) Luce replied, "Mr. President, good news isn't news. Bad news is news."[32]

When things are going well, there seems less of a reason for a news story. The news instinct is triggered by things going badly. As Israeli media scholar Tamar Liebes wrote, "Western journalism is a social warning system, exposing the exception rather than the rule, the deviant rather than the norm, disorder rather than order, dissonance rather than harmony."[33] Robinson and Sheehan found that television news covering the 1980 presidential campaign was neutral or ambiguous in its evaluation of candidates most of the time. But in the one story out of five that could be judged "positive" or "negative," coverage was negative 70 percent of the time (wire service news was more evenhanded).[34] In 1992, television coverage of the three leading presidential contenders proved more negative than positive in every case not because journalists are adversarial or nihilistic, but because they are professional.[35] News tends to emphasize conflict, dissension, and battle; out of a journalistic convention that there are two sides to any story, news heightens the appearance of conflict even in instances of relative calm. Reporters try to see through rather than observe politics. While this keeps them from being bamboozled by the politicians they cover, it strips political leaders down to their worst stereotypes, people possessing no motive other than political advantage.

As we saw in the introduction, news can portray crime waves even when there is no increase in crime. The media are much less likely to highlight waves of civil harmony, even if they exist. Sociologist Christopher Jencks observed that the chance of an African American's being murdered in the United States in 1985 was about the same as it had been in 1950, despite the considerable alarm about growing crime in America. "When crime declines, as it did in the early eighties, editors assume the decline is only temporary and give it very little air time. When crime increases as it did in the late eighties, both journalists and editors see it as a portent of things to come and give it a lot of play."[36]

Third, news tends to be detached. Increasingly, journalists take a distanced, even ironic view of political life. In fact, they are enjoined to do so by both the tenets of their profession and the cynical culture of the newsroom. Obviously, this does not apply to the sports story that takes partisanship for granted, or the human interest feature that depends on human sympathy in the reporter's and readers' hearts, or investigative reporting that presumes the audience's capacity for moral indignation. But in election campaign news, for instance, objectivity is the guiding principle, often religiously practiced. Robinson and Sheehan found journalists scrupulously avoiding color, bias, or judgment. They told CBS reporter Susan Spencer that their analysis of the entire corpus of CBS coverage of Senator Edward Kennedy's 1980 candidacy for president found that CBS did not once venture to draw so much as an inference from any aspect of Kennedy's positions on the issues. She replied, "Good."[37] U.S. journalists are typically proud of their detachment.

This relates to a fourth tendency in American journalism— the emphasis on strategy and tactics, political technique rather than policy outcome, the mechanical rather than the ideological. Focusing on the technical side of politics enables journalists to be professional, because they can remain apart from "the conflicts of interest, perspective, and value that are the dangerous stuff of political life."[38] Political reporters tend to be politics wonks rather than policy wonks, absorbed by "inside baseball" analysis rather than fascinated by the question of how the government should run the country. Their emphasis is on campaign strategy and tactics and on the prospects of candidates for winning, not on the candidates' policies or even on their capacity for leadership. In the 1980 presidential campaign, journalists made explicit evaluations of the candidates' qualities, leadership, or ideas in less than 5 percent of stories. Nonetheless, reporters felt free to judge candidates' likelihood of winning the election in more than a quarter of all stories.[39]

Journalists choose the experts they rely on accordingly. When national television journalists seek out experts, they seek out those who can satisfy what media scholar Janet Steele dubs the "operational bias" of the press. In covering foreign policy, for instance, journalists want experts who know or are close to the key diplomatic players, who can authoritatively explain the policy choices at hand, and who are willing to make predictions about how events will unfold. They lean toward former public officials, retired military leaders, and think-tank policy adepts who frame issues in a narrow, technical way rather than scholars who have done primary research on the country or conflict at hand or leading religious spokespersons who would address issues in moral rather than strategic terms.[40] A study of reporting on national security in leading U.S. newspapers found only 1 story out of a sample of 678 that cited a religious source.[41]

News professionalism in contemporary political culture tends to be event-centered, negative, detached, and strategic, but these qualities can take several forms. Take the time when President Ronald Reagan, after vacationing in California, flew back to Washington, D.C., but stopped en route in flood-ravaged Louisiana. There he made a brief radio broadcast from a flooded town, encouraging local citizens and promising federal aid. An AP photo, accompanying the *New York Times'* coverage, showed the president with a shovel helping to fill sandbags. The *Los Angeles Times* headline read, "Reagan Pitches In to Help Flood Victims." The *New York Times* played the story straight and neutral. The *Los Angeles Times* began the same way, but in the sixth paragraph noted that this was just "the type of event Reagan's advisers constantly are on the lookout for." It was a chance to show the president "in a highly photogenic setting expressing concern for those in distress," and it came at "an opportune time for White House strategists" by drawing attention away from Reagan's "holiday with wealthy friends in Palm Springs." This departs from a "just the facts" approach, but it is exactly the kind of strategic and political framework that political reporters reach for and feel justified in providing on their own authority as close observers of political means and motives.[42]

Of course, the image of human generosity in Reagan's gesture was undercut by this attention to political motive. Was the *New York Times* derelict in failing to provide the strategic and political context the *Los Angeles Times* offered its readers? Or was the *Los Angeles Times* unduly cynical? Was this a case where the show-biz president, struggling in the polls in a weak economy early in 1983, could help himself while genuinely helping the community? Perhaps the *Los Angeles Times'* stance of assertive political expertise went too far, but it has come to be accepted as a legitimate alternative to the deferential objectivity of the *New York Times* story. This is the general range of possibility within which most political reporting operates today. Reporters and editors seek what feels to them like a comfortable path between stenographic objectivity, on the one hand, and assertive professionalism, on the other.

The fifth tendency in the news is that it is official and dependent on legitimate public sources, usually highly placed government officials and a relatively small number of reliable experts. News is as much a product of sources as of journalists. Does this contradict the observation that professionalism leads to negative news? Not really. We can distinguish the routine news from official sources that occupies most of the paper most of the time from the more occasional news in which official pronouncements are questioned or undermined by accidents, scandals, leaks from other officials, or the ironic reservations of the journalist. In any event, officials remain the subject of news as well as its source, even though news often entangles them in negative coverage.[43]

Officialness makes the news "statist"; that is, it contributes to a tendency to cover government voices rather than nongovernmental or "civil" ones, to bow to the state's sense of national security, however narrow or self-serving it may be, to seek to be patriotic as well as truthful, and sometimes to be patriotic rather than truthful when the two conflict. When pacifist Oswald Garrison Villard published the text of secret Allied treaties during World War I in the *New York Post*, few other papers picked up the story, and the *New York Times* condemned Villard's action. In World War II, the press failed to report the increasingly detailed and authorized evidence of the ongoing Holocaust. This had several causes, but one was certainly that the press in both London and Washington accepted the assurances of government officials that focusing on the Jews could sidetrack the paramount aim of winning the war.[44]

In 2010, a very different *New York Times* joined with France's *Le Monde*, Spain's *El Pais*, Britian's *Guardian*, and Germany's *Der Spiegel* in publishing reports culled from a huge trove of U.S. State Department cables that the online organization WikiLeaks had obtained without authorization and shared with these news organizations in advance of making any of the documents available on its own website. Obama administration officials, including Secretary of State Hillary Clinton, quickly condemned the documents' release, defended the necessity of confidential communication in diplomacy, and warned that the leak could put lives at risk. This story is ongoing and how WikiLeaks or other organizations like it will affect the practice of journalism is yet to be determined.

Event-centered, negative, detached, technical, and official: in this view, the problem with the press is professionalism, not its absence. Professionalism produces its own characteristic angle of vision, and it can be argued that it is one that helps reinforce a view of politics as a spectator sport. It tutors readers in the cool and professional gaze that sees through policy pronouncements and rhetorical appeals and focuses on the strategies and tactics of the political trade. The "implied reader" of election news is a consumer in the political supermarket, someone with the time, interest, and attention to comparison shop, to read the lists of ingredients on each package, to check the store's information on unit pricing, to attend to advertising as a form of information while learning to discount it as a type of propaganda. This ideal political consumer will then make a reasonably rational preference for one candidate or the other. The trouble is that he or she will not have any incentive for turning that preference into a vote. The careful reader and watcher of the news might well be moved to stay at home, interpreting the lesson from contemporary campaign reporting to be "a pox on both your houses."

This is largely speculation. While there is some evidence to support this view, we do not really know how much the cynical undertow of political reporting influences its audience and how much it partakes of a broader culture of cynicism that the news audience already shares.[45] What, more generally, can we say about the influence of the news on its audience?

First, even when there is a demonstrably causal influence, it is important to identify what the causal agent is. If it is information from official sources, and if the media are primarily neutral transmitters of the information, then there is in fact a media effect, but it is one that masks the real influence—that of the source of the information. The media can be the messenger and little more.

Consider sociologist Todd Gitlin's book *The Whole World Is Watching*, the best account of the influence of media on social movements. Gitlin's study of Students for a Democratic Society (SDS), the major student organization of the New Left and the anti–Vietnam War movement, is widely taken to be a key illustration of the power of media framing or bias in affecting society. But this conclusion is equivocal. On the one hand, Gitlin demonstrated that news coverage of early SDS activism contributed significantly to the rapid growth of the organization. Such is the power of information: by simply distributing the news that SDS existed, news reports made the phone ring off the hook at SDS headquarters. But this is not the main emphasis in Gitlin's study or in the commentary on it. Gitlin's emphasis is on framing. He argued that later news coverage of SDS "trivialized" and "marginalized" the students' efforts and contributed to the breakdown of a relatively resource-poor movement. Buffeted by the growth of richer and more "legitimate" protest efforts of conventional liberals opposed to the Vietnam War, SDS lost control of the antiwar movement. Gitlin may be right that media framing contributed to the disintegration of SDS, but there is no real evidence one way or the other. It is easier to see how the early, rather sympathetic coverage could have hurt SDS more than the later, marginalizing coverage did: The early coverage was an advertisement for SDS that brought in many new members. These members displaced the old guard and shifted the orientation of SDS from an agency of the organized left to a coordinating center for a mass student movement. New members were more volatile, more impatient, and less politically seasoned. The shift to a new leadership fractured the organization. Perhaps it was the influence of new members inside SDS rather than later condescending news coverage from outside that made the organization implode.

This interpretation is consistent with the information provided by Gitlin. He showed that the media exercised influence in distributing to the general public the information that a new national organization was taking direct action to protest the Vietnam War. But he focused his analysis on a framing rather than an informational effect, pointing out that the press treated SDS protests as trivial and marginal. If I am right, the media hurt SDS less by framing it negatively than by reporting its existence in a straightforward manner, bringing it throngs of new and inexperienced members. The usual internal bickering of left-wing, splinter-prone groups did all the rest.

Another example: In the 2000 presidential election, Ralph Nader ran as a candidate for the Green Party. The Green Party had never elected a president. It had never elected a candidate to the House or the Senate or even to a statewide office. There are good reasons, then, that the news media might have chosen to spend little or no time covering Nader. On the other hand, Ralph Nader is arguably one of the most influential public figures of America's past half century, a pioneer of the consumer movement, a stalwart critic of the corporate establishment, a tireless and inventive crusader for the little guy. To have Nader heading the Green Party ticket energized sentiment on the left, put the Green Party ticket on the ballot in forty-four states, and led to poll ratings as high as 5 percent nationally. How should the press have responded?

Nader complained both during and after the election that the media systematically ignored him. "No matter what our campaign tried or accomplished, the media remained stuck in a cultural rut, covering the horse race and political tactics of [Al] Gore and [George W.] Bush rather than the issues."[46] The *Washington Post*, Nader observed, could find space for 750 words to cover a Gore family vacation but could not send a reporter across the street to cover a Nader press conference on Social Security. When the Nader campaign did get coverage early in the campaign, reporters "consistently viewed it as an occasional feature story—a colorful, narrative dispatch from the trail with a marginal candidate"[47] rather than a hard news story about campaign issues or events. Toward the end of the campaign, when it became clear that the outcome would be extremely close, Nader voters became part of the horse-race story and reporters repeatedly asked Nader if he was a "spoiler" whose persistence in the campaign would throw the election to George W. Bush.

Was there bias here? Nader certainly thought so: "No democracy worth its salt should rely so pervasively on the commercial media. And no seriously pro-democracy campaign will ever get an even break, or adequate coverage, from that media."[48] But at the same time Patrick Buchanan, a prominent national figure on the right, was representing the Reform Party, which (with businessman Ross Perot as its leader) had won nearly 20 percent of the vote in 1992. Buchanan was not getting any more coverage than Nader. The reporters and editors were not betraying a conservative political bias guided by capitalist ownership. They were not acting out of political ideology but rather out of what Gitlin called a "little tacit theory." Their little tacit theory went something like this: "Our job is not to determine campaign issues or to promote political dialogue across the whole spectrum of ideas but to give the public a fair-minded account of the candidates who have a reasonable chance of becoming president.

Nader might well be right that major-party candidates like Al Gore and George W. Bush disagreed on too little and buried too much of what really mattered to public life, but who is to say? Reporting that is not the job of the press, at least not in the news columns. Our political system coughed up Gore and Bush as the viable candidates in 2000; our task is to cover that, not to change it on behalf of Nader's views or Buchanan's or our own views of what the real issues are."

Is this little tacit theory correct? Who knows? The point is only that it is a theory or, rather, an implicit and never fully articulated position—one view of journalistic responsibility among several, and one ordained by traditions and routines and tacit assumptions. Journalists made a choice, even if it seemed to them a perfectly obvious and apolitical choice. That it may have been an entirely conscientious choice is beside the point. If the press had held to a different theory of reporting and of presidential politics, and if reporters believed it their obligation to get vital issues aired and not simply to follow the staged events and speeches of the leading candidates, they might very well have covered Nader differently or used Nader as a way to raise broader issues.

Was there framing? Yes, of course. Did it hurt Nader and Buchanan? That is plausible. By how much? That is not measurable.

There are other systematic biases in the news media. There are biases toward conventional over dissident opinions, toward science over religion, and toward upper-status and upper-income groups over the poor. There is a bias toward what sociologist Herbert Gans described as the core values of American journalism: ethnocentrism, altruistic democracy, responsible capitalism, small-town pastoralism, individualism, and moderatism.[49] These unquestioned and often unnoticed background assumptions govern the way news in the United States is gathered and framed.

There is a racial bias toward people who look like the majority of journalists over people who do not. *Washington Post* reporter and past president of the National Association of Black Journalists Vanessa Williams considered why the killing of a white middle-class person generates more news coverage than does that of a black lower-class person and concluded, "Because the people who make decisions about what is newsworthy more readily identify with victims who look like them and live like them and are utterly frightened or outraged when bad things happen to them. The coverage reflects that fear and outrage."[50]

Fifty years ago, racial bias was direct, open, obvious, and unembarrassed. In the past half century, it has become a more complicated matter. There may be more to Williams's point than even she suspects. One of the key features of news, after all, is unusualness. Even if half of the staff of a metropolitan daily were African American, the relatively common incidence of homicide as a cause of death among African Americans and its relative rarity among whites could explain the disparity in news coverage without reference to racial bias at all. Black journalists as well as white ones would recognize that the more unusual incident is more newsworthy. Now, why is murder more common among blacks than whites? That is a vital question, and surely it has to do with several centuries of racism, but it would be rare for any journalist to explore such a question as part of ordinary news reporting.[51]

Robert Entman has argued that local television news reinforces what he calls modern racism—a general antiblack sentiment and resistance to black political demands, combined with
a general view that racism has been eliminated. He found in a
study of local TV news in Chicago that blacks appear most often
as alleged criminals. He also showed that the way a black candidate for county office was portrayed on television reinforced
racism. The black candidate was presented as preoccupied with
self-interest, whereas white political actors were more often pic-
tured as oriented to the public interest. Coverage emphasized
the black candidate's angry rhetoric, the whites' calm rationality
(unlikely as this may sound for any aspect of Chicago politics).
Why the contrast? Entman speculated that the sources of this
portrayal are twofold. Underdogs are forced by their subordinate position to adopt a kind of loud, histrionic, even uncivil
style. This contrasts with the conventions of public behavior
that middle-class journalists take as legitimate. The underdog is
forced to attack, where the incumbent can appear reassuring and
complacent. It may also be that African American culture tends
to favor a more emotional linguistic style than does middle-class
white culture. African American politicians often play to the
anger of their core constituency as well, which may rally blacks
while raising the suspicions of whites. This all suggests that
the broad structure of American racism and cultural differences,
not any unique complicity of the news media, leads to negative
portrayals of the black politicians.[52]

INFORMATION EFFECTS, aura effects, and framing effects cannot be sorted out fully. For our purposes, it suffices to say that
they exist and that sometimes they make a real difference in the

world, a difference that merits the attention of scholars and critics. It is plausible to argue that the news media's insistent negativism and attention to moments of danger, stress, and conflict alter and heighten public awareness and fear of risk. It makes sense to argue that the news media inform people; identify and consolidate community; orchestrate a public conversation; and play important specialized roles in the political system, from screening candidates to serving the purposes of government officials who carefully release and withhold information to shape public policy.

At the same time, it is not very plausible to hold that the media, in general, make people more conservative or more liberal. Nor is it plausible to see the media as generally preventing or promoting social change. The media do not routinely legitimate or delegitimate governmental institutions. What's important to keep in mind is that the influence of news is cultural. It can relay a certain body of information and a set of attitudes toward that information to people who are open to receiving it, but it cannot reward or punish the audience for taking the information to heart. This does not make the news unimportant. It simply makes the news a subtle, cultural influence on human affairs, not an overtly controlling force.

Chapter Four
WHERE NEWS CAME FROM:
THE HISTORY OF AMERICAN
JOURNALISM TO WATERGATE

A LARGE PART of the explanation of the present lies in the past. We are what we are because we were what we were. Thus, the sociology of journalism cannot be severed from the history of journalism.

Is news something human beings have always sought? Have they always, in all times and places, been curious about novelty and especially curious about sensational kinds of novelty—blood, guts, sex, and the frailty and dissipation of the rich and famous? The press claims to serve universal and timeless longings, to be the storytellers of the world, the bards and troubadours of everyday life and everyday people.[1]

There may be something, but I think not much, to the idea that a thirst for news is fundamental to human nature. What does such a proposition help us to understand? Almost all questions about news inquire about differences among competing styles and principles of journalism, alternative institutional structures of news organizations, or different systems of political control of news. Why do states censor news in some countries more than in others? Why do some countries' journalistic traditions encourage journalists to write literary essays while others prefer fact-centered reports? Why are sensational stories on the front page in some newspapers and not in others, even within the same city? Why are some countries dominated by commercial TV and others by public television? What differences do these differences make? Why is one story more interesting than another? Why is a sports reporter free to favor the home team but the political reporter not equally free to cheer for the home-grown candidate? What is better for our civic life—news that gives politicians more room to state their own views without interruption or news that journalists more actively manage with quick edits and short sound bites? Positing a universal and timeless human passion for news ("Oh, would that it were so!" one can hear newspaper business managers sigh) answers none of these questions.

This chapter begins with a wide-angle lens on the scene of journalism, reaching back into its history and well beyond the American scene. Media history has long been a backwater of the historical profession, but in recent years it has been taking great strides. In some measure, this is simply because of the rapid and radical transformation of the delivery of news. The growth of television news in the 1960s, the growing commercial competition faced by public broadcasters in Europe, the availability of cable and satellite-beamed news delivery, and the explosion of digital media and the Internet, have all contributed to the widespread sense that everyday life is increasingly oriented to information, habits, and social relations originating in or propelled by the mass media.

Recent interest in media history has circled around two works of social theory that emphasize the media's importance. In *The Structural Transformation of the Public Sphere*, published in

German in 1962 but not until 1989 in English, the German sociologist and philosopher Jürgen Habermas portrayed the eighteenth-century emergence of the newspaper in the context of world history. The press became "the public sphere's pre-eminent institution."[2] Before Habermas, of course, substantial works on the freedom of the press and works on the role of "the fourth estate" as a factor in political life had been published. Habermas added to this tradition, however, by placing the press within a broad framework of social theory.

For Habermas, the "bourgeois public sphere" that emerged in parts of western Europe toward the end of the eighteenth century encompassed a social space and set of attendant norms that enabled and encouraged private persons to discuss public issues without the sponsorship of or surveillance by their government. In this sphere, people could converse as equals. Individual reason, not social position, was the measure of an argument's worth. Newspapers, pamphlets, coffeehouses, and salons were among the key institutions that made a public sphere possible. What began in this free, sociable space would over time take on specifically political functions. In the 1700s, journalists in London were not permitted to take notes in the gallery of the House of Commons. Only in 1834 were places installed for reporters.

Unfortunately, as Habermas tells the story, the expanding public sphere began to collapse by the mid- to late nineteenth century, as the power of capital turned a realm of liberty into an opportunity for profit. A means of enlightenment became a marketplace of sensation. Capitalism "refeudalized" public life, even though capitalism had been a primary force in shattering feudalism in the first place. That is, the concentration of power in a small number of private profit-making news organizations centralized cultural authority and clamped down on the free flow of expression. Whereas at first the press "evolved out of the public's use of its reason," by the late nineteenth century the newspaper had become "a medium for culture as an object of consumption." Whereas once newspapers were identified with the spirited essays of their editors, now they became the tools of the publishers who appointed editors "in the expectation that they will do as they are told in the private interest of a profit-oriented enterprise."[3]

The particulars of this argument have been challenged again and again, and few scholars today accept Habermas's view as he originally proposed it. Habermas first presented his work in an exceptionalist vein: as the sociologist Max Weber asked why rational capitalism arose in the West and not elsewhere, Habermas inquired why a bourgeois order, and not any other, gave rise to a domain of reasoned public discourse about politics outside the control of church or crown. While Habermas's historical argument has been debated, his category of "public sphere" has been held up as a normative model of exemplary civic life. This idea has inspired research in a wide variety of nations and periods.

Another theoretical account of the media's role in modern times that has attracted interest across the disciplines is historian Benedict Anderson's *Imagined Communities: Reflections on the Origin and Spread of Nationalism*, a fertile and provocative essay that covers five hundred years of world history in fewer than 150 pages. Anderson proposed that all nations and, indeed, all communities larger than small villages (and maybe even these) are "imagined communities"—that is, entities that exist in people's minds as objects of orientation and affiliation. The emergence of national consciousness in the European nation-states was produced by a conjunction of capitalism, print, and the "fatality of human linguistic diversity" in Anderson's account.[4] Anderson gave special credit to newspapers and novels as instruments of national imagined communities. He also gave emphasis to intellectuals who produced grammars, dictionaries, histories, and high literature in a vernacular language. Creating the idea of a nation entails both elite and popular activity.

With respect to newspapers, Anderson stressed the ceremony of common readership, citing philosopher G. W. F. Hegel's remark that, for modern people, newspapers substitute for morning prayers. Each reader—or "communicant," to use Anderson's word—knows that "the ceremony he performs is being replicated simultaneously by thousands (or millions) of others of whose existence he is confident, yet of whose identity he has not the slightest notion."[5] Of course, newspaper circulations were small until late in the nineteenth century. Multiple, often party-oriented newspapers not only presented the same news from different perspectives but covered different news events altogether. Still, Anderson's claim is arresting, bringing to our attention the ways in which the newspaper became the central prop in a mass ceremony and so part of a kind of performance art that enacts nationhood and national consciousness.

There is all the difference in the world between a community (Anderson's focus) and a public (Habermas's concern). Community tends to imply a common emotional identity, whereas a public implies only a common set of norms for public conversation. Community indicates a feeling of fellowship on the basis of interaction (even if it is mediated or imagined interaction); a public suggests civil interaction around a common political subject even in the absence of fellowship. Where Anderson examined social membership, Habermas looked to criticism of the state in the formation of liberal institutions. Anderson's "imagined communities" have nothing to do with liberalism but instead concern national consciousness; the Habermasian "public sphere" has everything to do with liberalism, both its achievements and its limitations.

Anderson's work promotes a more expansive view of news than Habermas inspires, a recognition of news not as the raw material for rational public discourse but as the public construction of particular images of self, community, and nation. It implies that the study of news should be classified along with other studies of the literary or artistic products of human imagination more than with studies in democratic theory.

Although Habermas inspired many contemporary scholars, the utility of his framework for the history of journalism is constrained in two respects. First, its emphasis on what is common among bourgeois societies ignores the significant differences among them. Increasingly, media scholars are focusing on these differences. Second, his emphasis on the commercialization of the media in the nineteenth century picks up only one part of a two-part development: journalism as an occupational field became professionalized at the same time that it became commercialized as a business enterprise. In the past two centuries, news has become a professionally created and commercially distributed product in most parts of the world. The movement from a party or government press to a commercial press accelerated sharply in the 1830s in the United States, the 1850s in the United Kingdom, and in the 1880s and '90s in Japan. As the press separated itself from political parties and political movements, it grew more driven by commercial considerations and more organized by a set of self-governing professional norms and practices, although these norms and institutions differed from country to country. Parties retained a stronger hold on newspapers in many parts of Europe than in the United States; in China, the former Soviet Union, and eastern Europe, commercialization has taken off only in the past two decades, after several generations of state-controlled news. The journalism of France has been less oriented to reporting, investigating, and scandal-discovering than Anglo-American media, although in France, Latin America, and elsewhere, a growth of investigative journalism has accompanied a rise in "infotainment" journalism in the past decade.[6] Newspaper readership, relatively low and declining in the United States and Canada, has grown in Europe even in the past half century. The circulation of newspapers per capita is nearly three times higher in Japan and the Scandinavian countries than in the United States, Canada, France, or Belgium. The United Kingdom has a thriving tabloid sector, but the United States, Italy, France, and the Netherlands do not.[7]

With all this variability, global terms like "the public sphere" and "refeudalization" (or "imagined community," for that matter) are not going to be enough to explain the local terrain of media history. Habermas drew attention, both normatively and empirically, to the central issue of commercialization. What is commercialization and what are its consequences? The profit motive can have terrible consequences, as Habermas emphasized, but it is one of the forces powerful enough to push people ahead in the face of risk, tyranny, and physical and moral hazard. What, then, are the costs and benefits of commercialization, and how has it varied across national traditions?

The same questions should be asked of commercialization's parallel development, professionalization. This process included the differentiation of journalism as a distinct occupation with its own norms and traditions and, depending on the time and place, some degree of autonomy from parties and publishers. How has this process varied across nations? What have been its sources? What have been its consequences?

The primary institutional and cultural features of contemporary news have a relatively brief history—400 years at the outside. People have been paid to write true stories about current events and to publish them on a regular basis only for about 250 years and, in many places, for more like 150 years. This occupational group has had a normative commitment to writing political news to inform citizens and to make democracy work only since the emergence of contemporary democracies (roughly two centuries ago). The idea that these journalists should try to write news in a nonpartisan and professional manner is a development barely a century old. All of these features of contemporary journalism take a different shape in different national traditions. This chapter focuses on the history of news in the United States, while remarking, where relevant, on its differences from the history in other countries. The upcoming discussion will call attention to the two master trends—commercialization and professionalization—that have deeply affected the American and most other experiences of news around the globe.

THE EMERGENCE OF NEWS

In colonial America, printers were businessmen first, not journalists. They pretty much invented the newspaper as they went along, amid efforts to make money by selling stationery;

printing wedding announcements; running the post office; or even selling chocolate, tea, snuff, rum, beaver hats, patent medicines, and musical instruments from their print shops. Their newspapers were four-page weekly journals initially designed to advertise their printing businesses. Their contents, after a time, tended toward a common model: an assortment of local advertising, occasional small paragraphs of local gossip, and large chunks of European political and economic intelligence taken directly from London newspapers. Political news of other colonies rarely appeared, and local political news was nearly nonexistent. Printers understood themselves to be small tradesmen, not learned professionals. They did not at first imagine their newspapers to be either political instruments or professional agencies of newsgathering. None of the early papers reached out to collect news; they printed what came to them.

In the first half century of American journalism, from around 1690 to the 1760s, little indicated that the newspaper would become a central forum for political discourse. Colonial printers avoided controversy, preached the printer's neutrality, and printed primarily foreign news because it afforded local readers and local authorities no grounds for grumbling. The preponderance of foreign news was overwhelming. Out of a sample of nineteen hundred items that Benjamin Franklin's *Pennsylvania Gazette* printed from 1728 to 1765, for example, only 6 percent touched on politics in Philadelphia or Pennsylvania.[8]

The ordinary colonial newspaper stayed very far from politics, in other words. When it did report politics, it stayed as far away as possible from politics close to home. Newspaper proprietors who attacked the royal governor or the colonial legislature were likely to find themselves indicted for seditious libel. Eighteenth-century colonial Americans had a very strong sense of government as a precious and precarious entity that could be mortally wounded by angry words in a newspaper. Everything the founders knew of history taught them that republican governments were fractious and transitory. If social habit and custom could not keep people obedient, political order could quickly break down.

As conflict with Britain heated up after 1765, politics entered the press and "printerly fairness" went by the board. It became more troublesome for printers to be neutral than to be partisan; nearly everyone felt compelled to take sides. Print shops became hives of political activity. In the late seventeenth and early eighteenth centuries, colonial politics had been relatively private. When an occasional pamphlet took up a political issue, it addressed itself to the colonial assembly, not the general population. Pamphleteers began political campaigning more actively in the 1740s in New York City, Philadelphia, and Boston, but pamphlet publication reached its peak later, especially with Thomas Paine's *Common Sense* in 1776. Whereas the typical pamphlet was printed once or twice in editions of a few thousand, *Common Sense* sold an estimated 150,000 copies and was reprinted in newspapers up and down the Atlantic coast. Paine, like other professional pamphleteers of his generation, addressed the general populace, but he extended and perfected the practice, dropping esoteric classical references for familiar biblical ones and seeking a less formal language.

In the same era, the American newspaper began its long career as the mouthpiece of political parties and factions. Patriots had no tolerance for the pro-British press, and the new states passed and enforced treason and sedition statutes in the 1770s and 1780s. By the time of the state-by-state debates over ratification of the Constitution in 1787–88, Federalists (those who supported a strong national government) dominated the press and squeezed the opposing Anti-Federalists out of public debate. In Pennsylvania, leading papers tended not to report Anti-Federalist speeches at the ratification convention. When unusual newspapers in Philadelphia, New York City, and Boston sought to report views on both sides, Federalists stopped their subscriptions and forced the papers to end their attempt at evenhandedness.[9]

Some of the nation's founders believed that outspoken political criticism had been well justified when they were fighting a monarchy for their independence. But open critique of a duly elected republican government, they felt, could be legitimately curtailed. Samuel Adams, for instance, the famed Boston agitator in the struggle for independence, changed his views on political action once republican government was established. This great advocate of open talk, committees of correspondence, an outspoken press, and voluntary associations of citizens now opposed all hint of public associations and public criticism that operated outside the regular channels of government.[10] As one contemporary observed, it did no harm for writers to mislead the people when the people were powerless, but "to mislead the judgement of the people, where they have all power, must produce the greatest possible mischief."[11] The Sedition Act of 1798 forbade criticism of the government, making it a criminal offense to print "any false, scandalous and malicious writing . . . against the government of the United States." As many as one out of every four editors of opposition papers was brought up on charges under this law. But this went further than many Americans of the day could stomach. Federalist propaganda notwithstanding, Thomas Jefferson won the presidency in 1800, the Sedition Act expired, and party opposition began to be grudgingly accepted. Only at that point did the famous 1791 First Amendment declaration that "Congress shall make no law abridging freedom of speech, or of the press" begin to accrue a legal tradition consistent with the broad protections of its language. Until then, it could be argued, the First Amendment was more a protection of states' rights than of the rights of individuals or the press. Only the federal Congress, not the state governments, was prohibited by it from abridging freedom of speech and of the press.

IN THE FIRST DECADES of the new nation, newspapers were identified with the editorial voice. Intensely partisan, newspapers were frequently founded as weapons for party or faction, like Alexander Hamilton's *New York Evening Post*, begun in 1801 to recoup Federalist power after the loss of the presidency to Jefferson. Jefferson, well remembered for his statement in 1787 that he would prefer newspapers without a government to a government without newspapers, was, as president, a prime target for the vituperation of the Federalist press. So it is not surprising that while president, he wrote more caustically about newspapers, telling a friend in 1807, "The man who never looks into a newspaper is better informed than he who reads them, inasmuch as he who knows nothing is nearer the truth than he whose mind is filled with falsehoods and errors."[12] Editors attacked one another as viciously as they attacked politicians and sometimes carried rivalries into fistfights and duels in the street.

Reporting of news was incidental, unorganized, and obviously subordinated to editorial partisanship. Politicians objected to the other party's papers but still favored the press as a whole. The Postal Acts of 1792 and 1794 established preferential mailing rates for newspapers, including free use of the mails to send copies of a newspaper to other newspapers around the country. From the republic's first days the press was the beneficiary of laws that offered significant subsidies to the newspaper business in order to promote the circulation of political information.

PARTIES, PROFITS, AND THE PRIMACY OF NEWS

In the 1820s, several New York papers began to send small boats out to incoming ships in order to get the London news more quickly. This practice was indicative of a turn toward reporting in newspaper work. But as late as 1833, the largest paper in the country still had a circulation of only forty-five hundred—and that was more than double a typical city paper's reach. The newspaper was distinguishable, by then, from the post office and the print shop, at least in some cases, but was not so easily separable from the party, faction, church, or other organization it served. Journalism was not yet an identifiable occupational path. Few papers hired reporters. A "correspondent" was just that—a friend or acquaintance of the editor whose writing was that of an unpaid amateur.

But like other institutions in Jacksonian America, newspapers were about to undergo a democratic revolution. Beginning with the *New York Sun* in 1833, a new breed of newspaper sought commercial success and a mass readership. Between 1833 and 1835 in New York City, Boston, Baltimore, and Philadelphia, venturesome entrepreneurs began "penny papers," each issue of which sold for a penny rather than six cents. The new papers were hawked on the street by "newsboys" rather than being sold only by subscription or at the newspaper office itself. The penny press aggressively sought out local news, assigning reporters to cover the courts and even "society." They also actively solicited advertising and engaged in vigorous competition to print the very latest news. Their business-minded assertiveness made penny papers the earliest adapters of new technologies. In 1835, already selling twenty thousand copies a day, the *New York Sun* became the first newspaper in the country to purchase a steam-driven press. Another penny paper, the *Baltimore Sun*, made early use of the telegraph and helped encourage its public acceptance. In the U.S. war with Mexico in 1846, penny papers in New York City and Philadelphia made the first and fullest use of the telegraph. Technology was available, and the competitive news-hungry, circulation-building penny papers made quick use of it. The penny papers brought a broadened, robust sense of what counts as news to American journalism and added dedication to using news to make profits rather than to promote policies or politicians.[13]

The penny papers were at the leading edge of journalistic innovation before the Civil War, but the most widely circulated papers of the time were still country weeklies or other nondailies with local circulations. These papers were invariably boosters of economic development in their own towns and regions. But they would in time face competition from the aggressive journalism of the cities. Horace Greeley, like many other journalists of his day, began his career on a small-town weekly. He moved from Vermont to Pennsylvania to what was already becoming journalism's mecca, New York City. There he first issued a literary magazine, then ran the Whig Party's campaign newspaper, and finally in 1841 began a penny paper of his own, the *New York Tribune*. The *Tribune* became one of the most influential papers of the mid-nineteenth century. Although it never rivaled the circulation of the *New York Herald*, James Gordon Bennett's penny paper, its weekly edition established a significant circulation beyond New York City. It was widely known in rural communities throughout New York State, New England, and the West.

The pluralism of American society was reflected in the press. The German-language press flourished in the antebellum years, when Germans represented a quarter of the country's foreign-born citizens. In 1828, the *Cherokee Phoenix* began as the first Native American newspaper, published in both English and Cherokee. The African American press began with *Freedom's Journal* in New York City in 1827. Former slave Frederick Douglass began the *North Star* in Rochester, New York, in 1847. African American–run papers before the Civil War participated in the abolitionist movement, to which William Lloyd Garrison and his Boston-based *Liberator*, first published in 1831, contributed prominently. The abolitionist press served as a vital part of a growing social movement.

In the conventional daily press, news gathering became the papers' central function. As late as 1846 only Baltimore and Washington, D.C.–based papers assigned special correspondents to cover Congress. But as politics heated up in the 1850s, more than fifty papers hired Washington correspondents. The correspondents typically wrote for a half-dozen or more papers and earned further salary as clerks for congressional committees or speechwriters for the politicians they were covering.

They often lived at the same boardinghouses as did members of Congress, and the boardinghouses tended to divide along party lines.[14] Journalism was only thinly differentiated from politics. Despite the proud, independent, commercial-mindedness of the penny papers, it was generally taken for granted for most of the nineteenth century that journals were financially supported by one party or another and dedicated to rousing the party faithful as much as to reporting the news. Not only did parties sponsor newspapers, so did factions of parties and sometimes individual politicians.

But the connection between party and paper began to weaken late in the nineteenth century. After the Civil War, newspapers rapidly expanded as large profitable, industrialized businesses. By 1870, every major daily in New York City had at least a hundred employees. Advertising became a more central source of income, and new advertisers, notably the urban department stores, became a major source of advertising revenue.

Competition for news grew intense. So did competition for readers, with new campaigns and stunts to promote circulation and court new audiences, particularly women. Crowd-pleasing features such as simpler language, larger headlines, and more lavish illustrations helped to extend readership to immigrants and others whose knowledge of written English was limited. By 1880, New York City had a half-million foreign-born citizens; a decade later, 40 percent of the city's population was foreign born. Economic changes made a new mass journalism possible, the prospect of profit made it desirable, and the changing populations of the cities made it necessary in the eyes of publishers.

The most celebrated publishers of mass-circulation dailies were Joseph Pulitzer, an immigrant himself, of the *New York*

World and William Randolph Hearst of the *New York Journal.* Pulitzer pioneered most of the new crowd-pleasing developments when he entered into New York journalism in the 1880s. When Hearst arrived in 1895, he quickly introduced pages of comics, sensational news coverage, and a self-promoting crusading spirit to the faltering *Journal.* Several hundred thousand people read Hearst's paper as he battled Pulitzer for the biggest circulation among the city's population. Hearst, followed somewhat more gingerly by Pulitzer, pushed for a war with Spain and sent correspondents to Cuba to cover the developing crisis there. Coverage of the Spanish-American War was a high-water mark of sensationalism. Still, the common view that yellow journalism "caused" the war owes a lot to Hearst's delight at receiving credit for the war. Many other leading papers, including those with the greatest influence in elite circles, opposed U.S. involvement.

The pull of dollars toward sensationalism helped move newspapers away from the political parties. So, too, did a growing reform movement that questioned the worth of parties altogether. In the 1870s and 1880s, liberal reformers began to criticize the very notion of party loyalty, first among Republicans and then among Democrats. They promoted new forms of political campaigning, urging an educational rather than participatory or "spectacular" campaign. They demanded a change from parades to pamphlets and urged voters to make a rational choice among candidates, parties, and policies rather than to demonstrate emotional allegiance to a party label. Newspapers became more willing to take an independent stand. By 1890, a quarter of daily newspapers in the North, where antiparty reforms were most advanced, claimed to be independent of any party.[15]

As late as the 1890s a standard Republican paper that covered a presidential election not only would deplore and deride Democratic candidates, but very often it would simply neglect to mention them. In the days before public opinion polling, the size of partisan rallies was taken as a sign of likely electoral results. Republican rallies would be described in Republican newspapers as "monster meetings" while Democratic rallies often were not covered at all. And for Democratic papers, it was just the reverse. Partisanship ran deep in nineteenth-century American journalism, and into the twentieth century objectivity was far from an established practice or ideal.

Still, several factors would soon bring it to the fore. First, antiparty reforms loosened the hold of parties on the press. Second, reporters came to enjoy a culture of their own, independent of political parties. They developed their own mythologies (reveling in their intimacy with the urban underworld), their own clubs and watering holes, and their own professional practices. Reporters' status, income, and esprit de corps rose at the end of the century. Popular acclaim for dashing reporters and their exploits—Elizabeth Cochrane's going around the world in eighty days (under the alias Nellie Bly), Henry Morton Stanley's finding ailing explorer David Livingstone in Africa, the handsome Richard Harding Davis's reporting on war and football— added to the appeal of the field.

Third, the work of reporting increasingly developed practices, routines, and disciplines that identified journalism as a distinct occupation with its own patterns of behavior. Interviewing, all but unknown in 1865, was widely adopted by 1900. By World War I, it was the mainstay of American journalism, although it was still rare in Europe. Its rapid diffusion among American journalists seems to have been unaccompanied by an ideological rationale. It fit effortlessly into a journalism that was already fact-centered and news-centered rather than devoted primarily to political commentary or preoccupied with literary aspirations.

The growing corporate coherence of journalists generated social cohesion and occupational pride, on the one hand, and internal social control, on the other. By the 1920s, this pattern produced a self-conscious professionalism and ethic of objectivity.[16] Journalists began to articulate rules of the journalistic road. The general manager of the Associated Press News Wire, Kent Cooper, announced his creed in 1925: "The journalist who deals in facts diligently developed and intelligently presented exalts his profession, and his stories need never be colorless or dull."[17] Newspaper editors formed their first nationwide professional association, the American Society of Newspaper Editors, in 1922–23. At their opening convention, they adopted the "Canons of Journalism," a code of ethics that included a principle of "Sincerity, Truthfulness, [and] Accuracy" and another of "Impartiality," which included the declaration "News reports should be free from opinion or bias of any kind."[18]

This newly articulated doctrine was related to the sheer growth in news gathering. Rules of objectivity enabled editors to keep lowly reporters in check, although they had less control over foreign correspondents. The ideology of objectivity was a kind of industrial discipline. At the same time, objectivity seemed a natural and progressive ideology for an aspiring occupational group at a moment when science was God, efficiency was cherished, and increasingly prominent elites judged partisanship a vestige of the tribal nineteenth century.[19]

While seeking to affiliate themselves with the prestige of science, efficiency, and Progressive reform, journalists also sought to disaffiliate themselves from the public relations specialists and propagandists who suddenly surrounded them. Journalists had rejected parties only to discover their new-found independence besieged by information mercenaries hired by government, business, politicians, and others. Early in the twentieth century, businesses and government agencies increasingly sought to place favorable stories about themselves in the press. A whole new occupation, public relations specialists or "press agents," emerged and got a boost from President Woodrow Wilson's attempt to use public relations to sell World War I to the American public. The war stimulated popular public relations campaigns for war bonds, the Red Cross, the Salvation Army, and the Young Men's Christian Association (YMCA). One journalism critic noted that by 1920 there were nearly a thousand "bureaus of propaganda" in Washington, D.C., modeled on the war experience. Figures circulated among journalists that 50–60 percent of stories, even in the venerable *New York Times*, were inspired by press agents. The new Pulitzer School of Journalism at Columbia University in New York City was churning out more graduates for the public relations industry than for the newspaper business. Philosopher John Dewey wrote in 1929 that the publicity agent "is perhaps the most significant symbol of our present social life."[20] Parajournalism was born.

Journalists saw how malleable and manipulable information in the propaganda age had become. Suddenly bombarded by parajournalists, they felt a need to close ranks and assert their collective integrity. At this point, objectivity became a fully formulated occupational ideal, part of a professional project or mission. Far more than a set of craft rules to fend off libel suits or a set of constraints to help editors keep tabs on their underlings, objectivity was finally a moral code. It was asserted in the textbooks used in journalism schools and in codes of ethics of professional associations. It was a code of professional honor and a set of rules to give professionals both guidance and cover.

At the moment that journalists claimed "objectivity" as their ideal, they also recognized its limits. In the 1930s, there was a vogue for what contemporaries called interpretive journalism. Leading journalists and journalism educators insisted that the world had grown increasingly complex and needed to be not only reported but explained. Political columnists such as Walter Lippmann, David Lawrence, Frank Kent, and Mark Sullivan came into their own in this era. Journalists insisted that their task was to help readers not only to know but to understand. They took it for granted that this understanding had nothing to do with party or partisan sentiment.

A BROADER VIEW

Some of the sociological conditions that affected journalistic norms and practices in the United States were absent or less pronounced elsewhere. The strong desire of journalists to distinguish themselves from public relations practitioners was absent in Europe, since public relations developed more extensively and influentially in the United States than in Europe. Moreover, the antiparty bent of American political life, intensified in the Progressive Era, went further than efforts to contain party corruption in Europe. In the United States, a civil service tradition had to be invented, and one finally emerged as the result of a political movement. In Europe, on the other hand, a

degree of bureaucratic autonomy, legitimacy, and professionalism could be taken for granted, so there was less cause for European civil servants to ideologize themselves the way American
reformers did. The ideological virtues of a journalistic divorce
from party, so readily portrayed against this American background of political reform, had no comparable political ballast
in European journalism.

To come at the comparative question from a different angle, it
may also be that the psychological space occupied by "objectivity" as a professional value in American journalism was already
occupied in Europe by a self-understanding among journalists
that they were high literary creators and cosmopolitan political thinkers. European journalists did not share the American
down-and-dirty self-image as laborers whose standing in the
world required upgrading. If there was to be upgrading, in any
event, for the Europeans it was to a literary rather than a professional ideal.

Media historian Jean Chalaby went so far as to observe that
journalism is an "Anglo-American invention." British and
American journalism became information- and fact-centered
in the mid-nineteenth century, but French journalism did not.
Until late in the century, when leading British and American
newspapers employed numerous foreign correspondents, the
French press drew most of its foreign news straight from the
London papers. The French were much less concerned with
drawing a line between facts and commentary. Journalism in
France and other continental European countries did not expe-
rience the "unique discursive revolution" that characterized
British and American journalism, and so would not develop an

objective orientation until many decades after the Americans—and, even then, less fully.[21]

This sketch brings us up to about fifty years ago. By the 1950s, at least in the higher reaches of American news organizations, journalists became committed professionals, not political partisans. The triumph of professionalism was neither so early nor so complete in Europe, where journalists were more self-consciously political and ideological. In the United States, however, publishers increasingly left the editorial staff alone to do its work. There is no mistaking the outrage of *Washington Post* publisher Katharine Graham when she recalled how President Lyndon Johnson and later his successor, Richard Nixon, assumed that she herself determined what *Post* reporters wrote. When an aide explained to Johnson that Graham did not direct *Post* staffers to write the stories he found so objectionable, he replied, "Well, by God, if I owned a goddamn newspaper, I ought to have some people around me who are going to do what I want." Graham observed, "This is such a classic politician's attitude about a publisher—every politician probably believes publishers sit in their offices doling out orders to reporters about what to write when."[22] Johnson did not understand that the genius of American journalism is the symbiosis of professionalism and commercial organization, not the subordination of the former to the latter.

In this first full flowering of journalistic professionalism, from World War II into the 1960s, journalists seemed to be at once "independent, disinterested, public-spirited, and trusted and beloved by everyone, from the corridors of power around the world to the ordinary citizen and consumer."[23] The rakish self-image of the urban journalist gave way to a buttoned-down image of the White House correspondent, one who might even give occasional political counsel to an aspiring senator or presidential candidate.[24]

It was not quite so clean as such images suggest. Vestiges remained of the bad old days, when publishers actively directed or censored reporters and favors were liberally exchanged between reporters and their sources. News about women, blacks, and others outside the narrow vision of the establishment press continued to be neglected. Liberals in the 1950s decried the "one-party press," pointing out that the vast majority of newspapers that endorsed presidential candidates supported Republican Dwight Eisenhower over Democrat Adlai Stevenson in both 1952 and 1956. Still, both Republicans and Democrats rallied behind a cold war consensus in foreign policy, and sociologist Daniel Bell could reasonably posit a coming "end to ideology" in American society as technical solutions were located for problems once regarded as political.[25]

This world of complacent consensus began to change with the explosive civil rights movement and with the inner-city riots of the early 1960s. It changed utterly as the nation became bogged down in a war of uncertain aim on behalf of a notably corrupt government in Vietnam, a country that few Americans could even locate on a map. For journalism, habitual deference to government officials, especially in foreign policy, came to be seen not as professionalism but as occupationally induced laziness, naïveté, or worse. In both Washington, D.C., and Saigon, the capital of South Vietnam and the command center for the U.S. military in the war, reporters became increasingly aware that officials in the field and at the State Department, the White

House, and the Pentagon—their primary sources for news about the war—routinely lied to them. Reporters dubbed the military's daily briefing for the press in Saigon the "Five O'Clock Follies." In Washington, journalists felt mounting distrust of the officials who misled them (and who themselves were sometimes misled by overoptimistic reports from the military authorities in Saigon). These journalists gained growing access to officials, usually lower in the hierarchy, who whispered their own doubts about the prosecution of the war. They watched with increasing alarm and interest as antiwar protests moved from college campuses to tense congressional hearings. At the same time, movement activists developed their own "alternative" media as instruments of oppositional politics—angry, feisty, irreverent, and innovative.

Journalism would never be the same. News organizations that had once cooperated routinely with the government began to see "national security" as a government euphemism for "stay out of my business because I could be embarrassed by publicity, whether it has anything to do with the nation's defense or not." In two dramatic moments, the government and the press faced off. In 1971, the *New York Times* began to publish the "Pentagon Papers," a secret Department of Defense–commissioned history of the Vietnam War. When the Nixon administration went to court to block further publication, the media dodged by passing the baton from one news outlet to the next. The *Washington Post*, the *Boston Globe*, and the *Chicago Tribune* took on the responsibility to publish the Pentagon Papers until they, too, were enjoined by court orders to stop. When the dust cleared, the U.S. Supreme Court found that the newspapers had been within their rights. The establishment press instantly became a hero of the antiwar movement and of First Amendment activists.

The second complacency-shaking episode, of course, was Watergate. This time the *Washington Post* was out in front, sometimes in lonely isolation. *Post* reporters pressed to uncover the story behind the story of why burglars with a shadowy connection to President Nixon's reelection campaign had broken into the Democratic National Committee headquarters in the thick of the 1972 campaign. In the end, one high-level White House official after another was marched off to prison, and President Nixon, after two years of denying any knowledge of the burglary or of the attempt to cover it up, resigned in disgrace. Tape recordings of his Oval Office conversations made it perfectly clear that he had been involved in the crime of obstruction of justice through his cover-up efforts from the beginning.[26]

Vietnam, the Pentagon Papers, and Watergate electrified journalism and utterly changed the field. *Washington Post* editorial page editor Meg Greenfield recalled that the generation of journalists that reigned in the 1940s and 1950s was "more obliging to its government sources, much more willing to keep its secrets, and much more involved in its actual policymaking than it ever should have been—and than the successor generation in Washington today would dream of being."[27] Journalists and those they covered in government had shared in a sense of common purpose in both World War II and the cold war; after Vietnam it would never be the same, not even after September 11, 2001.

Chapter Five
IN RECENT MEMORY: NEWS FROM WATERGATE TO THE WEB

HISTORY KEEPS HAPPENING, and the media keep changing. If a major effort of the sociology of journalism is to explain why news is the way it is, a concurrent effort seeks to understand why news changes. Our explanation of the news cannot preclude that it changes.

In the decades between Watergate and the Internet's liberation of written texts from paper, revolutionizing both the production and consumption of news, news changed in important ways. Two themes dominated criticism of the changes. First, when observers looked at the media's role in politics, they saw political reporting as increasingly and dangerously critical, even cynical, and tending to promote cynicism in the audience. Second, many critics viewed the product of news institutions as "soft news" or "infotainment," a concoction governed more by entertainment values than news judgment. Sometimes referred to as tabloidization, this was decried as an intrusion of marketplace values into the professionalism of journalists.

Both of these claims have merit. Media scholar Thomas E. Patterson documented trends in soft news. Soft news—which he defined as stories with no evident connection to policy issues—rose from 35 percent of all stories in 1980 to 50 percent by

1998, based on a sample of more than five thousand news stories from two television networks, two newsmagazines, three leading national newspapers, and twenty-six local dailies. In the same two decades, Patterson found, there was an increase in sensationalism, human-interest reporting, and crime and disaster news.[1]

Patterson also traced changes in news that might be judged cynical. In 1980, 25 percent of the press coverage of presidential candidates was negative; by 2000, it was over 60 percent negative. From Jimmy Carter on, each president has received progressively more negative coverage. At the same time, trust in government and trust in the honesty of politicians has declined. Patterson sees a causal relationship: "Negative news has weakened Americans' attachment to politics."[2]

But should these trends be presented, as they normally are, as grounds for complaint and concern? Or could they also be understood as an opening to an improved journalism? Can "cynicism" be read as brave critique? Can the trend toward soft news be seen not as a submission to market forces but as an expansion of an overly narrow, rigid definition of news to encompass a wider range of important topics? Let us reserve judgment, and try to understand the trends before trashing them.

TOWARD CYNICISM AND INFOTAINMENT

Anxiety about the news responds to the sense that a system once governed by professionalism and conscientious news values is being corrupted by an entertainment complex. This trend is all the more alarming because of the sense that it is happening at a time when the news media are more and more central to the way we govern ourselves. As political parties weaken, the news media fill the vacuum left behind; as politicians reduce their deference to established legislative hierarchies and routines, they lean more and more on publicity as the best path to their goals. I take up these matters in chapter 8 because they take us outside the news as such and into changing interinstitutional relations. Here it is best to focus on the changes in news reporting itself.

In his book *Out of Order*, as in his "Doing Well and Doing Good" research report cited above, political scientist Thomas E. Patterson made a strong case that cynicism in political reporting has grown, arguing that the press has developed an "antipolitics bias."[3] Three of his points seem especially telling. First, he finds that news weeklies from 1960 to 1992 increasingly reported bad news rather than good. In 1960, 75 percent of evaluative references to presidential candidates John Kennedy and Richard Nixon were positive; in 1992, only 40 percent of evaluative references praised Bill Clinton or George Bush.[4]

Second, journalists leave the impression that politicians will promise anything to get elected. They neglect to mention the political science studies that show that politicians generally work hard for and make good on their campaign pledges. This biased reporting is not in itself new: when political scientist and writer Edward Jay Epstein interviewed network television journalists in 1968 and 1969, he found that almost all of them had contempt for politicians and that they invariably attributed any act by an elected official to the ultimate motive of winning elections.[5] Patterson's data indicate that this underlying assumption has increasingly found its way into patterns of news prose.

Patterson's third point is that journalists see political careers as more oriented to politics as a game than to politics as policy.

The "game schema" that reporters create directs attention to conflicts and to a few individuals, not to social conditions and the larger interests that individuals may represent. Take, as a simple example, the lead story in the *New York Times* for June 15, 2001. It reported that the Senate passed a bill to require annual testing of student achievement in public schools. Because this appeared to be a significant innovation in educational policy, the question of whether annual testing would help or hurt schoolchildren or have no impact was important. However, it received not even passing notice until the final four paragraphs of a thirty-two-paragraph article. What the reporter focused on, instead, was clear from the opening sentence: "In a victory for President Bush, the Senate today overwhelmingly passed a bill to require annual school testing and penalize failing schools if they do not improve."[6]

The tendency of reporters to emphasize the game rather than the policy implications has increased over time. Patterson finds, for instance, that journalists have shifted from reporting candidates' speeches to reporting the strategic moves behind them (often saying little about the speeches themselves). From 1960 to 1992, Patterson found, there was a progressive increase in the proportion of *New York Times* political stories that emphasized a "game" framework rather than a "policy" one.[7]

As for the plunge of journalism into the entertainment business, this is an old complaint, going back to the charges of sensationalism hurled at penny papers in the 1830s and to the steady stream of complaints about mass-oriented, profit-minded newspapers since the 1890s. In the first years of its existence, TV news was so limited and low profile that it did not provoke this kind of attack, but when local stations in the 1970s figured out that news could be cheaply produced and yield large audiences, the trend toward entertainment-oriented news programming became manifest. The trend toward soft news in both print and broadcast journalism has only accelerated over the past few decades. A 1998 study produced by the Committee of Concerned Journalists found deterioration in the coverage of complex issues on television and in newspapers and newsmagazines between 1977 and 1997, with a declining attention to policy issues and an increasing attention to lifestyle, entertainment, and scandal. Even when politics remained the subject, the approach was increasingly "featurized and people-oriented."[8] Personnel move back and forth between TV news programs and the tabloids, and tabloid TV production techniques were adopted by legitimate news programs.

Twenty-five years ago, early signs of the trend toward soft and critical news were sometimes attributed not to large market forces but rather to a stylistic innovation in campaign reporting traced back to one individual, Theodore "Teddy" White. White was a veteran journalist who wrote a best-selling book about the 1960 presidential election. *The Making of the President, 1960* took readers behind the scenes of the campaign and showed the strategizing of the candidates, campaign aides, party officials, and consultants.[9] Readers saw how politics dealt not just in policies but in egos, not just in rhetoric for the ages but in the nitty-gritty, day-to-day grind of the campaign machinery. Editors literally handed White's book to their reporters as a model of how to cover campaigns.[10]

White himself would come to rue the trend identified with him. In 1972, covering George McGovern's hapless campaign for the White House, he told another reporter, "We're all sitting there watching him work on his acceptance speech, poor bastard. He tries to go into the bedroom with Fred Dutton to go over the list of Vice Presidents . . . and all of us are observing him, taking notes like mad, getting all the little details. Which I think I invented as a method of reporting and which I now sincerely regret. If you write about this, say that I sincerely regret it. Who gives a fuck if the guy had milk and Total for breakfast?"[11] But candidates' choices for both bed and breakfast became an enduring part of political coverage and opened vast new territories not only for trivia but for scandal.

The trend toward covering politics as scandal and toward opening the private lives of public figures to greater scrutiny reached its pre–Monica Lewinsky zenith in 1987 with coverage of the Democratic presidential candidate Gary Hart of Colorado and his extramarital affairs. His was not the first sex scandal concerning a president or presidential aspirant: others of note concerned presidents Thomas Jefferson, Andrew Jackson, and Grover Cleveland. The modern floodgates, however, opened in 1969 when Senator Edward "Ted" Kennedy drove his car off a bridge on Chappaquiddick Island at Martha's Vineyard in Massachusetts. Mary Jo Kopechne, a young campaign aide riding in the car, drowned. Kennedy left the scene and failed to report the accident for some hours; he never offered a full explanation of what happened. The accident raised serious questions about the senator's character and thereafter prevented him from becoming a viable presidential candidate. The Watergate scandals revealed in 1973 and 1974 involved nearly every kind of discreditable behavior by President Richard Nixon and his closest advisers and campaign aides—*except* scandalous sex. Congressional investigations of the intelligence agencies then retroactively unleashed another set of scandals. Investigations in 1975 brought to light evidence of President John F. Kennedy's White House sexual escapades, including an affair with Judith Campbell (who simultaneously carried on an affair with Sam Giancana, boss of a major organized-crime syndicate). The *Washington Post* ran the Kennedy story in its back pages, and others in the press did not pick it up until political columnist William Safire took it on as "a virtual one-man crusade."[12] Safire was motivated not only by a "good story" but by what would become a years-long effort to demonstrate that Democrats were just as guilty of sordid behavior as was Republican Richard Nixon, for whom Safire had served as a speechwriter before becoming a *New York Times* columnist.

Intrusive coverage of Hart during the 1987 prelude to the presidential primaries was by no means isolated. Yet it had a raw, naked quality, as no previous sex scandal had, and it raised the question, endlessly discussed, of whether the scandalizers in the press were themselves—even more than Hart himself—the real scandal. Should a reporter for the *Miami Herald* have staked out Hart's Washington town house to reveal that he spent the night with a young model, Donna Rice? Were rumors of Hart's womanizing sufficient grounds for such an invasion of his privacy?

Despite the stakeout and the public revelation of his affair, Hart continued in the next few days in his quest for the presidency. His campaign began to unravel, however, at a press conference in New Hampshire, where the *Washington Post* reporter covering the Hart campaign, Paul Taylor, asked an electrifying question. Taylor had been pondering not only the *Miami Herald*'s revelations but also a subsequent speech Hart gave to the American Newspaper Publishers Association in which he talked about the high moral standards of both his public and his private conduct. With that in mind, Taylor came to a small lounge at the Hanover Inn on the Dartmouth College campus, where 150 journalists crowded together to question Hart. When Hart called on him, Taylor asked, "When you said you did nothing immoral, did you mean that you had no sexual relationship with Donna Rice last weekend or at any other time you were with her?" Hart answered, "That is correct, that's correct." Taylor persisted: "Do you believe that adultery is immoral?" "Yes," Hart replied. Taylor asked, "Have you ever committed adultery?" Hart sidestepped the question but not before suggesting that the fairness of our system for electing presidents was in greater jeopardy than his marriage.[13]

But that question torpedoed Hart's campaign for the presidency and sent the world of journalism into a self-criticizing tailspin. It was a moment of drama and intense pain, Taylor recalled: "Hart was standing no more than six feet from me, with no lectern or podium or stage separating us. We both had trouble keeping our voices from breaking, and neither of us spoke much above a whisper."[14] For Taylor, who defended his question in the ongoing controversy in the press, it was nonetheless a deeply troubling moment. "Here I was, a child of the live-and-let-live 1960s, trying to force a presidential candidate to tell me how he had spent his private moments."[15] He had no idea that he (along with the *Miami Herald*) would unleash such a wave of revulsion at the press. The news media were no longer ringside but in the ring.

Criticism of the entertainment-oriented press complained of "sensationalism" in the nineteenth century, of "yellow journalism" at the turn of the century, and of "tabloid news" or "jazz journalism" in the 1920s. In the 1990s, a whole series of new terms emerged, such as "infotainment" and "tabloidization." Although this language began in the United States, within a few years it had spread elsewhere. In the United Kingdom, these terms focus on print rather than broadcasting; in Germany the term *Boulevardisierung* has been applied primarily to television.[16] German tabloidization in any form is relatively recent and modest. As was noted in the German newsmagazine *Stern*, "If [a member of the parliament] is caught with a lady in unambiguous circumstances, one laughs but does not print it. We are not in England after all."[17]

The most famous tabloid traditions are the American and the British, although they developed in very different ways. The British tabloids began a century ago, and their descendants are in many instances still going strong. The American tabloids, or "picture newspapers," as they were known when first introduced in the 1920s, faded fairly quickly, losing their mass audience to radio; in the United Kingdom, the more high-minded BBC did not compete with the tabloid press. The American supermarket tabloids, unlike the British mass press, make little effort to cover conventional news; they are devoted almost exclusively to gossipy accounts of celebrities (more often from the world of movies and pop music than from that of politics) and a smattering of health news and UFO sightings.

If the shift to cynicism and infotainment were solely an American story, we would need an explanation in terms of exclusively American developments. If the shift is more widespread, we need to look to cross-national factors. In fact, the shift is global. Reporting styles around the world have grown more informal, more intimate, more critical, and more cynically detached or distanced over the past two generations. Swedish evidence shows that news coverage has grown more critical of politicians over the past thirty years. Jörgen Westerstahl and Folke Johansson looked at broadcast news, including public broadcasting, where market considerations have little direct influence. In the 1940s, 1950s, and as late as 1960, less than 1 percent of the sampled news items contained criticism. By 1972, this had changed dramatically, and by 1980, 25 percent of news items were critical.[18] The Swedish scholars warn against romanticizing earlier journalism—traditional journalism "does not stand out as an ideal: the role of the media is reduced to that of a megaphone, amplifying the voices of the dominant actors in society."[19] British television interviewing changed from a formal and deferential approach to politicians to a more aggressive and critical style that makes politicians more visibly and immediately answerable to the public.[20] Japanese broadcasting changed similarly when TV Asahi, a commercial channel, challenged the dominance of state-supported NHK. In 1985, TV Asahi launched "News Station" with the very popular radio and TV host as its maestro, Kume Hiroshi. Hiroshi read the news scripts provided to him by the program's journalists, but he then responded to them with his own opinions. "I'm not a newscaster," he said, "I'm a representative of the viewer." As political scientist Ellis Krauss put it, Hiroshi's "alienated cynicism and critical stance toward society and government" appears to have charmed a younger, more urban, and more alienated generation.[21] His style moved toward a type of politics "more cynical and populist" than the old bureaucratic conservatism, but one that "offers little in the way of the framing of real political alternatives." Norway's most popular newspaper, *Verdens*

Gang adopted the melodramatic framework of tabloid journalism, in which "politicians . . . become human beings, while the voters become customers."[22] Meanwhile, a new investigative aggressiveness emerged in Latin American journalism. In Brazil, Argentina, and Peru, revelations of government scandals emerge not from old-fashioned partisan journalism but from a new, more entertainment-oriented journalism that adopts stock narratives and a personality-focused, moralizing style like that in the Latin American soap opera, the *telenovela*. Perhaps this contributes to a public accountability of the political order, but it is also possible that it arises from and reinforces cultural pessimism.[23]

There is something at work here consistent with what Dutch media scholar Liesbet van Zoonen calls the "intimization" of the news.[24] It is also a part of the modern feminist consciousness. Paul Taylor, among others, made this observation about his Gary Hart "adultery" question. He quoted Suzannah Lessard of the *New Yorker*: "A feminist sensibility has seeped into public consciousness sufficiently to make philandering appear to many at best unattractive, maybe unacceptable, and possibly even alarming where the candidate's emotions and psychology are concerned."[25]

Many factors contribute to the changing sensibility of political news, including economic changes wrought by cable television, cultural changes that have accompanied increasing ethnic and gender diversity in the workplace, and political changes in response to Watergate and the women's movement. In the United States, several of these factors were jointly at work in the saturation coverage witnessed during the Bill Clinton–Monica Lewinsky scandal. Monicagate was unleashed by the special prosecutor's office, which was created by the Ethics in Government Act of 1978, which itself was part of the legislative legacy of Watergate. The Monica story also depended on the media's overlearning of a Watergate lesson: that where there's smoke, there's fire. This mentality has long been visible in leading news outlets. The *New York Times* for years relentlessly promoted the Whitewater story, which involved allegations that President Clinton and his wife, Hillary Clinton, had knowingly been involved in a fraudulent real estate deal in Arkansas. The *Washington Post* and the *New York Times* repeatedly wrote editorials in favor of pursuing the impeachment inquiry that arose out of Monicagate. Finally, Monicagate depended on the erosion of a distinction between public and private that once was widely accepted. This, in turn, is a result of a variety of other factors, first and foremost the successful entrance of a feminist agenda onto the political scene. Feminists took as their watchword in the early 1970s that "the personal is political." From the politics of the bedroom to the politics of washing dishes or caring for children within families to gender discrimination in hiring and promotion, sexual harassment, rape and public safety, and many other issues, women made the case that there are political and public policy dimensions to matters once deemed entirely private.

The conditions that made Monicagate possible, then, included the institutionalization of high standards for government ethics alongside new operations to root out government corruption; aggressive investigative journalism; and the recognition that domains once considered part of private life have public dimensions and public implications. In other words, three developments one might well judge as improvements in public life contributed centrally to one of the most sordid episodes of modern media culture. What are we to make of this?

We have a politics of scandal today because democracy and the media put before us the scandal of politics. Politics—especially democratic down-in-the-dirt and out-on-the-stump politics—has long been viewed as unseemly. It was beneath the dignity of most of the founders of the American republic to solicit votes. In the eighteenth century, a man serious enough to serve in office would "stand" for office, not "run" for it, and such a gentleman would consider political office as part-time, temporary work. Most elections in colonial days were uncontested; local elites determined by word of mouth who should serve, and generally the yeoman voters fell into line. A candidate did not have to display sincerity before the masses or make promises to them—or have these promises tested.

Once a more full-bodied democracy arrived in the nineteenth century, borne on the shoulders of mass-based political parties, enthusiasm for the parties grew hand in hand with a countercurrent of derision and dubiousness about politicians. Distrust of politics became an essential element of U.S. political culture and the driving force behind reform movements from the Progressive movement at the turn of the century to campaign finance reform a century later.[26]

Why are scandals so prominent in the contemporary news media? British sociologist John Thompson has so far offered the most thoughtful and comprehensive analysis, particularly in showing how *not* to understand the topic. Are scandals simply collective shaming rituals that in the end reaffirm society's moral standards? This Durkheimian perspective captures a feature of some scandals, but as Thompson observed, not all:

other scandals reverberate primarily within elite political circles, touching the general public only as distant entertainment. These scandals reaffirm political cynicism, if anything, and not moral values.[27]

Do scandals trivialize public discourse and focus popular attention on incidental matters rather than the economic and political issues that really count? This view is also commonly advanced. The Durkheimian view presents scandals as centrally important to society, even a necessary mechanism of moral regathering; this second view, however, casts scandals as nothing more than distraction, or worse, a major contributor to the demoralization and degeneration of public life. This view of scandals as a distraction fits some kinds of scandals, notably sex scandals, but not others, such as scandals of financial mismanagement, campaign financing, or corruption.

Thompson offered instead what he called a "social theory of scandal," which simply takes scandals to be "struggles over symbolic power in which reputation and trust are at stake."[28] This is not a dramatic claim, but it is the most reasonable one anyone has offered. Thompson's theory implies that reputation and trust are complex social resources and the contest over them delicate. Those reporting scandal can be sullied by their revelations as much as the people whose reputations they seem to wound; this happened to special prosecutor Kenneth Starr in Monicagate and also in some measure to congressional Republicans as a group. The media can profit from reporting scandal, but they can also lose, when their audience finds the reporting unpersuasive, as happened in the end with both Whitewater and Monicagate. But Clinton lost, too, in his legalistic maneuvers to hide his infidelity, and Vice President Al Gore lost as well in his subsequent unwillingness to make use of the adept, charismatic Clinton as a campaigner or to make the successful Clinton record a primary thrust of his campaign in 2000. Even after a scandal has been buried, the smell of putrefaction persists.

Representative democracy is a political system built on distrust of power and the powerful. But politicians in a democracy rely on their reputation and the public's trust. Even a democratic public may long for leaders with charismatic appeal; even in an age of apparent cynicism and disenchantment, people need to see, personified, the ideals for which they want the collective will to stand. Democracies are therefore as vulnerable as other forms of government to the imperfection and corruption of their leaders, and perhaps more so, because the press in democracies can often be aggressive and because a democracy's political leaders are not perceived as distant gods but as elevated versions of the people themselves.

For all of the faults of media, Americans eventually came to have more information, and more credible information, than ever before. Twenty years after Watergate, people had unprecedented access to careful, conscientious, analytically sound, crisply presented information about national and world affairs. Local news was never very good, and remains so, but the quality of national news, on the other hand, has improved. Elites gained access to especially rich information. Twenty-four percent of college graduates "sometimes" listened to news from National Public Radio (NPR); there was no NPR before 1970. Twenty-eight percent of college graduates "sometimes" watched the cable channel C-SPAN, which televises the proceedings of Congress; there was no C-SPAN until 1979. Some two-thirds of college graduates "sometimes" watched CNN, which did not exist until 1980. Half of college graduates "sometimes" read the *Wall Street Journal*, the *New York Times*, or *USA Today*; the *Times* did not have national distribution until the 1970s, and *USA Today* began publishing only in 1982.[29] The news grew more cynical, more infotainment-oriented, and at the same time, more comprehensive and credible. Three underlying trends in journalism help account for these developments: growing professional interventionism, increasing narrative or thematic coherence in news reporting, and an increasing interinstitutional news consensus.

As discussed in the last chapter, journalism experienced a growth in professionalism in the past century. The ties between news institutions and parties weakened near the end of the nineteenth century, and with more and more news institutions run by corporations rather than by egomaniacal capitalist adventurers, the use of the press to advance the political interests of an individual, faction, or party was reduced. Reporters and editors have since taken on greater autonomy vis-à-vis their publication's owners and their own sources, and they are less likely to defer to official authority than they were even a generation ago. The professionalism of the 1940s and 1950s was a complacent sort, and journalist insiders were all too comfortable reporting exactly what high-level government officials told them, even when the journalists had good reason to know the officials were lying. Vietnam changed that, and on its heels, Watergate provided the most visible seal of approval on journalistic distrust of government. There is always a tendency for members of the press to revert to the comfort of being friendly insiders, and with a growing sense among leading journalists by the late 1970s that a Watergate-crazed journalism had become too critical, too cynical, and too scandal-happy, the media were eager for a honeymoon with government during the Ronald Reagan presidency. However, many journalists came to feel manipulated by Reagan's photo opportunities and his successor George H. W. Bush's cynical flag-waving victory over Democratic candidate Michael Dukakis. This sentiment contributed to a heightened self-consciousness about the possibilities and pitfalls of journalism.

Whether journalists are manipulated or manipulators (and of course they are both), they take pride in their professionalism and, when possible, exercise their own judgment about what news to cover and how to cover it. One sign of their confidence in their own autonomy and their own legitimacy as professional political analysts is the shrinking of the sound bite in television news. In national network coverage of elections, the average length of time a candidate spoke uninterrupted on camera was 43 seconds in 1968; by 1988, it was 9 seconds. This trend has generally been understood to mean that television news has grown more trivial. That was not the conclusion of communication scholar Daniel Hallin, however, who did some of the original research regarding sound bites.[30] His conclusion was simply that TV news had become more "mediated," that is, that journalists intervened with growing frequency in order to provide a compact and dramatic story. What did this mean for the overall quality of television news? Hallin found an increase in "horse race" coverage from 1968 to 1988—a measure of the growing "game" or "strategy" orientation that others have criticized. In this sense, he confirmed everyone's worst fears. But he also found an increase in the coverage of "issues," showing that television news is doing exactly what the media critics think it should be doing. How can both kinds of coverage increase at the same time? The answer is that TV journalists offer a "more highly structured, thematic" story.[31] There is less wasted motion, less silence, and more rapid-fire editing.

As professionalism in broadcast news manifested itself in shorter sound bites, professionalism in print produced longer stories. In 1964, according to a study of news in ten major daily papers, on average only one front-section story a day ran twenty inches long or longer; in 1999, there were three; in 1964, there were typically thirty-six front-section stories less than six inches long, and in 1999, there were only thirteen. Local, national, and international news represented only 24 percent of the news in 1999's papers, as opposed to 35 percent in 1964's, but the total space devoted to news doubled during that period, making the amount of news in the daily papers in 1999 significantly greater than it was in the early 1960s.[32]

When journalists believe themselves legitimately empowered to frame news according to their own best judgments, they produce more thematically coherent news narratives. Media critic Paul Weaver has observed that television news is more inclined to "tell a story" than is newspaper news. Both TV and newspaper news are "essentially melodramatic accounts of current events," Weaver wrote.[33] But TV news is more tightly structured than newspaper stories, which still have an inverted pyramid structure in which the news account ends with a whimper, not a bang. The newspaper story has no teleological drive to wrap things up; in fact, after the opening paragraph or "lead," which can be read as a complete capsule story in itself, the rest of the story may be presented in very loose and only semicoherent order. The newspaper story is designed not to be read in its entirety, whereas the TV story is meant to achieve its significance only as a full and finished piece that keeps the viewer attuned throughout. The newspaper story may confine itself to reporting an event, uninflected by any effort to give it meaning or analysis. The TV story, in contrast, "inevitably . . . goes into, beneath or beyond the ostensive event to fix upon something else—a process, mood, trend, condition, irony, relationship, or whatever else seems a suitable theme in the circumstances."[34]

Thematic television news stories are unsatisfying in an age suspicious of grand narratives and one in which the cold war no longer provides a default narrative frame. So news institutions work overtime to put what they print into some kind of coherent analytic framework. Very often, this means putting the news into historical perspective. Where we do not have master narratives, we at least have some residual faith in the coherence of chronology. There is an increase, not a decrease, in news institutions' framing of current events in historical terms.[35]

By the 1990s news institutions were paying more attention to one other than ever before. The stories one read in one publication were more likely to bear a strong resemblance to the stories in the next publication than in the past. A century ago, competing newspapers in the same city featured front-page stories that their rivals did not even carry in the back pages. There was little urgency in journalism about coming up with "the" picture of that day's reality. But by the 1990s news institutions monitored one another all the time and across the divide between print and television. CNN became a permanent presence in the newsrooms of daily newspapers with the first Gulf War. Newsrooms kept CNN on "and it has stayed on ever since, changing the consciousness of the people who put out newspapers."[36] By 2000, newsmagazines and newspapers previewed their next editions on websites that reporters and editors at other news institutions could examine as soon as available. Newspapers advertised the next day's stories on cable news stations. The result is interinstitutional news coherence.

One consequence of this practice is that journalists not only know what is going on in other media outlets but also—and this is "the CNN effect"—they assume their audiences do, too. This assumption may be wrong, media analyst Tom Rosenstiel has suggested. Most Americans are not watching "all the news, all the time.³⁷ Still, the assumption leads reporters to push ever more insistently toward writing news with greater punch, more "attitude," and more evident interpretation, since they tend to assume that their readers already know the basics of the story from TV. Literary and film critics have talked of intertextuality for a long time. Now news intertextuality is reality, not an accidental outcome of wars that draw reporters to the same hotel or of power centers that draw them to the same bars in a capital city. News is a widely distributed, seamless intertext.

This situation is in part a result of the domination of the news system by television. Weaver contended that because TV journalism insists on thematic coherence, it "gives credence to the idea that there exists in America a single, coherent national agenda which can be perceived as such by any reasonable and well-intentioned person."³⁸ This idea intensified with national news distribution (via the *New York Times* News Service, CNN, *USA Today*, NPR, and others) and with the growing importance of news from Washington, D.C., since the Kennedy administration. The Vietnam War created modern television news as nothing else had before it. Since Vietnam, even more news comes from Washington. Various factors contribute to the primacy of the nation's capital in setting the news agenda: the growing role of the federal government in everyday life, the growing celebrity of national television journalists, the improved technological capacity of satellite-borne television signals, and the growing corporatization of the press. More newspapers are owned and run by outsiders who have few ties to the indigenous power structures and no sentimental attachment to local roots. All of this not only nationalizes news but enlarges the possibility for cynicism. When news is local, it typically remains personal, friendly, upbeat, gossipy, and homey. It very rarely probes local power structures or the assumptions of local cultures—religious, ethnic, or otherwise. Nationalizing news distances journalists from their audiences, for better and for worse.

Growing *inter*institutional news coherence is matched by an increased *intra*institutional news coherence. In each news institution, reporting seeks a new comprehensiveness and cultural inclusiveness. If you had walked into a newsroom fifty years ago, you would most likely not have seen any racial minorities, and the only women you would have encountered would have been writing the society page. The first nonwhite reporter on network television news, Malvin Goode, was hired by ABC in 1962. Goode, like nearly every African American journalist of his generation (he was born in 1908), began his career with the black press, in his case the well-known *Pittsburgh Courier*. As black journalists began to find employment in the mainstream press, and as the number and circulation of black newspapers fell, mainstream media reported on a broader scope of society and covered minorities less parochially. By the same token, one paper became more like the next.

At first, diversifying the newsroom seemed primarily a matter of assuring equal opportunity in employment. Not everyone conceded that this might, or should, change the nature of news. Prominent women in journalism long denied that gender could, let alone should, influence news judgment. The proposition that they might see news differently from their male colleagues seemed an affront to their professionalism. This is no longer true. The mainstream press conscientiously, if belatedly, sought to hire and promote women, black Americans, and other minorities to cover news and views of those segments of society. The diversification of the newsroom has been slow, troubled, and incomplete, but it came to be accepted that stories of special interest to women and minorities are legitimate general-interest news stories.[39]

MY PORTRAIT OF AN increasingly national, coherent, intertextually informed news product runs counter to what one hears from many media analysts in the digital era. Today there is concern about media "fragmentation."[40] This concern is driven by two developments. First, the rise of cable television and especially of an ideologically driven cable channel, FOX News, launched in 1996, troubles many people. Liberal critics point to the unrelentingly conservative cast of FOX news commentators, and surveys show that FOX viewers are more likely than others to be misinformed on issues that suit a conservative agenda—no, the U.S. did not find weapons of mass destruction in Saddam Hussein's Iraq, but FOX viewers are less likely than others to recognize this.[41] But this may be the very old story that people hear what they want to hear and know what they want to know. It is more likely that conservatives are drawn to FOX than that FOX creates conservatives. Still, are there not grounds to worry that people can, thanks to cable, inhabit cognitive hothouses where their conservative views (FOX) or their liberal ones (MSNBC) can luxuriate and where they lose contact with opinions or data that may challenge their preconceptions? And, if this is true with cable, is it not a thousand times more true with the endless number of ideologically narrow and insular news sources available online?

I do not presume to have the last word on this question, but offer simply two remarks that suggest to me that media fragmentation is less of a problem than many critics believe and that liberal concern about FOX News is a "moral panic," that is, a symbolic focus for anxieties whose root cause lies elsewhere. First, despite the rapid rise of FOX News, and despite the decline of audience size for the broadcast networks ABC, CBS, and NBC, the latter still have a vastly larger audience than FOX for the evening news. These networks do not, of course, air news-related programs around the clock, and FOX News does. It is thus difficult to know how to compare the appeal and influence of 24-hour cable news channels and the broadcast networks.

Second, despite the availability online of every imaginable viewpoint (and many one never thought imaginable), the vast majority of people who go online for their news go to the websites of leading mainstream news organizations that adhere to reputable professional values. In 2010, the most visited news sites online were (in this order) Yahoo, CNN, Google, MSN, local news sites, FOX, AOL, MSNBC, New York Times, and internet service providers.[42] Online, FOX is prominent but by no means overwhelming. What is striking is how ordinary people's choices are; they seem to be looking for updates and quick news items, not ideological reinforcement. It may not speak well of Americans that when they access these sites, they typically spend just a minute or so scanning headline news, but it at least indicates that they are not opening themselves to indoctrination that is likely to separate them from their neighbors.

It is difficult to separate the scholarly act of observing change from the moralist's task of documenting changes one has already judged to be dangerous. The latter activity dominates much media research. Sociology helps confirm that one important change in news reporting in our time has been toward critical rather than obligingly deferential professionalism, and this trend grew more intense from about 1970 on, in the United States and in other parts of the world, too. Are we worse off for it? On that question, there is no consensus. Another change that has intensified in the past decades is a move toward a more audience-centered approach to news. Critics see this as the corruption wrought by commercial motives, but this is only part of the story. News has grown deeper, more investigative, less deferential, more critical, more attuned to interests of women and minorities, more likely to stray from politics and economics to science, medicine, education, family, sexuality, religion, and other topics once largely ignored by mainstream news media. Are we worse off for these changes? Was not the sainted journalism of the 1950s and 1960s just what Meg Greenfield, longtime editorial page editor of the *Washington Post*, said it was—"too gullible and complaisant"?[43]

To this point, I have said little about the Internet. The economic havoc it has wrought with the standard business model of the advertising-supported news media and the cultural crisis it has engendered in practically every phase of news production require the rethinking of what journalism is and what it means. What is a journalist? What is news? Who is an editor and what is editing? What is the difference among reporting, aggregation, and commentary? Among straight and satiric and snarky? All of this is up for grabs as the digital revolution shapes both the production and reception of news (and blurs the line between them)—as chapter 12 will consider.

PART II

THE COMPONENTS OF NEWS MAKING

Chapter Six
NEWS IN THE MARKETPLACE

CONSIDER THE FOLLOWING RIDDLE: When should a profit-seeking newspaper seek fewer readers? Answer: When the readers it loses have, on average, less income than the readers it keeps. American newspapers make the lion's share of their income—typically around 80 percent—not from subscriptions but from advertising. Advertisers are attracted to the perceived quality, not just the quantity, of the newspaper's circulation. "Quality" means "wealth"; with a higher average income among its readers, the newspaper becomes more attractive to upscale advertisers.

So in the early 1980s, when the low-brow *New York Daily News* was struggling to survive, the high-brow *New York Times* hoped very much that it would. If the *Daily News* folded, some of its readers would certainly move over to the *Times*, but they would in most cases be readers with lower incomes and less desirable "demographics" than the traditional *Times* reader. This would water down the upscale profile of the *Times* reader and make the *Times* a less cost-effective "buy" for some advertisers. Advertisers would find themselves paying to reach readers that they did not really want. Some elite advertisers would begin to worry about the "advertising environment." The upscale department store Bonwit Teller's sales promotion director at the time expressed concern that Bonwit ads might appear next to ads for discount retailers and price slashers, which would place their advertising in the *Times* if *Daily News* readers began reading it.[1] The *Daily News* survived its crisis. But this tale reveals what has happened to American newspapers in the past half century. When the *Philadelphia Inquirer* in the 1980s and 1990s kept losing readers, advertisers did not complain: the "demographics" of the remaining readers were better than ever. Readership in leafy suburbs was growing; readership in poor neighborhoods was falling away. News coverage, many observers in and out of journalism agree, tends to mirror these patterns: less coverage of delayed welfare checks and more coverage of where to get the best cappuccino.[2]

The profit motive at the heart of the commercial newspaper can work in mysterious ways. Not that money is the only motive in the news business. Eugene Meyer, the longtime publisher of the *Washington Post*, lost a million dollars or more every year during his first twenty years of ownership. Meyer had grown up during a time when many publishers still sought newspaper ownership for the sake of the political platform it gave them, not for the sake of making money. Meyer did not need the *Post* to make money; his money was already made. He ran the paper to make a statement. This kind of motivation has grown more rare in recent years, but it is by no means obsolete. The profit motive is at the heart of the commercial newspaper, but this does not necessarily mean that market logic dictates news outcomes.[3]

How can we understand these complexities? How can we acknowledge that profit matters and motivates but that its pursuit conflicts with other demands inside and outside the news organization? That profit can be sought in a variety of ways through a variety of strategies, some of them consistent with good journalism? That profit matters more today than a half century ago, but that it is not the only god in which news organizations believe?

It has been difficult to ask such questions in the study of news because ideology has made them so contentious. One camp sees anything said in favor of capitalist ownership of the news media as a surrender to rapacious, profit-hungry owners who would sell any kind of news in any kind of way in order to make a buck. The other camp takes anything said against private ownership to be an invitation to government control and ultimately government censorship and the collapse of American liberties. Neither view, as I emphasize again in later chapters, comes to terms with the many faces of private ownership or the many variations in government involvement in the media across democratic societies. Neither view recognizes how complex a news institution is or how many constraints, quite apart from the profit motive, press upon it. Neither view, then, is credible or illuminating. They both close off the central questions of how, how much, and under what conditions economics influences news judgment. There is reason to worry that not just the state but the market, too, can threaten press freedom, but it does not follow from this that capitalism is necessarily the enemy of free expression. What should follow, if we are to understand the news media, is an examination of the ways different news institutions have insulated editorial decisions from business pressures. We can look at different sources of economic constraint (for instance, the difference between the demands of advertisers, the demands of the audience, and the demands of investors) and their various consequences. We can investigate how different media place hurdles between news judgment and balance-sheet requirements.

The issue of market-driven censorship, rather than state censorship, is made urgent by troubling evidence that news judgment is growing less and less protected from commercial concerns. In the United States, especially in strong, ambitious, and financially well-managed media organizations, the business office has traditionally stayed clear of the newsroom. Studying *Time, Newsweek,* and CBS and ABC network news in the 1970s, sociologist Herbert Gans concluded that journalists were not pressured to choose news to attract the most profitable audience: "In the news media I studied . . . editorial and business departments operate independently of each other."[4] The business side sometimes wanted to influence news decisions but was generally powerless to do so.

In the years since Gans's study, family ownership has increasingly given way to ownership by publicly traded corporations; correspondingly, more newspapers have come to be managed by executives with little or no experience in journalism. As reporter David Halberstam observed, "a proprietarial generation has been replaced by a managerial generation."[5] Control does not necessarily follow ownership; in fact, in some publicly owned newspaper corporations (i.e., corporations controlled by owners of its publicly traded stock), stock is issued in two or more classes, and ownership of the stock that provides the most powerful voting rights is restricted to members of the newspaper's founding family. The number of directors elected by owners of common stock is frequently limited, so that family members hold majority voting power. Structurally, then, even the publicly owned news organization is to a degree insulated from the bottom-line preoccupation of Wall Street investors. Nonetheless, these family directors are obliged, like other corporate directors, to listen to Wall Street, and they are influenced by Wall Street analysts and investors.[6]

Along with the move from family-owned to publicly traded corporations has come a change from local ownership to chain or group ownership. This trend goes back to the early twentieth century but has accelerated in recent decades. A few large corporations own hundreds of the nation's newspapers. In the past decade, a time of great economic distress for many news organizations, even some of the largest and most powerful media giants have disappeared, big fish swallowed by whales. News Corporation or NewsCorp, the company run by the Australian press baron Rupert Murdoch (who became a naturalized American citizen in 1985 to meet legal requirements for owning U.S. television stations) bought Dow Jones and Company in 2007, the owner of the *Wall Street Journal* and many smaller papers. NewsCorp also owns the *New York Post* and, more important still, the FOX television network that launched the FOX News Channel in 1996. In 2007, the Tribune Company (Chicago) bought the Times-Mirror Company, the publisher of the *Los Angeles Times*, *Newsday*, the *Baltimore Sun*, the *Hartford Courant*, and other papers. The Tribune Company was soon thereafter bought by businessman Sam Zell, and Tribune Company declared bankruptcy in 2008 (its papers still operating). The McClatchy Company bought Knight Ridder and thereby gained some 4 percent of the national newspaper market share (by circulation), similar to the Tribune Company's share and exceeded only by Gannett with about 9 percent (2007 figures).[7]

The newspaper industry is not highly concentrated, in comparison to many other industries. Moreover, newspapers obviously compete not only with other newspapers but with other sources of news in television, radio, and online. So it is not surprising that the long-term implications of the concentration of ownership in the news media are not clear, although on the face of it, having vast information outlets under the effective control of a few dozen firms is worrisome. Still, research on the impact on news content of chain ownership compared to independent ownership has been either inconclusive, as media scholar David Demers found,[8] or, as the late law professor C. Edwin Baker put it, "tepid, hardly motivating any strong critique of chain ownership or prompting any significant policy interventions."[9] The chains can harm the news product by a more rigid commitment to high-profit margins than independent papers typically have. But at the same time the chains can provide their papers greater resources; protect them from local political, business, and advertiser pressure; and sustain important capital improvements.[10]

Perhaps more important than the national concentration of the newspaper industry is the emergence of local newspaper monopoly power. In 1920, 579 American cities—45 percent of all cities in the country, had two or more newspapers. By 1960, this had been reduced to 239 cities (16 percent of cities) and, by 2000, just forty-nine cities (3 percent of cities). Most daily papers in the vast majority of population centers had become local monopolies by the time the Internet began to offer new forms of competition for advertising dollars and new forms of competition—and opportunity—for reaching readers.[11] Corporatization of the media brought to journalism executives from businesses outside journalism. In 1995, Mark Willes, whose business experience was in packaged foods, became the chief executive officer of the Times Mirror Company, then the parent of the *Los Angeles Times*. Willes was outspoken about breaking down the wall between the business side and the news side—with "a bazooka, if necessary."[12] He was the most prominent executive to endorse what had become a general trend, in which editors planned marketing strategies with advertising and circulation chiefs, developing projects or even whole sections for their financial potential, not for their news value.

Journalists watched Willes with concern, wondering what would happen to their cherished "wall of separation" between the business and editorial sides of news organizations. In 1999, they found out. The *Los Angeles Times* produced a special section of the newspaper to celebrate the opening of a downtown sports arena, the Staples Center. Presented as news, the section was essentially an advertising supplement paid for by the Staples Corporation.[13] This was a disturbing symptom of the erosion of management regard for professional values in journalism. At the same time, the response to the Staples supplement demonstrated that people who honor news values above business values were not about to roll over and play dead. Protest was fierce. Management was deeply embarrassed and battered by indignant protest among journalists, including many in the *Los Angeles Times* newsroom, and among the broader public.

This suggests that the desire of journalists to produce news according to their own best judgment can be a significant constraint on commercial motives. Professional values do not always triumph, of course, but as long as journalists are needed to report the news, they will have a measure of power in media organizations. They may maintain this power through their vigilance or they may lose it through their fears. When media critic Steven Brill asked *CBS Evening News* anchor Dan Rather why in July 1998 he had devoted more time to a story on the demolition of O. J. Simpson's Brentwood, California, home than to a story of thousands killed in a flood in China, Rather responded, "Fear. Fear runs strong in every newsroom in the country right now, a lot of fears, but one fear is common—the fear that if we don't do it, they will get a few more readers, a few more listeners, a few more viewers than we do."[14] Economics matters indeed—but only because its force can crush the spirit of journalists who come to their work with much more than profit in mind. Sometimes journalism still wins, not because virtue trumps greed but because journalists build the newsroom culture on which the entire organization depends.

If journalists themselves are the first line of defense against commercialism, the management of the audience is a second defense. Ever wonder why there are so many Hollywood celebrities on the covers of *Time*? Probably not—because there aren't. People who buy at newsstands typically buy an issue because of what is on its cover, but 95 percent of newsmagazine readership is by subscription. Business departments like newsstand sales because they yield more profit per sale, but news departments rarely take this into account. Newsstand sales records were set by some Watergate covers and by some sex covers, but sex covers are rarely used. In 2000, political topics accounted for twenty *Time* covers, science and medicine seven, social problems or social trends eleven, and technology and media topics five. Of the fifty-two weekly issues published that year, only six focused on entertainment and sports personalities or topics. *Time* covers were not very different from the ones used forty years earlier.

The change from 1960 to 2000 was not an increase in nonpolitical topics but instead a shift away from foreign affairs topics, as might be expected after the end of the cold war.[15]

Because most newspaper readers are subscribers, newspaper circulation does not fluctuate greatly from one day to the next, and most news decisions will not affect circulation one way or the other. Of course, this is especially true in monopoly markets where one newspaper dominates, as is nearly ubiquitous in the United States today. Readers can switch from newspaper to radio or television or online news, or they can defect from local coverage altogether and switch to the *New York Times*, *USA Today*, or the *Wall Street Journal*, but most do not have the option of expressing dissatisfaction by reading a rival local newspaper. In many other parts of the world where multiple newspapers serve a single city or region, readers of a particular newspaper typically remain loyal to it because it has a distinctive political orientation. If one lives in London or Paris or Tokyo, one can easily turn to another newspaper, but different political orientations keep papers from being perfect substitutes for one another.

The advantages of reader loyalty for a newspaper are enormous. Most of the news decisions that matter to journalists are decisions to which readers are relatively indifferent; that is, these choices will not drive readers to cancel their subscriptions. In these terms, the relative sluggishness of readers is a great asset to journalists. In fact, a newspaper is more likely to find readers rebelling, protesting, or canceling subscriptions if it drops a favorite cartoon than if it gives too much or too little coverage to foreign affairs or too critical or too deferential an account of the president's activities. Readers are bound to a paper by a variety of hooks—among them supermarket coupons, classified advertising, cartoons, puzzles, sports, and wedding announcements. The more genuine pleasure these different departments provide, the less the news department has to fret about catering to the whim of the audience.

This logic does not work so well for television, however. Television does not have the advantage of a magazine or newspaper's long-term contract (a subscription) with the audience. Television news is therefore obliged to win loyalty in other ways. The best formula for an implicit long-term contract TV news provides is encouraging the viewer to develop a strong emotional attachment to the news anchorperson. This attachment keeps viewers with one station rather than another; it also gives TV news anchors a special power and responsibility in times of public crisis or danger: the audience trusts anchors not simply as professionals but as people they feel they have come to know.

Pressure from advertisers is another source of potential constraint on news judgment. In a 2001 survey of 118 local television news directors, 53 percent acknowledged that advertisers had pressured them to run positive stories or to kill or "spike" negative ones.[16] Evidence from other surveys indicates that often advertisers succeed in directly influencing the news, even though some news directors held that they did not buckle to advertiser coercion and that even when advertisers threatened to withdraw their sponsorship, management backed up a principled news department.[17]

There is a paradox here: the desire for profit makes a news operation vulnerable to influence by advertisers, but the more profitable a news outlet is, the more it is able to withstand such pressure. If commercial news organizations fail to make profits, they will go out of business or will limp along at a level that prevents them from investing in news gathering. A small TV news station or newspaper with limited financial resources may steer clear of news stories that might elicit libel suits or other legal action because it cannot afford to retain its own lawyers. Profit, then, is not only a potential source of corruption but a potential force that insulates a news organization from corruption as well.

Journalists have the power to stand up to corporate executives in the name of traditions of independence and free inquiry, news organizations can cement long-term relationships with their audiences, and the news media, if financially successful enough, can tell meddlesome advertisers to lay off. A fourth way the news media may protect themselves from market-driven censorship is to educate the audience on the benefits and pleasures of reliable, in-depth news reporting, analysis, and commentary. This is the longest, slowest, but most enduring strategy for keeping the business office at bay. This idea suggests an elitist attitude on the part of journalists toward their audiences: "We know what is best for you." Sometimes the audiences educate the journalists, however. Part of the effort at education is an effort to stay in touch with a changing audience and a changing social world, which is necessary to good reporting, in any event.

None of these strategies for keeping news free from business pressure works completely. Privately owned news media seek profit and they will cut corners to get it. They will seek to reduce costs even at the risk of limiting the quality of journalism. They may reduce the size of the editorial staff or close an overseas bureau. They may be reluctant to assign a reporter to an investigation that will take weeks or months to yield a story.

One reason local television news devotes more attention to crime than to any other single topic, as one TV executive acknowledged, is that crime news is "the easiest, fastest, cheapest, most efficient kind of news coverage for TV stations."[18] Almost every time a reporter is assigned to a crime story, the news director can be confident it will turn into a broadcast story; there is "a one-to-one ratio between making the assignment and getting a story on-air." The police will have marked off the crime scene, so the chance of good video images is high. Disparaging local television news, former NBC News president Lawrence Grossman wrote, "Just get to the crime scene, get the wind blowing through your hair, and the rest will take care of itself."[19]

Capitalist ownership limits news in a much broader sense, too. As publisher Edward W. Scripps shrewdly observed, the capitalist proprietor is corrupted not so much by a drive for profits but by the ways in which wealth isolates a person from his or her fellows. "This isolation results in a constantly diminishing sympathy for humankind."[20] The personal character of the wealthy is so modified by wealth itself that the rich cannot be intimate with the poor, who are too different from them. Scripps continued, "A social capitalistic class quickly crystallizes and solidifies into a social caste, and the journalist who has become a capitalist is inevitably estranged from the larger community."

Scripps, who published cheap newspapers aimed at working-class readers at the beginning of the twentieth century, noted that newsprint by itself costs more than the reader pays for the written and edited newspaper. As mentioned earlier, most of the expense of producing a newspaper is borne by advertisers, not by readers. Well, Scripps reasoned, you don't get something for nothing. "The readers of newspapers can only surely secure reliable advocates and, to them, friendly newspapers, by employing and paying their own journalistic servants, and not accepting gratuities from the capitalistic and advertising class."[21] That is one solution: for interests critical of capitalism to run their own media—which, of course, they do. There is a long history of radical journalism in the United States, including socialist dailies and weeklies. The Internet makes it more possible than ever for dissident journalism to find a place but not necessarily an audience. Media supported more by wealthy benefactors than by advertising (as are many political magazines such as the *Nation*, the *New Republic*, and the *National Review*) escape the constraints of the marketplace. Some of them have been enormously important outlets for views and voices that eventually find their way into the mainstream but could not have started there.

Some scholars write as if corporate ownership and commercial organizations necessarily compromise the democratic promise of public communication, but from a global perspective the worst-case scenarios involve the absence of commercial organizations or their total domination by the state. In Latin America, government officials benefited more from state-controlled media than did the public; for Latin American policy makers in the recent wave of democratization on that continent, "strong control, censorship, and manipulation of the mass media during authoritarian and democratic regimes have deeply discredited statist models."[22] Since political democratization in South Korea began in 1987, journalism there is more free than it was under the military regime of the early 1980s, when seven hundred antiregime journalists were dismissed, security agencies kept the media under constant surveillance, and the Ministry of Culture could cancel any publication's registration at will and routinely issued specific guidelines on how reporters should cover events.[23] Still, in the new South Korean media system, old cultural expectations persist—that the president should receive favorable media treatment, for example—and newspapers run by right-wing families and business conglomerates are closely aligned with political authorities and the state bureaucracy and themselves act as part of a conservative establishment.[24]

Not that market-dominated systems and state-dominated systems are always easy to distinguish these days. Media scholar Yuzhei Zhao has written a detailed and persuasive account of the blending of commercial and state-controlled media in post–Tiananmen Square China.[25] After the violent suppression of student protests in Beijing's Tiananmen Square in 1989, the Chinese government tightened controls on the media, closed down three leading publications whose coverage it judged too sympathetic to the protesters, replaced editors at other newspapers, and required all news organizations to engage in self-criticism. Even today, the Communist Party continues to monitor political news, but it does not closely scrutinize coverage of economics or of social and environmental issues. Self-censorship, rather than heavy-handed party control, is the operating system.[26]

Despite the tightening of party control in China, there was a rapid commercialization of the Chinese popular press in the 1990s and a proliferation of sensational, entertainment-oriented tabloids that compete with the established press for advertising revenues. Party-operated media respond largely or exclusively to the demands of the party. Media outlets in the "commercial" sector cater first to the party's propaganda needs but are obliged by their dependence on the market to try to "establish a common ground between the Party and the people" through the selection of what topics to cover and how to cover them.[27] The commercial media have grown rapidly while the circulation of the traditional party media has dropped. While party control of the media remains powerful everywhere, even at Central China Television, the most influential station in the country, some news formats have tested the limits and sought to please the public as well as the party leadership. *Focus*, an innovative discussion-format program launched in 1994, has raised critical issues, spoken on behalf of the poor, and investigated corruption in both business and government. Still, *Focus* refrains from airing any segment that could induce political instability. Chinese journalists are "dancing with chains on."[28] The blend of state, independent, and commercial news media and the mixed pattern of ownership and control are so new that they do not even have names, let alone theories to explain them. Zhao, for lack of any better term, describes the Chinese system as a "propagandist/commercial model" of the media.

Returning to the American case, where market constraints on free expression are more threatening to the diversity of public expression and debate than is state control, it would be a shock to find the mainstream press or broadcasting a hotbed of radical thought. In all political and economic systems, news "coincides with" and "reinforces" the "definition of the political situation evolved by the political elite."[29] This basic generalization seems incontestable. The cause of free expression and the greatest research interest lie in determining the generalization's limits and specifying what structural and cultural features of the media can work to keep news porous, open to dissident voices, and encouraging of genuine debate.

Critical or radical thought in any society at any time is exceptional. Who would expect it to be happily sponsored by a society's most established institutions? And yet it happens. For example, why did a local TV news station in Houston in 2000 unearth the unusual number of accidents that Ford Explorer owners were experiencing with Firestone and Bridgestone tires? Why not the appropriate government regulatory agency? Why not a university-based academic or a radical scholar? Why not PBS? One might have been able to explain this if the news institution involved had been the *New York Times* or the *Wall Street Journal*—elite institutions with a vested interest in sustaining their reputations as tough, serious-minded institutions of journalism. But local television news, generally treated by media scholars as beneath contempt? Even in this arena, a part of the news business that bows obsequiously to market pressure, strange things can happen.[30]

To give credit where it is due, the commercialization of the news media in the long run helped shield news production from government control and later helped liberate it from the sway of political parties. Commercialization has encouraged the development of professionalism among journalists in the very act of commodifying news. When news could be bought and sold as a commodity, when it was separated from state propaganda, on the one hand, and party programs, on the other, journalists could develop professional standards and practices for news gathering and news writing across news institutions. Moreover, the drive for profit was even more potent a factor than the party drive for political power in orienting newspapers to a mass public and imbuing news writing with a broad democratic rather than elitist appeal. Thus a case can be made in favor of commercial media. Commercial forces have historically encouraged good journalism—that is, popular and critical journalism—even if they have not intended to do so. In the nineteenth century, the commercial drive to please audiences helped make news relevant to a broad population and helped wrest it from a journalistic mandarinate that spoke only to political insiders.

Profit is not the only important factor and it is not invariably the decisive factor in commercial news organizations, but it looms large. In parts of Asia, Latin America, and eastern Europe where the transition to democracy has been dramatic and energizing in the past two decades, a realization has dawned that the marketplace offers constraints as well as freedom. Great dangers lurk within market-driven media. Sheila Coronel, a pioneer of investigative journalism in the Philippines, even suggested that "tyranny of the state may be better than tyranny of the market. As journalists we know what to do with the state—you topple it. But what do you do with the market?"[31]

What do you do with the market? You follow where others have led, asserting journalistic values against corporate assault, building formal economic structures that reduce dependence on Wall Street, developing a range of audience loyalties that enables you to bore or offend some of the audience some of the time without losing them. You become profitable enough, with your sources of profit diversified enough, to resist pressure from any particular advertiser or group of advertisers. You do your job of reporting well enough to educate the audience about the worth of journalism while allowing that audience to educate and change you. None of these strategies separately or together will end the threat that dollars pose to news, but the evidence shows that they have helped, even in recent years, to contain it.

main source of information, that everything that happens with it is important. . . . That's the journalistic law of the least effort. It's faster and easier to practice journalism based in the world of government than putting emphasis on what's happening in society."[3] Studies of media that see the process of news production beginning in the newsroom rather than in the halls of power have been criticized as "too media-centric," and rightly so.[4] Very few studies have looked at the whole development of a news story, starting with the news source rather than the news reporter.

Government sources are not alone in seeking to satisfy the media's hunger. You may be reading this sentence for a class in a college or university. Colleges and universities maintain public information offices that manage information for their institutions, trying especially to put the best face on negative news (a plagiarism scandal, a toxic-waste disposal problem in the science labs, a rape or murder on campus). They also provide the news media with a stream of press releases about positive news (a faculty member wins a Nobel Prize, test scores of the new freshman class are up from the year before, the women's volleyball team goes to the national championship). It serves the university's interest to keep its name in the news when good things happen. Colleges and universities are not ivory towers; they must compete in a marketplace of opinion to attract students, to keep gifted faculty content, to maintain a corps of satisfied employees who could find rewarding work elsewhere, to win the favor of philanthropists, to impress the officers of foundations and government bureaus that support research, and even to please municipal officials who act on land-use issues that directly concern the institution. News is crucial to these efforts; it is the currency of community standing. Similarly, private corporations, hospitals, professional associations (such as the American Sociological Association), voluntary associations, and others seek a favorable public image. Public relations units in government, large corporations, and major nonprofit organizations are typically staffed by people with experience in journalism.

Many different kinds of organizations try to control their image in the media through offices of public information and through cultivating good associations with reporters and editors. Despite this, government sources predominate. They include not only federal, state, and local U.S. governments, but foreign governments who hire spokespeople and public relations (PR) firms to shape their image in the American news media. Herman Cohen, a longtime official in the U.S. State Department who served as ambassador to Senegal and Gambia and as assistant secretary of state for Africa, after leaving government service established a business to represent various clients, including some African nations, to the U.S. Congress and the American public. His clients included Gabon, Tunisia, the Ivory Coast, Mozambique, Angola, and Liberia. Other Washingtonians who combine lobbying and public relations have represented dictators such as Saddam Hussein of Iraq and Nicolae Ceauşescu of Romania. Money, no matter how bloody, can buy public relations in Washington.[5]

Among government sources, routine government sources matter most. That is, most news comes to the news media through ordinary, scheduled government-initiated events such as press releases, public speeches, public legislative hearings or deliberations, press conferences, and background briefings for the press. "Your time is taken up by the large, regular flow of presidential news announcements, the campaign, summit meetings," said Robert Donovan, Washington bureau chief for the *Los Angeles Times* in the 1970s. "There's almost always something going on that deprives one of the time to dig underneath."[6] In the 1950s and 1960s, nearly 60 percent of foreign and national news in the *New York Times* and the *Washington Post* relied entirely on government-initiated contacts. Only 26 percent entailed "enterprise"—that is, reporters' using initiative to conduct an interview or otherwise seek out information that did not come to them on a platter.[7]

There is nothing surprising or shocking about any of this. In fact, it follows directly from the way the press organizes its daily efforts. Reporters take on certain "beats"—the Supreme Court or the White House or the police department—and they maintain regular telephone and face-to-face contact with their key sources on these beats. The higher up in the hierarchy they can maintain a source, the better, because they are always looking for sources who can speak for their institutions with full legitimacy. Reporters may learn more from someone in the mayor's secretarial pool than from the mayor's press secretary, but the clerk-typist does not speak for the mayor, whereas the press secretary does. Reporters need to interview not just sources but authoritative ones.

This need, of course, gives great power to high-level government officials. Access to them is a scarce resource, and they control journalists by granting or denying access. They typically will favor journalists from leading news outlets over journalists from less prestigious—and less predictable—publications. They thereby help maintain the advantage in news gathering held by the already established leading institutions and they help solidify class distinctions among journalists.[8] In fact, the Canadian scholars Richard Ericson, Patricia Baranek, and Janet Chan have even said that sources "function as 'reporters,'" doing all the work necessary within their organizations to provide a news account that the media organization will accept. "The reporter for the news organization then functions as an 'editor,' determining what aspects of this material will be used along with accounts tailored for the purpose of news discourse by other sources."[9] This is an unconventional way to talk about these social roles, but it makes good sense. Sources work to make what they reveal to journalists as newslike as they can. They have to think like reporters, and it is therefore not too much to suggest, as I have earlier, that they are parajournalists.

In some countries, relations between reporters and officials are even more routinized. The most famous case is that of the Japanese *kisha* clubs. These clubs of reporters, which date to early in the twentieth century, are maintained by the news organizations that provide their membership. They are formal associations of reporters from different media outlets assigned to a particular ministry and granted privileged—but highly controlled—access to the minister and other high-level officials. Since most clubs are connected to government agencies, news takes on an official cast. The daily association of reporters at the clubs contributes to a uniformity in the news pages; reporters are driven by what is described as a "phobia" about writing something different from what all the other reporters write.[10]

At the other end of the continuum are the foreign affairs journalists in the Netherlands: "They do not pound the halls and knock on doors in the Foreign Ministry, as American journalists do. Rather, they work for the most part at home, reading, thinking, perhaps phoning an official whom they know, writing if the muse visits, and not writing if she does not. Since their output is personal and thus explicitly subjective, there is little basis among them for the competitive spirit that animates American coverage of foreign-affairs news and that results in a convergence of judgment of what that 'news' is."[11] In fact, the independence of these correspondents is so striking that they do not generally know one another and are generally ignorant of or indifferent to the work styles of their nominal peers.

In the United States, conditions that tend toward *kisha*-like group journalism are derisively labeled pack journalism, where reporters covering the same beat or same story tend to emphasize the same angle and adopt the same viewpoint. Pack journalism happens most when journalists literally travel in packs, as they do in covering the White House or in covering a presidential campaign. In these cases, a single significant source brings the press together and commands their constant attention. This very fact creates a new relationship—not of journalist to source but of journalist to the rest of the corps of reporters. The traveling corps of reporters becomes a set of companions, even comrades, sharing a long, intense, emotional experience together. Theodore "Teddy" White described this well in his pathbreaking book on the 1960 presidential campaign: "The talk of the corps of correspondents who follow the candidates is not simply gossip; gossip is only its surface form. It is consensus—it is the tired, emotional measuring of judgments among men whom the weeks on the road have made into a brotherhood that only they understand. And the judgment of the brotherhood influences and colors, beyond any individual resistance to prejudice or individual devotion to fact, all of what they write. For by now they have come to trust only each other."[12]

Reliance on government officials does not guarantee the officials get favorable news. As sociologist Silvio R. Waisbord wrote, "Official wrongdoing is another form of official news and as such is more likely than other forms of wrongdoing to become the subject of journalistic investigations."[13] It is difficult to muckrake the government without the government's cooperation. Journalists may have rumors, leads, leaks, or near-certain knowledge of a government misdeed, but normally they can't go to print within the conventions of the craft without first getting confirmation of the story from a well-placed figure. Government officials cooperate with the press for various reasons, and not always to advance a unified government interest. Officials may leak information to the press to deliver an official administration message, but they may also be seeking to undermine rivals in the government by passing on embarrassing information. They may use the media to communicate not with the public but with a senior official or the president's staff when going directly to the president is too difficult.[14] In any case, sources use the press to their own advantage. In Latin American journalism, the practice whereby one insider uses the press to spread scandal about another insider even has a name: *denuncismo*. From the reporter's perspective, this is simply quick-and-dirty journalism; from the source's perspective, it is a form of ventriloquism through which to try to dictate the news and advance his or her own interests.[15]

There is no doubt that reliance on government officials is solid ground for criticism of a progovernment or statist bias in the press. Philip Geyelin, who served as editorial page editor of the *Washington Post* during the Vietnam War, wrote, "For all the talk of their awesome power and responsibility, our news-gatherers are remarkably pliable."[16] During Vietnam, he observed, what the press provided the public was "determined to a large extent by what it gets openly or in carefully calculated, thoroughly managed 'background' official briefings for supposedly faithful delivery to the public" In his judgment, "what the press was getting from the government during the Vietnam War was not to put too fine a point upon it—trash."

In U.S. journalism, manipulation is practiced daily. One journalist who attended the Democratic National Convention in Los Angeles in 2000 was invited to an off-the-record Kennedy family party. There she was surrounded by celebrities galore from both the political arena and Hollywood. It was hard not to be overwhelmed; she found it all "far too seductive" and recalled, "Walking the line between working press and elite partygoer was just too hard to do. I went, I saw, and I wanted to write. At the same time, I went, I drank wine, and I wanted to be an insider."[17] James Warren, the Washington bureau chief for the *Chicago Tribune*, offended fellow journalists by writing about the subtle corruptions of schmoozing. "Early on," he recalled, "I wrote about the fawning over White House staff members at Bill and Hillary Clinton's annual Christmas party, where journalists lined up dutifully for twenty or thirty minutes before they got to the head of the line and met the president and first lady, turned around, and had their glossy color photo snapped, the photo arriving at their homes about ten days later, most suitable for framing. After the photo, it was on to the huge tables of free food and booze and schmoozing with the folks many routinely covered."[18]

Seduction by proximity to power is serious business when the stakes of national and international policy making are as high as they are in Washington, D.C. "So many reporters are smitten by having access to key decision-makers" who can provide them a little scoop and make their career.[19] Likewise, the source can shut someone out, and the reporter's bosses will get nervous when the competitors are getting the inside story and their reporter is not.

The temptations of the reporter-source relationship are real; efforts to protect journalistic chastity in the face of them have contributed to an elaborate etiquette and code of ethics. This code centers on gifts from sources to reporters, mostly meals and transportation. The general rule is to accept no gifts. At ABC News, for example, employees may not accept transportation, meals, or any other consideration from sources that is intended to compromise their "responsibilities as objective newspersons, or which gives the appearance of doing so."[20] The ABC policy goes on to recognize that there are certainly some situations, such as a business lunch, that would be embarrassing or silly to avoid, "but the rule holds: Accept no favors which might compromise or even appear to compromise, the independence and integrity of ABC News and the individuals involved."

At ABC, commonsense exceptions to the ethics policy are recognized. The case gets trickier when what is at stake is not merely dinner or a pair of cuff links but significant amounts of income instead. Some journalists, for example, make large sums by lecturing. Among star U.S. journalists in the 1990s, lecturing for a fee became a widespread and highly lucrative practice. When ABC News anchor Ted Koppel's fee for a lecture reached fifty thousand dollars, he finally declined to speak for pay. But others continue to rake in large sums. To whom is it acceptable to lecture for pay? Some news organizations have decided that it is acceptable for a journalist to speak to an organization if that organization is not specifically part of the reporter's beat. Lesley Stahl of *60 Minutes*, then, could receive a large fee to moderate a program for an insurance company during congressional debates over health-care reform because she was not the CBS health reporter. And ABC's Cokie Roberts could accept thirty-five thousand dollars for a speech to Toyota automobile dealers at the time of a major U.S.-Japan trade dispute because although she reported on the politics of trade, she was not on the trade beat as such. All three major networks by 1995 had cracked down on this kind of activity, but journalists at many other news organizations are free to speak to special-interest groups for pay.[21]

A different kind of case arose in 2001 when *CBS Evening News* anchor Dan Rather gave a speech at a Democratic Party fund-raiser in Austin, Texas. He was invited by his daughter, a Texas business executive who is active in Democratic Party politics. He reportedly did not realize that the event was a fund-raiser, and afterward he apologized for his actions: "I made an embarrassing and regrettable error in judgment in going to this event. It was a serious mistake, which I acknowledge."[22] Rather clearly violated CBS's ethical guidelines, but was this a serious breach? Alex Jones, a former *New York Times* media reporter and now director of Harvard University's Joan Shorenstein Center on the Press, Politics and Public Policy, said it was grounds for a "wrist slap" but nothing more. "He was doing it for his daughter, for Pete's sake. . . . This is sort of in the 'C'mon, let's get real here, we've got other things to worry about' category."[23]

In too many countries, there are no subtleties about payments to journalists to buy influence. In China, for instance, the degree and extent of corruption is legendary. News sources in China routinely pay for journalists' travel, hotel, and meals when they report out-of-town events (a practice called "three-warranty reporting"), some journalists moonlight as public relations agents for businesses, and journalists and news organizations receive cash, negotiable securities, personal favors, and gifts not only from business clients but even from government officials who seek favorable coverage.[24] Journalists' salaries are low and "few can resist the temptation offered by one paid news report that can bring in a red envelope as much as a whole month's salary, not to mention an advertising deal worth years of salary."[25]

Another famous case is the *gacetilla* system in which the Mexican government pays reporters to print the information they provide. This practice is so well institutionalized that Mexican newspapers pay very low salaries to reporters, expecting their reporters to bring in income for themselves and for their newspapers from *gacetillas*. In fact, a reporter's proven ability to bring in *gacetilla* revenue is a basis for promotion through the ranks, usually to covering a government agency where still more *gacetilla* revenue can be expected.[26] This and related forms of bribery are known in various parts of the world as envelope journalism, a very common problem in emerging democracies.

In the United States, most of the influence sources exert over reporters has nothing to do with money or favors changing hands. It is instead a matter of pleasure, the sheer pleasure journalists feel at having access that other mortals are denied.[27] It is a matter of human relations. Journalists manipulate sources, and sources manipulate journalists. "In my experience," commented reporter J. Anthony Lukas, "the relationship between reporter and source, particularly one of long term, is filled with collaboration and manipulation, with affection and distrust, with a yearning for communion and a yearning to flee."[28] In Washington, in state capitals, and even more in the capitals of other countries where journalistic and political elites naturally intertwine, the trouble is not one of mutual manipulation but rather of living in a common social world. In France, for instance, Thomas Ferenczi, associate editor of *Le Monde*, complained that journalists and politicians—and it does not matter if they are left wing or right wing—belong to the same "microcosm." "When they are young they go to the same schools, later they live in the same areas, go to the same holiday resorts, and so on." Ferenczi warned, "There is real danger for democracy here: namely, that, journalists and politicians, because they are so closely linked, have their own narrow idea of what the media should cover . . . and ignore the interests of the people."[29]

In 1980, columnist and network commentator George Will helped presidential candidate Ronald Reagan prepare for his television debate with President Jimmy Carter.[30] This assistance did not come to public notice until three years later, when the *Wall Street Journal* ran a front-page story titled "Should a Newsman Be Active Participant in Partisan Politics?" Some journalists castigated Will, and for a time the *New York Daily News* dropped his column; other journalists came to his defense. Will, of course, defended himself: while confessing that he would not do something similar again because "it makes so many people anxious," Will also wrote that as a columnist he had more license than a straight political reporter would have and that he was glad for the opportunity to see behind the scenes of the political machinery. Also defending Will, the *Washington Post*'s Richard Harwood reminded readers that "everybody does it." As he put it, "If you sat all the political reporters in Washington down in a room and told them that only those who had never given advice to a politician should stand up, hardly a soul would dare rise. . . . Scratch a scribe in this town and you find a campaign manager. The candidate has no more seductive, nay irresistible, gambit in wooing the press than asking, 'What do you think I should do?'" David Broder, Harwood's *Washington Post* colleague, wrote that the answer to the flattering "What do you think I should do?" question should be simple: "You want to know what I think? Buy the paper. It only costs a quarter. You get all the ball scores and comics—and they toss in my advice for nothing. Which is probably what it's worth."[31]

The reporter's reliance on sources keeps taking on new twists and new language. Critics of the way government handles the media have attacked "government by press release" since World War I, but the language has changed. The 1950s brought criticism of "news management," especially the clever manipulations by President Dwight Eisenhower's powerful press secretary, James Hagerty. In 1968, writer Joe McGinniss's *Selling of the President* presented a powerful analysis of the image-management efforts of the Nixon presidential campaign. In the early 1980s, with Reagan's presidency, the phrase "photo opportunity" came into the language, as Reagan's staff would set up situations in which the president would make himself available for news photographers. In the 1990s, the term "spin" was introduced in the lexicon of Washington journalism. (It first came into use in the late 1970s.)[32] The 1990s brought criticism of advisers to presidents and presidential candidates, known as spin doctors or spinners. Spinners are campaign aides available to talk to television and print interviewers to "spin" the news of the day in a direction favorable, or less harmful, to their candidate.

Everybody tries to deliver news that places them in the best possible light: in that sense, everybody spins, beginning with the student who explains why his or her homework assignment is late. Well before the language of spin was invented, historian Robert Darnton reflected on his own experience as a *New York Times* reporter. Darnton wrote about how government spokespersons and public relations people try to influence the angle or tone of a reporter's work. He emphasized that "amicable familiarity over a long period of daily contact" works better than outright manipulation. "After a year or so on a single beat, reporters tend insensibly to adopt the viewpoint of the people about whom they write."[33] Nevertheless, spinning seems to be more common today than in the past. At any rate, campaign communications are more centrally planned and more dependent on professional experts. "As a result," wrote German scholar Frank Esser and his colleagues, "elections have become increasingly media affairs rather than party affairs."[34] This is especially true in the United States and also in the United Kingdom, where the language of spin doctors had arrived within a few years of its American birth. In Germany, even though campaigns are becoming more professionalized, the stage managing of them is not yet a subject of media inquiry itself, as it has become in both the United Kingdom and the United States.[35]

From the White House on down, spinning is growing more elaborate, more plotted, more carefully tested. The process is known by more vulgar terms: political columnist David Broder refers to it as "the White House propaganda machine."[36] Media critics Tom Rosenstiel and Bill Kovach say even more plainly that when their fellow journalists accept spinning, they are just providing legitimation for lying.[37] Of course, as politicians grow more expert, journalists grow more resistant and able to deflect or redirect at least the most obvious manipulations. But this resistance is easier for the experienced national press than for local news outlets. The latter are flattered by attentions from national politicians and are generally not skillful at challenging them.

Spinning is a parajournalistic practice at which Americans seem particularly adept, having more or less invented the modern PR industry early in the twentieth century. But recently, professional PR has grown rapidly elsewhere in the world, too. In the United Kingdom, it expanded in the 1980s and 1990s, accentuating the disproportionate government and corporate-sector control over the media in that country, where these institutions have the greatest PR resources. More than 90 percent of PR professionals in the United Kingdom work for government or businesses, whereas only 9 percent work for nonprofit organizations.[38] Even so, public relations as an institution does not necessarily favor the establishment. Organizations with modest resources have successfully used PR and information campaigns to upset establishment apple carts. PR resources are preponderantly in the hands of establishment institutions, but PR is relatively less capital dependent than are other forms of public communication. For instance, British news beats are so deeply mired in ongoing government and media relations that PR is one of the few resources available to resource-poor nongovernmental associations to gain media attention.[39]

One study after another produces essentially the same observation. It does not matter whether the study is at the national level or the local level. Journalism, on a day-to-day basis, is the story of the interaction of reporters and government officials, both politicians and bureaucrats. Most analysts claim officials have the upper hand. Some media critics, including many government officials, say reporters do.[40] But there is little doubt that the center of news generation is the link between reporter and official.[41]

This link between reporters and officials is apparent in the daily practices of journalists. "The only important tool of the reporter is his news sources and how he uses them," one U.S. political reporter explained.[42] Media scholar Stephen Hess confirmed this in his study of Washington correspondents: he found that reporters use no documents apart from press releases in the preparation of three-quarters of their stories.[43] What journalists do on an ordinary day, even in the era of e-mail and the Internet, is talk to people, although now the convenience of the Internet brings them to consult more documents and to be in touch with more reports from other media than in the past. Even so, they retain as an ideal what columnists Joseph and Stewart Alsop urged upon them a half century ago when they recommended that reporters live by the rule of the feet: "In Washington terms, the rule of the feet means that a reporter should try to see—not telephone—at least four officials or politicians every working day. This works out to about 24 major interviews a week, which should be further supplemented by casual contacts."[44]

In practice, the rule of the telephone may be more common. This is supported by a study of Israeli journalists by journalism scholar Zvi Reich as is his general conclusion that news reporting is "more about trust than about knowledge." As he writes, "Heavy reliance upon human sources, by a series of contacts that are usually relatively short, remote, technology mediated, and purposive, shows that news is much more a phenomenon of trust between people than independent fact-finding."[45] A corollary to the power of the source is that resource-poor organizations have great difficulty getting the media's attention.[46] If they are to be covered, they must adjust to modes of organizational interaction more like those of established governmental and business organizations.

The advent of online journalism changes these generalizations, but there is both change and continuity. Journalists may pick up more news from surfing the web, from (in unusual cases) "crowdsourcing" (systematically or opportunistically enlisting dozens or hundreds of amateurs as unpaid research assistants), and from communications with their own readers, now much more available than in the past. Online, they may use documents and databases more than before. These changes add to, without replacing, the old-fashioned ways. Consider the case of reporters Bettina Boxall and Julie Cart in their Pulitzer Prize–winning series in the *Los Angeles Times* that sought to explain why the incidence and intensity of forest fires in California was growing. Once their broad plans for the story emerged, they began to interview people. Then they turned to the Internet for additional sources, and this proved useful. They came upon relevant research from a University of Wisconsin scholar cited in other news stories, found more about him from his website, read his research, and then interviewed him. The reporters decided it would be fruitful to pursue recently retired Forest Service personnel as sources: "We knew those fresh retirees were the most likely to give us candid, on-the-record interviews about the political pressure fire commanders encounter." They picked up some names from other sources but also "just typed 'Forest Service and retired' into Google and found former commanders who were consulting—along with their phone numbers and e-mail addresses." The Internet matters. "I think the Internet is a great aid," Boxall wrote. "You stumble across documents and sources that you didn't even know existed and with a few key strokes, they are rolling off your computer printer. . . . It has made basic research faster, easier and richer. But it can't displace interviews, being there, or narrative."[47]

THE SIGNIFICANCE of reporter-source studies is twofold. First, they detail the dynamics of news production as it is usually practiced. Second, they implicitly put the power of media institutions in perspective. Media power looms large if we assume that the portrait of the world the media present to audiences stems from the preferences and perceptions of publishers, editors, and reporters unconstrained by democratic controls. However, if the media typically mirror the views and voices of established and democratically selected government officials, then the media are more nearly the neutral servants of a democratic order. To note one well-studied instance, policy experts widely attacked American television news for pushing the U.S. government to intervene with military force in Somalia in 1992 by showing graphic scenes of starving people. But research shows that the networks picked up the Somalia story only after seven senators, a House committee, the full House, the full Senate, a presidential candidate, and the White House all publicly raised the issue. When the networks finally got to it, they framed it very much as Washington's political elites had framed it for them.[48] This does not mean the TV stories made no difference; clearly they rallied public interest and public support for intervention. But where did the TV story come from? Not from thin air, and not from reporters, but from established, official sources.

Does the consistent finding that official sources dominate the news damn the media? If the media are to fulfill their democratic role, shouldn't they offer a wide variety of opinions and perspectives to encourage citizens to choose among them in evaluating public policies? If the media allow politicians to set the public agenda, they may unduly narrow public discussion and diminish democracy. This is the argument made by W. Lance Bennett in his account of the "indexing" function of the press. For Bennett, the media "tend to 'index' the range of voices and viewpoints in both news and editorials according to the range of views expressed in mainstream government debate about a given topic."[49] Bennett argued that this perpetuates a "world in which governments are able to define their own publics and where 'democracy' becomes whatever the government ends up doing." He proposed, instead, that the media defer to government officials under normal circumstances, granting them "a privileged voice in the news" except where the range of voices in official debates "excludes or 'marginalizes' stable majority opinion in society, and unless official actions raise doubts about political propriety." Under such unusual conditions, the press may reasonably reach out to present other voices "as checks against unrepresentative or otherwise irresponsible governments."

Of course, this is not very practical advice. How are journalists to decide when "stable majority opinion" has been marginalized in official debates? (And when, if ever, are journalists to make room for serious and considered minority opinions?) How are journalists to determine when political propriety is in question? These questions suggest that Bennett's proposal does not go far enough in releasing news professionals from their dependence on government officials. Yet another perspective suggests that his proposal goes too far.[50] What if the best hope for a mass democracy is that people evaluate leaders, not policies? What if asking the press to offer enough information, history, and context for citizens to make decisions on policies before politicians act is asking the impossible? It may be more plausible, and more consistent with representative democracy, for citizens to assess leaders after they have acted.

Chapter Eight
THE POLITICAL CULTURE OF NEWS

PEOPLE WANT TO KNOW what impact the media have on politics. If it were only so simple! Political institutions and media institutions are so deeply intertwined, so thoroughly engaged in a complex dance with one another, that it is not easy to distinguish where one begins and the other leaves off. In the broad ecology of public life, the media do not define politics any more than political structures dictate news. Parties, electoral systems, structures of political financing, and the work of interest groups are involved just as much as the news media are in shaping, organizing, and setting the agenda of public discussion about politics.[1] True, the media have grown more visible and more independent of traditional political power centers, most notably the parties. In Europe, this change has taken place only in the past half century, a "Copernican revolution," as two European scholars put it: "Yesterday everything circled around the parties, today everything circles around and in the space of the media."[2] In the United States, the revolution is about a century old, although here, too, there has been a marked shift toward media influence in political life in recent decades. In Europe this process has been called a "mediatization" of politics—indeed, a mediatization of social life in general.[3] But the relationship between media and parties is only one part of a complex interplay of political institutions, political culture, and political reporting.

Take, for instance, media coverage of Supreme Court nominations in the United States. This process has become, many
observers fear, too politicized and too unseemly. Many saw the
carefully orchestrated 1987 campaign to block the confirmation of federal judge Robert Bork as Supreme Court justice as
a turn in the wrong direction. The subsequent circus of hearings around the eventually successful nomination of Clarence
Thomas in 1991 became a cause célèbre. Was Thomas guilty
of the sexual harassment of Anita Hill? What, indeed, is sexual
harassment in the workplace? Could an all-male Senate committee ever give fair consideration to that question? The matter was
discussed for weeks in a media frenzy and, for years thereafter in
academic studies, off-color jokes, and serious theater pieces. One
cannot doubt that this massive publicity has influenced how
presidents conceive of their judicial appointments, how people
consider whether they are willing to have a president submit
their name, or how the Supreme Court itself operates. The Bork
and Thomas cases gave the impression that the media had waded
into a territory where their scrutiny could do more harm than
good; more recent nominations, as in the confirmation hearings
of Sonia Sotomayor in 2009 and Elena Kagan in 2010, seem to
indicate that nominees and their advisers have adapted to the
media glare by revealing as little as possible about themselves.

Yet a closer look reveals something different. Public scrutiny of judicial nominations arrived because of changes in the
way judicial confirmation is conducted. During the first century of U.S. history, Supreme Court nominations were certainly
political, but the politics took place behind closed doors. Deliberations in the Senate over confirmation were secret. Neither
special-interest groups nor the general public participated.

In the late nineteenth century, interest groups began to make their voices heard about appointments to the Supreme Court. The effect was muted, however, because the key decision maker, the Senate, was well insulated from punishment at the polls. Until the passage of the Seventeenth Amendment in 1913, senators were elected by state legislatures, not by popular vote. Only after Progressive Era reform provided for direct election of senators did judicial decision makers become vulnerable to and responsive to public opinion.

Even the direct election of senators had limited impact until a 1929 Senate rule change made floor debate on nominations routine. Not until then did full-fledged public hearings before the Senate Judiciary Committee become standard practice. Hearings remained perfunctory, however, until 1949, when the full Judiciary Committee met to consider President Harry Truman's nomination of Tom Clark. Confirmations grew more elaborate, especially after President Richard Nixon's nomination of Clement Haynesworth in 1969. From that point, it became routine for interest groups to offer public testimony. This practice expanded after 1981, when television coverage of the hearings made these occasions a great publicity opportunity for various interest groups.[4]

Today, public opinion is a prize to be sought in the confirmation process. President Nixon orchestrated public appeals to support his nominees, including a direct-mail information campaign that targeted local newspapers, and sought to avoid the more critical and probing national press. The Ronald Reagan administration used speeches by cabinet officers, satellite-transmitted interviews with local television stations, radio interviews, and op-ed articles in the print media. All subsequent administrations have also taken their nominations to the public as part and parcel of the Supreme Court appointment process.

What is at stake, then, is not a one-way campaign of media aggrandizement designed to distort a once pristine process that should have been left alone. What we see instead is a range of changes in government, media, the private sector, and the broad political culture. These changes all interact to create a system in which the role of the media is central—not supreme, not paramount—but indispensable.

A hundred years ago, presidents made little effort to court public opinion. The public mood was of little or no influence on their legislative program, if they even had a legislative program. President Franklin Roosevelt pioneered the practice of appealing over the heads of Congress to a broad public and over the heads of newspaper publishers to their Washington correspondents. Still, fifty years ago Washington politics remained insider politics. The successful president was adept at a chess game in which Congress sat across the board. But increasingly, presidents have tried to pressure Congress not directly but through their constituents and through that broad, amorphous entity known as public opinion.

Only in the second half of the twentieth century did the fundamental strategy of presidential leadership shift from "bargaining" with Congress to "going public."[5] This has meant that presidents require a permanent entourage of media consultants. It has also reoriented governing to become a form of campaigning, bringing a notable increase in presidential travel, both at home and abroad. President Herbert Hoover, who came into the White House in 1925 with a reputation for international humanitarian activity, averaged just a day a year of foreign travel and six days a year of domestic travel in his first three years in office. A half century later, President Jimmy Carter averaged fourteen days of foreign travel and more than twenty days of domestic travel.[6]

What accounts for a presidential strategy of "going public"? Multiple factors have to be considered. First, the federal government has grown more and more important as the modern welfare state has developed. The government's growing influence in daily life created large, interested political constituencies outside of Washington. More constituencies listened in on a regular basis, so there was more of a reason to speak to them. Second, it became easier to reach those burgeoning constituencies. Radio and television greatly enhanced the capacity of the president to speak to the whole nation immediately and dramatically, while jet aircraft have enabled presidents to move quickly to disaster sites, national gatherings and conferences, and other sites of political opportunity. Third, the decline of popular allegiance to political parties limited public adherence to a particular party standard and weakened relations between party professionals and political elites that had once made political bargaining convenient and apparently natural. Fourth, Congress—the center of bargaining in national politics—grew more democratic and egalitarian in its structure, and each member of Congress became more entrepreneurial in conducting politics. The politics of bargaining rested on clear hierarchies in Congress and on a relatively restricted number of power centers for the president to manage. The multiplication of committees, subcommittees, caucuses, and affinity groups inside Congress compounded the effects of weakened parties and of a broad distrust of hierarchy, seniority, and almost any established cultural authority. These changes weakened the attractiveness and even the feasibility of a bargaining system.[7]

The place of the media in society, and especially in political life, depends on the rules of the political game at a given place and time. These rules can vary greatly from one place to another. In Sweden, as compared to the United States, the country is so small (with a population about the size of Los Angeles County's) that a few news outlets have a very large degree of control over public discourse. In the 1960s, to be part of Sweden's public debate meant one had to read and write for *Dagens Nyheter*, the dominant daily newspaper. In 1965, one article in that newspaper set off a wave of essays in the paper criticizing U.S. policy in Vietnam. "Before the article, little serious discussion of Vietnam had occurred. After the outpouring, Vietnam became the object of a campaign that lasted until the war ended. Reporting became extensive, and it took on a propagandistic tone. No prominent voice was raised again in defense of American policy," wrote political scientist Steven Kelman.[8] It is relatively easy, he observed, to call attention to an issue or even one side of an issue in Sweden: "All that is required is to convince a small number of key intellectuals or media people."[9] It is not as simple as that today, but surely a large nation will by its very size have a different media dynamic and different political culture than will a small nation. In the large society, the press will be both more necessary and at the same time less effective in fostering coherent communication among elites.

In the United States, foreign policy decisions are often made in interaction with public opinion. Officials have to consider how their actions will be viewed by the public. Bernard Cohen, a longtime analyst of the media's role in American foreign

policy, wrote that the U.S. media impose on foreign-policy officials "a set of priorities and perspectives that are frequently different from the priorities and perspectives that would otherwise
inform their judgment."[10] This would seem obvious, necessary,
and natural in a democracy—only it is not at all the same in
the Dutch democracy. In the Netherlands, officials of the Foreign Ministry operate almost entirely outside the context of
news coverage and public opinion. Cohen wrote, "The Dutch
media . . . only very rarely play an agenda-setting role in foreign affairs, and they make no major contribution of their own
to any ongoing public debate about foreign policy."[11] To the
limited extent that there is any press coverage of foreign policy
making before decisions are made, it is reporting of parliamentary debate, led invariably by top party officials. Whereas the
U.S. media sometimes play an agenda-setting role in foreign
policy by providing "a widespread and persistent media focus on
an issue," Dutch media attention to foreign policy is "limited,
often accidental, random, even idiosyncratic."[12]

The United States has a more decentralized and participatory
political structure than does any other democratic nation except
Switzerland. America has more elective offices, more frequent
elections, more initiatives and referenda, more overlapping and
practically indecipherable districts than other countries. One
of the consequent difficulties in covering American politics is
that "there's too much politics," as a veteran reporter of local
politics in California remarked.[13] In many urban areas, where
television does not cover local election campaigns, the dominant
metropolitan newspaper has to cover races for mayor, city attorney, county boards, state representatives, school boards, judges,
and so forth. Any one story—apart from the few citywide or

countywide offices—will be irrelevant to a large majority of voters and readers. Chances are, in fact, that with overlapping districts and redistricting every ten years, voters will not even know for which offices they are eligible to vote. Nothing has worried media analysts more during the past few years of severe economic crisis among metropolitan daily newspapers than the problem of covering local politics. Only the metro dailies have invested significantly in local political reporting and now, as many of them reduce newsroom employment by a third or a half or even more, local political coverage has declined.

Anglo-American media studies have generally taken liberal democracy for granted and so have often been insensitive to political and legal determinants of news production. Increasingly, this is being recognized as a serious deficiency. In the 1980s in Europe, in the face of a threat to public broadcasting from conservative governments sympathetic to commercialization, many scholars came to view public broadcasting as a pillar of a free public life.[14] New efforts have been made to articulate a view of "civil society" in which the media hold a vital place and attain a degree of autonomy from both state and market, as in the best public service broadcasting.[15]

This correctly suggests that among the world's market societies are a variety of different institutional forms taken by constitutional regimes governing the press. Knowing that a nation is capitalist, even knowing that the press is composed of private, profit-seeking firms, is not enough to predict the nature of a nation's journalism. State-operated media in authoritarian political systems serve directly as agents of state social control. But both publicly and privately owned media in liberal societies serve in a wider variety of roles: cheerleading the established order, alarming the citizenry about flaws in that order, providing a civic forum for political debate, and acting as a battleground among contesting elites. Performance of these functions varies with political culture and law. In terms of press law, Sweden and the United States protect free and open expression better than do the United Kingdom, France, and Germany. On the other hand, parliamentary systems with proportional representation, such as those in France, Germany, and Sweden, tend to accommodate a wide range of views in the central parliament, whereas the American two-party, winner-take-all electoral system normally (but not always) favors centrist positions and tends to prevent extreme or idiosyncratic views from gaining attention.

The distinction between "market" and "state" organization of media and the distinction between commercial and public forms of broadcasting are vital. Still, they mask important differences within each category. Public broadcasting may be operated by a quasi-independent corporation or directly run by the government. Its income may come from fees only (as in Japan, the United Kingdom, and Sweden), or also from advertising (as in Germany, France, and Italy), or from the government treasury (as in Canada). In the United Kingdom, cabinet ministries determine fee levels, whereas in Japan, France, and Germany, the parliament makes the decision.[16] Each of these variations creates and results from a distinct politics of the media. In Norway, Sweden, France, and Austria, the state has for several decades subsidized newspapers directly, especially newspapers offering substantial political information but receiving low advertising revenues. These policies, which I look at more closely in chapter 11, have sought to increase public access to diverse political viewpoints. The subsidies have fallen in recent years, as governments have come to place more faith in market principles and the virtues of economic efficiency.[17] The "state vs. market" distinction by itself gives no intellectual leverage for assessing or understanding any of these variations.

Consider another domain of variation that has become more and more important: how should the news media cover the private behavior of public officials? There is great concern, particularly in the United Kingdom and the United States, that commercial motives have led to a dangerous preoccupation with sex over politics. Yet in Germany, coverage of sexual behavior of politicians or other celebrities barely exists, because German civil law gives strong protection to personal privacy. News coverage of "the intimate sphere" is generally illegal. British and American law, on the other hand, give vastly greater freedom to report on private behavior, especially the private behavior of "public" persons such as politicians or celebrities.[18]

Or think about the relationship of the press to political parties. In American broadcasting, political parties are almost invisible. When newscasters cover a national political event, they most often portray it as a battle between the president and Congress. The implications of events for party strength are therefore much less likely to be noticed than are the implications for presidential stature with the public or with Congress. In Italian broadcasting, in contrast, newscasters less often provide their own political analysis and instead interview a spokesperson from each of the leading political parties. The news thus presents a range of partisan opinions and reinforces the central place of the parties in politics. The American style reinforces the relative weakness of political parties in the public mind.[19] French newspapers operate more like the Italian rather than the

U.S. media; more than a quarter of those quoted in political news in France are party spokespersons, whereas party officials are scarcely ever quoted in the United States.[20]

Or consider the extent to which journalists feel obliged to represent the news with an eye to the security and preservation of their country. In Israel, senior journalists see economic censorship (by media owners) as a greater danger to a free press than state censorship (by the military). The press in Israel began as a revolutionary Zionist press and to this day retains a deep, internalized commitment to Zionism. The result is that direct or overt censorship on matters pertaining to the military is very rare; the journalists exercise their own self-censorship. Although military censors and journalists will argue fiercely over particular stories, the arguments are rooted in fundamental, shared understandings. Israel's chief military censor said, "The editors have children just as I do, and my children and their children serve in the same army, for the same security reasons, for the same state."[21] With a generation of journalists now in charge who were not part of the original nation-building elite, with the presence of more foreign journalists covering the Arab-Israeli conflict, and with the increase of live television reporting, censorship has become much more difficult than it once was. Even so, while the Israeli-Arab conflict dominates Israeli political life, "journalists carry with them the concerns of any press at war, asking—Will this story serve the enemy? Endanger a hostage? Increase long-term risks of nuclear war?"[22] This kind of self-consciousness about the risks to national security of reporting and publishing has been rare although by no means unknown in the United States, especially at the height of the cold war. After September 11, 2001, however, American journalists individually and collectively shared in a wave of patriotic fervor and a deep sense of vulnerability. This led to some serious self-criticism about news stories that detailed the flaws in airport security, the vulnerability of subways to terrorist attack, and the technology of crop dusting. When reporters and editors begin to reasonably imagine that their audiences include mass murderers who seek to inflict as much damage on the country as they can, these journalists, too, carry out their work on a wartime footing.

Political culture is not a term meant to suggest that "everybody does it differently." Common elements are shared in the news media across nations. In some respects, a remarkable conjoining of cultural trends and styles has arisen in recent years across national borders. As this chapter has indicated, media professionals have become more central to political communication in one country after another. Party organization and loyalty have been weakening in most of Europe and in many other regions of the world, too. Party organizations direct more of their attention to winning elections rather than to building deep structures of political socialization. They rely more and more on affiliated interest groups. They trust increasingly in "capital intensive" campaign strategies built on political advertising and the fine-tuning of candidates' speeches, appearances, and ideological coloring. The "labor intensive" campaign of days gone by—the "ground war" of politics as opposed to the TV advertising "air war"—has not disappeared. Today, however, it is directed by campaign professionals whose voter databanks give them greater precision than in the past about which doors their armies of paid and unpaid workers should knock on and which phones they should call up.[23]

Globalization is not necessarily a mysterious process. Developing nations borrow patterns of journalism directly from the United States and the European countries. Nicaraguan newspapers in the 1990s had endured decades of censorship, first by the Anastasio Somoza regime and then by the Sandinista regime; they finally developed in a much broader and freer political environment. A wide variety of sources lavished assistance on them. Some Nicaraguan journalists gained formal credentials abroad. One editor earned a master's degree at a Chilean university; another attended a World Bank–sponsored seminar for journalists in Colombia; others studied in programs for Latin American journalists at Florida International University, which has trained thousands of foreign journalists. Still others visited U.S. newspapers under the sponsorship of the International Center for Journalists. The U.S. embassy in Nicaragua organized workshops for journalists. Spanish journalists and newspaper designers brought new ideas and plans to *La Tribuna*, one of Managua's dailies. Nicaragua's leading newspaper, *La Prensa*, hired U.S.-based consultants.[24]

No topic is more in need of new conceptualization than the relationship between news and politics. Daniel Hallin and Paolo Mancini took a big step toward it in their study of media and politics in eighteen western European and North American democracies.[25] They found three broad patterns, labeled "liberal" (or North Atlantic), "democratic corporatist" (or northern European), and "polarized pluralist" (or Mediterranean), which differ according to whether journalistic professionalism is strong (as in the first two models) or weak (as in the Mediterranean or southern Europe model), how closely allied the papers are to the political parties, and how much the state intervenes in the news industry. Hallin and Mancini understand fully that no conceptualization will be useful if it ignores variations in press laws, political institutions, and political culture. Students of the press have long recognized that journalism does not stand outside politics looking in; journalism is an element of politics. Frequently, this observation is offered up as a rebuke to journalists who have stepped across the observer-participant boundary. Understanding journalism as a part of politics should be not the closing line of a sermon but part of a continuing inquiry into how different political cultures and institutions shape different news cultures and institutions.

Chapter Nine
THE AUDIENCE FOR NEWS

IT IS NOT EASY to say what people do with news, because they do so many different things with it. Newspaper readers may quickly scan headlines, glance at a weather map, check the baseball scores, read a few paragraphs by a favorite columnist, read every word of a review of the movie they just saw for the pleasure of comparing notes, or read a movie review because they have just secured a babysitter for the first time in a month and plan to see a show. They may look quickly through the food section to find a recipe or to clip a coupon. If they are reading online, they may e-mail a story to themselves, for future reference, or to a friend who may find it funny or may have a special interest in it, or they may relay the news on Facebook or Twitter. The many uses and tastes for television news are likewise varied. One person may be dedicated to C-SPAN, in part because friends and acquaintances appear on it with some frequency, but will turn it off when his or her spouse, who finds C-SPAN a bore, enters the room. Another person may watch the evening "magazine" news shows, complaining through the entire hour about their smug superficiality.

All of these behaviors can be found in the same household, on the same day, within the same hour. Any news consumer has a range of consumption habits, a large repertoire of the ways he or she finds use and pleasure in news. Readers and viewers vary tremendously in the intensity of their engagement with news, even from one moment to the next, let alone from one person or occasion to the next.

This does not mean that news readers are fickle and that news institutions must work hard to seduce them. These same flighty readers may read textbooks with great patience and care, watch movies with effortless engagement, go over travel brochures or mortgage amortization tables with the avidity and acuity of Sherlock Holmes examining a telltale clue. The news media do not find and respond to an existing audience; they create one. There is no news consumer apart from the news. There is no "short attention span" apart from the kind of world that elicits certain types and qualities of attention.

News is one of the cultural forms that does not require people's constant concern. A distinction has emerged in studies of the history of books and reading that may be applicable here. Historians have argued that there has been a shift over time from a quality of reading termed "intensive" to one termed "extensive." In intensive reading, people typically read very few works or even just one work—most commonly, the Bible or another sacred text—read it over and over, memorize it, and assume others are familiar with it. In extensive reading, people pick up and put down a work, read and discard a wide variety of reading materials, read in a cursory rather than devotional fashion, and are more likely to read for pleasure than for instruction and spiritual well-being. A move from intensive to extensive modes of reading is coincident with the eighteenth-century development of the novel and the newspaper as widely distributed print genres. These new popular forms did not displace older ones but were added to them. Devotional reading continued. A close study of the reading habits of the celebrated eighteenth-century British man of letters Samuel Johnson found that Johnson read different texts for different purposes in different ways. He closely studied some texts and read others in a more cursory fashion. He was, in other words, both an intensive and an extensive reader.[1]

So are most readers. But the cheap and easy availability of popular, nonreligious forms of print moved the center of gravity in reading from intensive to extensive. True, many people's primary acquaintance with books these days is the textbook, and they may rarely pick up a book once they leave school. But they read magazines, newspapers, computer screens, medication-package inserts, contracts, technical manuals, websites, street signs, and much more.

As for the newspaper, it has intensive and even ritual qualities of its own. This fact was illustrated by one of the classic papers of media sociology, published by Bernard Berelson in 1949.[2] Berelson had the wit to see the 1945 newspaper strike in New York City as an opportunity for social research. The delivery workers of all the leading newspapers of the city went on strike for more than two weeks. What happened to New Yorkers who could no longer get their daily news?

Of course, there were alternative news sources, most notably radio news. And no doubt some New Yorkers could obtain newspapers from Hartford, New Haven, Philadelphia, or Trenton. Still, hundreds of thousands of people who normally read one or more daily newspapers suddenly had none. So what happened? Berelson and his colleagues interviewed sixty New Yorkers, distributed across economic and educational strata. They discovered that most people would quickly talk about how important it was to follow the serious news of national and international affairs and that they felt deprived when they were unable to do so. But only half of these could come up with a specific topic in the world about which they wished they had more information. Only about a third of respondents overall seemed to miss the newspaper's coverage of "serious" political and economic affairs.

And yet almost all the respondents truly missed the newspaper, for a variety of reasons. News assisted them in daily living—providing the schedule of radio programs or movie listings, advertisements for shopping, daily weather forecasts. News also offered welcome escape from the dullness of everyday life in the richness of its human interest content and its cheap, accessible delivery. People also used the paper as a respectable resource for entering into social conversation. For some readers, the newspaper was social contact in itself, especially for women who followed the gossip columns. They found in the newspaper a source of what scholars would later term "para-social interaction," interacting with characters in the media as if they were friends or acquaintances.[3] "You get used to certain people," one respondent told Berelson, "they become part of your family, like Dorothy Kilgallen" (a prominent gossip columnist).[4]

Berelson found that people liked the newspaper simply for the pleasure of reading. In the absence of the newspaper, they moved not so much to other sources of news as to other forms of reading, such as old magazines lying around the house. This alternative reading gave some satisfaction but did not replace the intensity of many readers' connection to the newspaper. Readers, Berelson suggested, shared a "ritualistic and near-compulsive" attachment to the newspaper. They read the paper at a particular time of day, often as a secondary activity to accompany eating or traveling to work. Half of respondents discussed the habitual nature of their attachment to the newspaper.[5] When they missed the newspaper, as media scholar Theodore Glasser has observed, they were not informationally unprepared to meet the day but *emotionally* unprepared. They were robbed not of information and advice about the weather, the stock market, or the news from Washington but of a "serenity" that the news-reading ritual provides.[6]

Very likely they also missed the time-filling function the newspaper or other stray reading matter can serve. This incidental use of the newspaper presented itself early on; in the 1850s novelist Fanny Fern wondered how people managed life before newspapers. "What did cab-drivers do, while waiting for a tardy patron? What did draymen do, when there was a 'great calm' at the dry-goods store of Go Ahead & Co.?"[7]

Not everyone could turn to other reading material when the newspaper was gone. It was part of life in many American homes for parents to read the newspaper comics to their children. The strike put an end to that for most New Yorkers. Fiorello La Guardia, New York's feisty mayor at the time, made a regular radio broadcast from City Hall. He closed a Sunday broadcast soon after the strike began by calling to children in the audience to "gather around and I will tell you about Dick Tracy today." He then read the comic strip, playing the roles of different characters with appropriate voices. While still on the air, he called to WNYC's program director, "Morris, every afternoon . . . I want a program . . . so long as the papers are not delivered, of the funnies for the children." The next week the newsreel cameras were rolling as La Guardia pulled out the comics and read again of the latest adventures of Dick Tracy. It was a gesture that endeared La Guardia to the citizens of New York.[8]

This is a reminder of the many features—including the comics—that have linked citizens to their newspapers. The newspaper for children has been a symbol of adulthood; for young children, the comics, and for some older children, the sports section, became symbolic transitions to adulthood.[9] Some of us retain these childlike tastes. Some people live for the daily crossword; others are enamored of the comics throughout their lives. Indeed, nothing attracts more letters to the editor than a change in the format of the funnies. On June 19, 2000, the fifty-two-year-old *Rex Morgan, M.D.* comic changed artistic hands, and readers bitterly complained that "the new artist has totally changed the faces of all the people in the strip."[10]

The ritualism of newspaper reading continues for many people. In the 1950s and '60s watching the network evening news was a ritual for many American families. A smaller number were ritualistically attached to the more lightweight morning news programs. Nothing appears to be more important for people who watch local television news than the look, sound, and personalities of the local news anchors (who are rewarded with vastly higher salaries than other local television news workers). None of this enters into the lore of journalism. Journalists want to astound, surprise, move, and motivate their audiences. But even crime stories rarely surprise; more often, they reassure, they restore, they offer vicarious cognitive control over the uncertainties of living.[11]

One might imagine it would greatly improve journalism if journalists knew what audiences wanted. But it may be that the less they know the better! In the 1980s and 1990s, as news organizations became more and more anxious about the bottom line, they increasingly turned to consultants to tell them how to cater to a bored, fickle public, ever ready to turn the page or change the channel. Consultants and their focus groups notwithstanding, journalists generally kept operating on their own intuitive judgments about audiences. Thirty-five years ago, sociologist Herbert Gans found that reporters and editors at U.S. newsmagazines and network television programs "had little knowledge about the actual audience and rejected feedback from it." They typically assumed that "what interested them would interest the audience."[12] Journalists still work in this way but less so; the ready availability of e-mail and other online feedback, especially for reporters and columnists who encourage it, increases journalists' knowledge of and interaction with audiences.

Nevertheless, journalists often write as much to impress their colleagues as to influence a broader audience. Historian Robert Darnton remembers that in his stint as a *New York Times* reporter in the 1960s, neither he nor his colleagues ever wrote for the audience of newspaper subscribers. "We wrote for one another. . . . We knew that no one would jump on our stories as quickly as our colleagues, for reporters make the most voracious readers, and they have to win their status anew each day as they expose themselves before their peers in print."[13] Not only are other reporters more likely than the general audience to read stories, they are more likely to respond. The sociologist Everett C. Hughes used to say that a quack is someone who succeeds in pleasing customers rather than colleagues. Reporters who are too eager to please their general audience, we might infer from this, are the quacks of journalism.

But times are changing in this regard. In the online world, it is much easier than it used to be to quickly respond to a news story with an email or a post on a journalist's blog. Audiences provide journalists much more direct responses than ever before—appreciation, applause, criticism, and correction. Journalists take note, take the general audience into account more than in the past, and can still keep their colleagues in mind most of all. The news media may reach hundreds of thousands or millions of people, but the journalists do not come face-to-face with the general public at the office the next morning. Instead, they face their sources; their editors; their fellow reporters; reporters from other news organizations on the same beat or story; and their spouses, parents, and children. These are still their most faithful, most regular, and most consequential readers.

To some degree, news is designed for insiders and is written in code. The general reader may not know who "a highly placed source close to the president" is, but this is the kind of phrase that Washington, D.C., elites will be able to decipher. Not only the phrase will allow them to determine which aide, if not the president himself, was the reporter's source, but they will be able to infer the person's motives for talking to the reporter. Like a children's book or movie, or like *The Simpsons* on television, a news story may be a complex construction that communicates one message to one audience and, by irony and innuendo, a very different message to a more sophisticated audience.

Amid a veritable deluge of public information, people— especially the young—exhibit a declining appetite for newspapers, newsmagazines, and the "serious" news presented on television. Disparities in the news audience by age, education, and income are familiar and long-standing, but the trends over time are disturbing for those in the newspaper business. In 1977, 67 percent of the American population read newspapers regularly. In 1997, only 51 percent did. For citizens with less than a high school education, 57 percent read newspapers regularly in 1977, but only 39 percent did so in 1997. For college graduates the trend was also sharply downward: from 77 percent to 60 percent.[14] Note how deep the decline in newspaper reading was even before the general availability of online news.

Today, the declines continue. A national survey in 2007, focused on young consumers, found that 49 percent of people over age thirty and 29 percent between the ages of eighteen and thirty read a newspaper every day or several times a week. Of the over–age thirty group, 80 percent watched national television news several times a week or more compared to 57 percent of the eighteen-to-thirty-year-old group. For local TV news, the figures were 81 percent and 61 percent; for radio, 58 percent and 44 percent; and for the Internet, 31 percent and 38 percent, respectively—the only medium where younger people were more attentive than their elders.[15] Among people 18 to 29 years old, the Internet equaled television as their "main news source" in 2008 and 2009 and surpassed television in 2010. TV is the main news source for all other age groups but the Internet is second, displacing newspapers, among people 30 to 49.[16]

The news industry is alarmed for obvious economic reasons, but in fairness, their concern is not exclusively economic; people in the news business, especially in newspapers, feel the move away from news and notably the move away from print is a sign of cultural decline. Still, it is all too easy to believe that "in my (older) generation and not in your (younger) generation, we did things right." Some critics resist this and see the coverage of politics as a topic of entertainment on daytime TV talk shows, late-night comedic monologues, cable television "fake news" programs like *The Daily Show* and *The Colbert Report*, and personality-oriented interview shows not as "dumbing down" political coverage but as opening political discourse to a wider audience while removing some of the stuffiness of conventional coverage.[17]

The general question about audiences is, who reads or watches? The next question, for many audience researchers, is, how can we keep these people in the audience and how can we get more demographically desirable people into the audience? This policy objective comes from the interest of news organizations in making money. It comes also from nonprofits such as the BBC in the United Kingdom or PBS in the United States, which justify themselves to their boards of directors and to the governments or organizations that subsidize their operations by showing that they are serving people in their communities. If no one is watching or reading, of course, it is hard to make a case for continued subvention. It comes, finally, from the conviction—and there are data to back it up—that people who follow the news are also more likely to be people who vote and in other respects attend to public life.[18] Encouraging more people to keep informed inspires more people to participate in public life.

Chapter Ten
NEWS AS LITERATURE AND NARRATIVE

A NEWS STORY is both news and a story. Because it is a story, readers can expect it to have a beginning, a middle, and an end and to operate by some standard conventions of narrative prose. It is purportedly a true story—that is, a story about something that happened. Because it is a true story, it is responsible not only to literary convention but to a faithful rendering and even a verifiable rendering of what really happened.

Journalists are often more aware of the claims they make to truth than of the fact that they present their work in the form of a story. "I guess usually I don't consider myself a storyteller," said *Philadelphia Inquirer* investigative reporter William Marimow. "I consider myself a gatherer of facts."[1] Still, the reporter's job is to make meaning. A list of facts, even a chronologically ordered list, is not a story and it is not a news story. From a list or chronicle, the writer must construct a tale, one whose understanding requires a reader or viewer to recognize not merely the sum of facts but the relationships among them. For this to happen, the news story must be recognizable as a certain type: straight or feature, sports or politics, human interest news or breaking news. Implicitly or explicitly, the writer learns to tailor the facts to a form and format in which their relationships will come to make sense.

That abstract process becomes concrete in the daily life of the working journalist. It takes shape around a number of basic, workaday questions:

Is this a story? Is there a story in that set of facts or events?
"All is calm but for a cat climbing a tree. The cat gets stuck in the tree. Firefighters are called. Neighborhood children gather to watch. Firefighters rescue the cat." This is a coherent story. It narrates a set of related events with a beginning, a middle, and end. It defines a problem or obstacles, describes a set of activities directed toward resolving the problem, and finally resolves the problem and returns the world to normal.

Is this a news story? Perhaps it is, at least to enterprising sixth-graders publishing a newsletter for the block where the cat drama took place. For them, this might be front-page news, a big break from routine life on their street. But the metropolitan paper or even the community weekly will not run the story. It is too familiar and too predictable. If ants published newspapers, it might be a headline every time you walked down the street and wiped out a few dozen of their leading citizens. But stepping on ants is so much part of even a sixth-grader's daily life and its victims so far from sixth-grade consciousness that it won't make their school paper.

What if the cat belongs to the mayor? Better still, what if the cat belongs to the city councilman who just voted to reduce the fire department budget, complaining that the firefighters "spend too much time rescuing cats and not putting out fires"? Now, suddenly, reporters have a story, and a rather delicious one at that. Why? Is it the pleasure of irony? In part. But if it had been an ordinary citizen who had just complained to neighbors that the fire department spends too much time rescuing cats, it would not be news. This citizen made a private statement, not a public one. And this citizen is not an elected official whose views are always potentially public acts, whose facial expressions will be scanned for their world import. The news story must not only be tantalizing but somehow impinge on or offer a kind of commentary on public life. What counts as public life, of course, is not obvious. It changes from time to time and it varies from place to place. Part of the unsettling transformation of news in our own day is that large domains of life have newly moved from private to public.

What's the lead?

Finding the most important element of the narrative is a subtle part of the task of story construction. The reporter seeks a lead when she knows she has a story but has not quite located the heart of it. This should be a familiar enough anxiety to anyone who has written a term paper in which he or she had to choose their own topic rather than respond to a set topic from the instructor. The student must arrive at an interesting question, interesting enough to be a topic for a paper. Reporters face the same challenge in finding a lead. Is there an interesting topic in this general array of facts? What stands out as notable and newsworthy? At the Democratic National Convention in August 2000, candidate Al Gore gave a forty-minute acceptance speech and nearly every newspaper across the country identified the same headline and the same lead, quoting Gore's claim "I stand here my own man." The lead provides a theme for the story as a whole. In narrating a complex event or one segment of an extended event, just as Gore's speech was one notable but small segment in a yearlong campaign for the presidency, the reporter must have an instinct for the heart of the matter. Sometimes it is obvious—which is to say, there is widespread consensus. Sometimes there is room for a variety of very different leads concerning the same set of events.

Does it have legs?

A reporter constructs a story for a particular day's edition of the news. But is it a one-day wonder or an ongoing story? In the jargon of journalism, does the story have legs? Our penny-pinching city council member's cat is most likely a one-day story, an amusing but incidental sidebar. It might suggest a follow-up on council members who take advantage of city services whose budgets they try to cut, but the story itself goes nowhere. A story with legs, on the other hands, strikes journalists as a palpable force with a momentum of its own that will generate follow-up stories. A story with legs plays the journalist as much as the journalist plays the story.

A REPORTER DIRECTS these questions and others in the first instance to editors and fellow reporters. The questions are anchored in general patterns and norms of journalistic culture. Only indirectly do reporters consider their audience of news readers and viewers, but in the end assumptions about what audiences want and what will please them are at stake. The response most journalists want to evoke in their audience is, as media scholar Peter Parisi has written, "astonishment, not understanding." He cited one reporter saying that she wanted to write stories that would make a man reading the front page at the breakfast table spit out his coffee and declare, "My God,

Martha, did you see this?"[2] Media analysts have called these "what a story!" stories. Editor Bob Woodward at the *Washington Post* advised the reporters he supervised to go after "Holy shit!" stories.[3] For all of the philosophizing one finds about news and democracy, the working journalist mostly seeks a spitting-out-the-coffee response, not an engaging-in-public-debate response. The reporter hopes for readers who will be scandalized more than enlightened, who will marvel more than learn, who will feel irresistibly compelled to say to the next person they meet, "Did you hear about . . . ?"

Reporters cannot manufacture "Holy shit!" stories. They can seek them out. They can have a nose for news and follow their nose toward holy-shit jackpots. They can craft the story in a way to heighten or highlight this effect. But that is as far as they can go. They have to hope they will be lucky enough to stumble on just the right set of events or to be the first on the scene when the Cessna crashes on the White House lawn.

Obviously, most stories do not produce the "what a story!" effect. Some do not even try. Investigative reporting seeks not a spitting out of the coffee but a sputtering "There ought to be a law!" The investigative story seeks to evoke moral outrage. As media scholars Theodore Glasser and James Ettema have shown, it carefully constructs an innocent victim and a guilty party, and it provides both a cognitive ordering of events for the audience and a moral ordering of responsibilities.[4] The outcome will reinforce the common moral order; news stories do not challenge fundamental moral assumptions, although the events they narrate or the sources they quote may do just that. "Events on city streets and in county jails are not merely represented but rather made compellingly real because they are shown to belong to an order of moral existence that renders them meaningful."[5] These stories enable readers to "judge the moral significance of human projects . . . even while we pretend to be merely describing them."[6]

WE TELL STORIES for various reasons. People may tell stories to children at bedtime to ease them to sleep or on a long car ride to keep them awake until they get home. People may tell stories to impart lessons or to entertain. They may tell family stories to keep a tradition and identity alive—that is, they may tell stories as homage to the past. Or people may tell stories with an eye to the future, to inspire or to motivate. Journalists tell stories professionally rather than as part of daily life, but they make use of all these possibilities, sometimes writing to soothe and sometimes to enliven, sometimes to honor and commemorate, and sometimes to embolden and impassion. They tell stories competitively, seeking to do better than their rivals at the next desk or on the next newspaper or television station. They may seek the astonishing spitting-out-the-coffee story or follow a community-building, ritually reaffirming story that covers a state funeral or a reconciliation of two political rivals, thereby inducing in the audience a sense of well-being and belonging.[7]

Most understandings of news generation merge two ideas: a "cultural" view, which centers on storytelling, and the various social-organizational views of news manufacturing that have already been discussed. These two kinds of accounts are analytically distinct. Organizational views take news to be a manufactured product created anew each day in interactions among firms, markets, and resources. A cultural view is more impressed with the things news workers inherit than with what they create; it emphasizes not social production so much as the symbolic determinants of news in the relation between facts and symbols. A cultural account of news helps explain generalized images and stereotypes in the news media—of predatory stockbrokers and hard-drinking factory workers—that transcend structures of ownership or even patterns of work relations.

For instance, in their analysis of British mass media coverage of racial conflict, media scholars Paul Hartmann and Charles Husband noted that "the British cultural tradition contains elements derogatory to foreigners, particularly blacks. The media operate within the culture and are obliged to use cultural symbols."[8] A 1973 article examining media coverage of homosexuals in Britain, took as a theoretical starting point the anthropological view that all societies like to keep their cultural concepts distinct. Societies are troubled by "anomalies" that do not fit the preconceived categories of the culture. Homosexuality is an anomaly in societies that view the opposition and relationship of male and female as fundamental. Thus homosexuals provide a culturally charged topic for storytelling that seeks to preserve or reinforce the conventional moral order of society— and its conceptual or symbolic foundation. News stories about homosexuals may be moral tales: "a negative reference point . . . an occasion to reinforce conventional moral values by telling a moral tale. Through these means tensions in the social system can be dealt with and 'conventionalized.'"[9]

A cultural account of this sort can explain too much; after all, news coverage of homosexuality has changed enormously since 1973. Recent studies of U.S. news coverage concluded that gays and lesbians appear much more in the news now than they did fifty years ago. They are covered much more "routinely" as ordinary news subjects rather than moral tales, and although coverage is not free of antigay prejudice, it is generally fair.[10]

Similarly, we must be cautious with broad cultural explanations of the prevalence and character of crime news as fulfilling deep societal needs for moral order. It makes sense that broad and long-lasting phenomena—like heavy news coverage of crime over two centuries across many societies—will have deep cultural roots. It is also important to recognize fashions, trends, and changes in coverage. For instance, sociologist Joel Best recounted how some newly defined crimes receive only occasional or episodic press coverage, and others, with better institutionalized support in a "victim industry," receive more systematic and ongoing treatment. What is at stake here is the interaction between general cultural and specific social-organizational dimensions of news.[11]

News is not one literary form but instead a set of literary forms. Some news forms are as predictable and formulaic as the unfolding of a mystery novel, a romance, or a limerick. Others are more complex, and neither the practitioner nor the reader is entirely conscious of what the aesthetic constraints are. Political news, for example, varies from the breaking story to the reflective news analysis to the investigative series run on three consecutive days. It also appears in the magazine essay and the full-length book that is often a second look at material the writer first wrote as hard news. Even within a single story variation can be found. In most newspapers the headline and lead tend to defer to official sources; in the body of the story, alternative interpretations may appear and (as in the *Los Angeles Times* story on President Ronald Reagan's stopover to survey flood damage in Louisiana, discussed in chapter 3) directly undermine the preceding official version.

Elements of content may fit conventional notions of ideology or, more or less consciously, more or less obviously, express widely accepted dominant values. Aspects of form operate at a more subtle level. By using the word "form," I refer to assumptions about narrative, storytelling, human interest, and the conventions of photographic and linguistic presentation in news production. For instance, there are systematic differences between the inverted-pyramid structure of print news and the "thematic" structure of television news. The inverted-pyramid form is the standard journalistic literary matrix, a form within which every reporter operates. According to this model, a news story begins with a "lead" that answers the basic questions "who," "what," "when," "where," and "(sometimes) why" in the first few sentences. In the most strait-jacketed version of the model, all of these questions are addressed in the first sentence. Following the lead, the story takes on the most important features of the reported event and moves from one topic to the next in descending order of importance. This form was a peculiar development of late-nineteenth-century American journalism. It seemed to fit the technology of the telegraph—an inverted-pyramid story "telegraphs" the most important news first. But it did much more than that. It fit not only a world of telegraphs but also a world of increasingly independent and cocky journalists who were prepared to name on their own authority what aspect of the news could be judged the most important. This feature of the narrative form, then, implicitly authorized the journalist as expert. In political reporting, it helped redefine politics itself as a subject appropriately discussed by experts rather than partisans. The "summary lead" just described is not the only way a news story can begin. Reporters may try an "anecdotal lead," easing the reader into the story with, say, an account of how the general issue that the story will discuss affects a particular individual or family. The real topic of the story and the particular development that has occasioned it will then appear some paragraphs further on, in what journalists call the "nut graph" or "nut graf." Or a story may begin with what might be called an "analytical lead," a paragraph that offers a general overview of the topic or issue the story will consider.

Most research on the culture of news production takes it for granted that, at least within a given national tradition, there is one common news standard among journalists. This is one of the convenient simplifications of the sociology of journalism that merits critical attention. Indeed, it might be a point at which a lot of current assumptions about journalism begin to unravel. Reporters may adhere to norms of objectivity in reporting on a political campaign, but they also will not hesitate to report gushingly about a topic on which there is broad national consensus or to write derisively on a subject that lies beyond the bounds of popular consensus. It is as if journalists were unconsciously multilingual, code-switching from neutral interpreters to guardians of social consensus and back again without missing a beat. Media scholars Elihu Katz and Daniel Dayan have noted how television journalists in the United Kingdom, the United States, Israel, and elsewhere who narrate live "media events" rather than ordinary daily news stories abandon a matter-of-fact style for a tone of hushed reverence or a lyrical language that certifies, not merely describes, the majesty of a coronation, a funeral, or an Olympic Games closing ceremony.[12]

Journalists, well aware of the formal and informal norms of professional practice, are less cognizant of the cultural traditions that specify when or how professional norms are called into play. Communication scholar Daniel Hallin distinguished three domains of reporting.[13] Each operates by different journalistic rules. In the zone of "legitimate controversy," recognition of a culturally sanctioned conflict (like anything on which the two leading political parties differ) guarantees a professionalism dedicated to presenting both sides. In the zone of deviance, coverage of issues or groups goes beyond the reach of normal reportorial obligations of balance and fairness. These topics— for instance, gang members, sex offenders, preteen girls who swoon over pop music idols, and those pop music idols whose primary fans are preteen girls—can be ridiculed, marginalized, or trivialized because reporters instinctively realize that mainstream culture treats them with derision or contempt.

The third zone involves reporting on topics in which values are shared. It includes most feature writing, human interest reporting, much sports reporting, and occasional hard news reporting that takes for granted a common human sympathy between reporter and reader. For instance, it is inconceivable that after expensive houses perched on the edge of canyons are destroyed by mudslides in California or elegant vacation homes in a flood plain are wiped out, a reporter would ask why the devastated homeowners had been stupid enough to build there in the first place. They might, however, ask the local zoning authority why it had allowed those homes to be built. A private citizen could not be interrogated with the kind of aggressive questioning to which public officials are routinely subjected. Moreover, by unspoken understanding, there are not two sides to human tragedies. Consider the code switching in Israeli print journalism in covering the assassinated prime minister Yitzhak Rabin. In life, Rabin walked in the sphere of legitimate controversy, but in death, he was absorbed into the hallowed sphere of consensus.[14] No one teaches this at a journalism school, but everyone knows it. It is part of the culture of news gathering, part of the etiquette of the profession.

U.S. journalists instinctively and willingly abandon the effort to report from a neutral stance under at least three conditions. First, in moments of tragedy, journalists assume an almost priestly role. On television, correspondents adopt an air of solemnity. This attitude is evident, for instance, in news coverage of assassinations of political leaders, in state funerals, and in coverage of the mourning of the victims of the terrorist attacks of September 11, 2001. Second, in moments of public danger, journalists replace professional objectivity with neighborly reassurance, whether danger comes from terrorists or hurricanes. They seek to offer practical guidance and to communicate fellow-feeling. They become part of a public health campaign, not just a public information system. Finally, journalists reject neutrality during threats to national security. When they are convinced that national security is at risk, they willingly withhold or temper their reports. American journalists did so at the time of the Bay of Pigs invasion of Cuba in 1961, for example. In 2010, when the *New York Times* joined the *Guardian* (U.K.), *El Pais* (Spain), *Le Monde* (France), and *Der Spiegel* (Germany) in publishing stories based on the trove of confidential U.S. State Department cables WikiLeaks provided them, the *Times'* staff worked hard to avoid publishing any information that might endanger American military forces or individuals in Iraq, Afghanistan, and other countries who had assisted the U.S. war effort and might become targets if their identities were revealed.

The events of September 11, 2001, brought together all three moments where journalists choose to abandon neutrality: tragedy, public danger, and a grave threat to national security. Journalists sought to honor the victims of the terrorist attacks, called attention to the firefighters and police officers working at the World Trade Center as heroes, and a month later, strove to reassure citizens when anthrax infection threatened public panic. In cases of tragedy, public danger, and threats to national security, journalists take it for granted that there are no "sides" and that "we are all in this together." There was a rush of feeling that, for journalists, felt quite wonderful after September 11—a sense that this group, often alienated and alien, was momentarily at one with the general public.[15]

Another crucial cultural distinction in journalism separates news into departments: local, national, and foreign; or general news, business, sports, and features. These divisions of the field covered by news reporting are powerful and consequential. Take the distinction between general news reporting—which centers on politics—and business reporting. Executives of large corporations, who may often have more influence on the daily lives of citizens than do government officials, are invariably less visible in general news. They may be highly visible on the business pages, but the way they are covered in that section is radically different from the style of general news. On the front page, journalists write in anticipation of readers who ask, "What is happening in the world today that I should know about as a citizen of my community, nation, and world?" On the business page, journalists presume readers will ask, "What is happening in the world today that I should know about as an investor to protect or advance my financial interests?"[16] The reporter may be scrupulously professional in both cases, but by the unspoken assumptions of the genre, the die is already cast as to what can or cannot become a story, what angle will or will not make sense.

Though news operates by narrative conventions, the conventions are not fully under the control of the reporter. News writing, then, is not just a matter of assembling the appropriate mix of elements: click on the icon for television, radio, or print, then select from column A "breaking news," "news analysis," "investigative reporting," or "human interest"; from column B, choose the sphere of consensus, the sphere of legitimate controversy, or the sphere of deviance; from column C, select an expert, insider audience or a general, easily distracted audience. It does not work so mechanically. Still, news is organized by a set of literary conventions, a part of culture that reproduces aspects of a larger culture that the reporter and editor may never have consciously articulated. News is produced by people who operate, often unwittingly, within a cultural system, a reservoir of stored cultural meanings. It follows conventions of sourcing—who is a legitimate source, speaker, or conveyer of information to a journalist. It lives by unspoken preconceptions about the audience—less a matter of who the audience actually may be than a projection by journalists of their own social worlds. News as a form of culture incorporates assumptions about what matters, what makes sense, what time and place we live in, and what range of considerations we should take seriously.

A news story is supposed to answer the questions "who," "what," "when," "where," and "(sometimes) why" about its subject. To understand news as culture, however, requires asking what categories of person count as a "who," what kinds of things pass for facts or "whats," what geography and sense of time is inscribed as "where" and "when," and what counts as an explanation of "why." Media scholar James Carey argued brilliantly that news incorporates certain modes of explanation and rejects or makes subsidiary others. For most news, the primary mode of explanation is "motives." Acts have agents, agents have intentions, and intentions explain acts. In covering politics, the agent is ordinarily a politician or candidate and the motive is ordinarily political advantage or political power. If this mode of explanation seems insufficient to understand a given act or event, reporters may look also to "causes," such as broader social or institutional forces at work. By unspoken convention reporters may ascribe motives on their own authority, but if they have recourse to "causes," they must find "experts" to make the case.[17]

The "what" of news is equally a product of cultural presuppositions. Metropolitan newspapers are dependent on their suburban readers and will sometimes cater directly to their presumed needs and interests. But as media scholar Phyllis Kaniss observed in an important study of local news in Philadelphia, the central city remains the heart of local news coverage. Although a majority of readers do not live, work, or vote in the city, "news of the city government and city institutions . . . takes premier position over policy issues facing suburban communities."[18] The development of suburban industrial parks is barely noticed while downtown development or the renovation of the old train station wins continuous coverage. "These projects are given a place of prominence in the local news media not because of their importance to the regional audience, but because of their symbolic capital."[19] The mass media carry a great deal of symbolic freight in urban and regional identity, more than they know, and certainly more than they self-consciously engineer. They help to establish in the imagination of a people a psychologically potent entity—a "community"—that can be located nowhere on the ground. News, in this sense, is more the pawn of shared presuppositions than the purveyor of self-conscious messages.

All news stories are stories, but some are more storylike than others. Some of them remind us of the novel, the joke, the campfire story, gossip, the moral caution, the various fictional or nonfictional but highly structured and purposive forms people typically associate with the word "story." The classic "hard news" story places all of the critical information in the first sentence and does not compel most people to read to the end. That end is never a conclusion or a moral; it is only the least important information of all the information that would fit in the allotted space. Thus, hard news stories aren't narrative-driven in the sense of a traditional work of fiction or film. The classic hard news story operates more to convey useful information efficiently than to build a shared world with readers emotionally. At this end of journalistic writing, the reporter mimics a piece of machinery that conveys relevant information with accuracy. At the other end, the reporter resembles a literary or photographic artist, connecting worlds more than conveying data. To return to the discussion that opened chapter 4, the mechanical model is in some ways more closely connected with Habermasian visions of rational democracy, whereas the artistic model is more closely linked to Andersonian visions of horizontal community. Storytelling in the latter sense is part of community building. This narrative view of journalism sees news as part of a process of producing collective meanings rather than as a process of transmitting information. It emphasizes the social rather than the mechanical feature of the news process.

The emphasis on stories, narrative, and story form suggests a functional rather than instrumental idea. That is, it shows that understanding the news does not require that we know who transmits information to whom for what reason and with what effect. Instead, it reveals the whole news process as part of a ritual beyond the ken of any of its participants. Journalists do not have to read a handbook to know to shift from declarative reporting to emotive prose when they do human interest reporting or to adopt hushed tones when covering a state funeral. They move from neutral interpreters to hometown celebrators to guardians of social consensus and back again. They may or may not catch themselves in this act, and it does not matter if they do. They are a part of a larger culture and they play their appointed role. For journalists to fail at this would not be a professional error— it would be a kind of cultural sacrilege. It would mark them as rebels or mavericks or, if they got away with it, as innovators.

Chapter Eleven
LAW, DEMOCRACY, AND NEWS

NEWS AND NEWS INSTITUTIONS exist even where democracy does not. Notifying the public about politics does not require or even imply including the public in politics. Organized, regular information and commentary on contemporary affairs is provided for the people of China or Cuba just it was for the people of the Soviet Union, Fascist Italy, and Nazi Germany. News in these settings may have various functions. It may recruit people to national purposes, rally support for the government, or provide a common text for subversive deconstruction and the "reading between the lines" that so famously characterized citizens' attitudes toward the news in communist Eastern Europe. News is everywhere democratic only in the sense of being nonexclusive, published information potentially available to anyone who wishes to attend to it. It does not necessarily promote or seek to promote active, empowered citizenship.

News has little to do with political democracy unless the state includes or tolerates a degree of self-government and criticism of state power. The colonial American press contributed something to democracy because monarchical though the British Empire was, it also had a parliamentary tradition; there were representative assemblies in each of the thirteen American colonies.

When a society enjoys an elected legislature and an independent press, the consequences can be great. Amartya Sen, the

Nobel Prize–winning economist who has studied world hunger, has written, "No substantial famine has ever occurred in a country with a democratic form of government and a relatively free press."[1] This is so even for poor democracies beset by crop failures. Famine is more a product of distributional failures than shortfalls in production, and electoral democracy, with the support of publicity, does not fail the most needy in the ways authoritarian regimes do. News can take politicians to task: this has long been its most critical role in a democracy.

There is no doubting, then, the importance of the press to a democracy. But the press by itself is not democracy and does not create democracy. It has coexisted decade after decade with undemocratic, authoritarian, and repressive regimes. So it is not the case that, as media scholar James Carey put it, "journalism as a practice is unthinkable except in the context of democracy; in fact, journalism is usefully understood as another name for democracy."[2] For Carey, journalism is justified by the fact that it builds a democratic social order. "There were media in the old Soviet Union just as there was communication and even something resembling a news business. There just wasn't any journalism, because there was no democracy, which alone gives rise to the social practice of journalism."[3] But this evaluation conflates an empirical description of journalism with a normative public philosophy. Carey would like there to have been (and still to be) a practice called journalism that is dedicated to circulating the voices of engaged citizens who debate the common good and so generate new arguments, engage new voices, and regenerate society through politics. At some points in history, something like this has happened: Thomas Paine's publication of *Common Sense*, William Lloyd Garrison's editing of *The*

Liberator, the unstamped press of the British working class in the 1830s, the outburst of free expression in Eastern Europe in the late 1980s and early 1990s between the fall of communism and the consolidation of new commercial media, the emergence of a more critical and watchful press in the United States and parts of western Europe from the Vietnam war on, and the uses of online communication for political argument and organizing in many parts of the world in the past decade. But if this is all that counts as journalism, what is everything else that goes by its name?

It is journalism, too. When Brazil moved to a representative democracy after twenty years of military rule, the leading television news network—the privately operated TV Globo—didn't miss a beat. Business pragmatism had led TV Globo to serve the military regime well; the same business pragmatism, not journalistic commitments, led the network to support the new democracy. Democracy opened up a wider range of political criticism, but TV Globo's news coverage tended to be progovernment in the new system just as it had been under the old military regime.[4] The private, profit-making newspaper industry in Spain during the military regime of Francisco Franco made ideological purity its first priority. After Franco, in the transition to democracy, the very same newspapers emphasized profits first while offering increased opportunity for freedom of expression.[5]

It is tempting to see the sheer quantitative power of the printing press or broadcasting or the Internet to disseminate information as a naturally democratic force. Historian Paddy Scannell has made an especially eloquent defense of broadcasting's influence in this respect, writing that "broadcasting has enhanced the reasonable character and conduct of twentieth century life by augmenting claims to communicative entitlements. It does this through asserting a right of access to public life."[6] However, it is a lot easier to make this claim if one has the BBC in mind as representative of broadcasting, rather than state radio in a third-world dictatorship, or Central China Television, or even the American commercial networks.

One thing that can be said in favor of a natural link between journalism and democracy is that job satisfaction among reporters and editors seems to be directly related to the amount of freedom journalists have to write and publish as they please, without censorship or ideological constraint. Journalists of all political stripes like free expression; if they don't have it, they seek it out. Journalists who ply their trade under repressive regimes sometimes have been brave champions of a free press, identifying their vocation as one committed to freedom and designed for democracy. In China, for instance, journalists have developed a professional devotion to freedom of expression and have formed a pressure group for the liberalization of press laws.[7]

When journalism operates within a liberal democracy, it may operate in a variety of different ways. "Congress shall make no law abridging freedom of speech, or of the press": this simple, categorical prohibition in the First Amendment has been the pride of American journalism. And that pride is not misplaced. The press is more free of government restrictions in the United States than in any other nation on earth. However, the First Amendment does not mean exactly what most journalists think it means, nor does it resolve all matters of censorship and constraints on expression. In particular, limits on governmental constraints in the United States have made the American news media more vulnerable to the censorship of the marketplace. That is, the diversity of expression in the press is limited not by government censors but by publishers' need to make money. With strong competition for people's attention, the managers of broadcast and print media may be pressed to play down or delete news and views that would bore or offend the audience. Marketplace censorship is reduced in countries with strong state trusteeship of an independent media, such as the United Kingdom, or state-subsidized support for diverse and minority viewpoints, as in the Scandinavian countries. In the views of a growing number of important critics, following the First Amendment rigidly does not provide the best environment for encouraging freedom of expression.

Consider Pat Tornillo, who in 1972 ran for a seat in the Florida state legislature. The *Miami Herald* wrote a couple of scathing editorials about him. Tornillo asked for space in the paper to respond, citing a 1913 Florida "right of reply" statute that required newspapers to provide comparable space for reply, upon request, when the newspaper assails the personal character of any candidate for nomination or for election. When the *Herald* refused to satisfy Tornillo's request, he sued. The circuit court sided with the newspaper and declared the old statute unconstitutional, but the Florida Supreme Court reversed and held that the right of reply served the "broad societal interest in the free flow of information to the public." Many democracies around the world would agree. Right-of-reply provisions are commonplace around the world, either as constitutional or statutory protections; the models of France and Germany have been particularly influential.[8]

The *Miami Herald* believed, in contrast, that the right-of-reply statute abridged the freedom of the newspaper to publish what it pleases. The *Herald* appealed the Florida decision to the U.S. Supreme Court, which sided with the newspaper. The case posed a classic problem: Could government constitutionally enhance public debate and discussion only by staying out of media regulation altogether? Or could it and should it endorse press laws to enhance free expression and to make good what the Supreme Court in 1964 described as "a profound national commitment to the principle that debate on public issues should be uninhibited, robust, and wide-open"?[9]

On the face of it, a right-of-reply statute would seem a boon to public debate. In 1972, local television news largely ignored local politics, and the only general news coverage of candidates for most state and local offices was provided by newspapers. This is even more the case today. The fact that most American cities boast only one daily newspaper would make a statute like Florida's seem desirable, even a necessary protection for democracy. But the Supreme Court unanimously declared otherwise. All government remedies, the Court argued, would be worse than the disease. Justice Byron White saw in Florida's statute "the heavy hand of government intrusion" and feared making the government "the censor of what people may read and know."[10] For White, this was not permissible: if the marketplace was to be the censor, that would be regrettable but also fully constitutional; it is state censorship that the Constitution forbids.

Whereas the Supreme Court came down unanimously against right-of-reply statutes, constitutional law scholars remain divided. One such scholar, Benno Schmidt, made a spirited attack on the *Miami Herald* decision, holding that the opinion was "almost devoid of reasoned support, its use of precedent . . . disingenuous, and the constitutional principle announced . . . not consistent with other rules grounded in the First Amendment."[11] Law professor Cass Sunstein offered some cautious support for right of reply as part of a general argument that the purpose of the First Amendment is to protect democratic deliberation, not freedom of the marketplace. The First Amendment's aim, Sunstein argued, is to protect media institutions and a media system that affords "broad and deep attention to public issues" and provides "public exposure to an appropriate diversity of view."[12] To maximize these two chief values of democratic deliberation, it may be vital for government sometimes, and within careful limits, to intervene. According to this view, the position that government should invariably keep its hands off the news media may actually undermine, rather than preserve, basic democratic freedoms.

In contrast, law professor Lucas Powe, Jr., defended the *Miami Herald v. Tornillo* decision. He argued that the authors of the First Amendment knew nothing about newspapers committed to fairness or objectivity. They knew outspoken, partisan, brawling, bickering newspapers, full of unrestrained personal invective attacking politicians they opposed. This was the press that the First Amendment sought to protect. The *Miami Herald* decision reaffirmed, in Powe's view, that "we can have a free press or a fair one, but . . . we cannot have both."[13] Any state intrusion, he believes, will in the long run hobble press freedom.

This is just one example of the many questions about press freedom and democracy that concern First Amendment scholars. Should broadcasting be treated differently from print? Broadcasters require federal licensing, whereas newspapers do not.

Should this enlarge government's right to intervene in broadcast regulation? For instance, should television be subject to a "fairness doctrine" to ensure that contending political sides all get a hearing? The Federal Communications Commission once said yes but now says no. Should actions for libel be made easier or more difficult to sustain? How should individuals' right to a fair trial be balanced against the community's right to learn about the proceedings of trials? Are there ways the state can or should intervene to equalize speech between unusually loud voices and those too weak to leave a mark on public discussion without subsidized access to the media? There are many other important legal issues, but the example of the Florida right-of-reply statute focuses on the basic question with clarity: is freedom best served when government stands aside or when government intervenes on behalf of open, diverse expression?

Consider the direct press subsidies that some nations maintain. Norway, Sweden, and Finland are among the countries that provide direct government financial aid to the press. In Norway, the system began in 1969 as an effort to stem the worrisome decline in the number of newspapers after World War II. The government directed subsidies to small local newspapers, to newspapers of cultural minorities, particularly those serving the Saami ethnic group and to the "nondominant" newspaper in a given newspaper market. The aim was to keep the financially weaker newspapers in business and thereby to contribute to a diversity of political opinion in the public sphere. The results of this system have been mixed. It did help to keep newspapers from folding, and there were more Norwegian papers in 1995 than in 1972. On the other hand, the weakening link between political parties and daily newspapers left increasing numbers of markets without ideologically diverse media. So subsidies by themselves have not been able to maintain diversity of partisan political opinion, but they have encouraged media outlets for cultural minorities.

Whatever the strengths or failures of the Norwegian subsidies, it is at least apparent that free expression was not damaged by government involvement in the independent press. There is no indication that subsidized Norwegian newspapers, for instance, are more docile than other newspapers or more likely to withhold criticism of the government. In fact, one study indicates that these newspapers are more likely than others to criticize government policy.[14]

Obviously, there is room to disagree on questions of the best legal framework for a democratic media. Constitutional scholar Owen Fiss has distinguished between market-determined speech (what the press becomes if the state simply opts out) and democratically determined speech (what people would choose after full deliberation and with neither state nor market limitations).[15] Even the latter may be an insufficient ideal, however, since it is conceivable that a democracy would choose a regime of censorship, particularly of minority viewpoints. So another ideal has been proposed: "uninhibited, robust, and wide-open" debate on matters of public importance. This is the standard that Supreme Court justice William Brennan articulated in his most famous opinion, the majority opinion in *New York Times v. Sullivan* in 1964.[16]

The Brennan standard suggests that the First Amendment aims not to protect the individual's autonomy of expression (in practice, the individual news organization's autonomy) but to serve the society's goal of rich public debate. This was the point made by legal scholar Alexander Meiklejohn in a famous book published in 1948.[17] In it, he offered the model of the town meeting that not only encourages individuals to speak but also allows them to choose a moderator who, when appropriate, abridges their speech. The moderator enforces norms of public discussion. For instance, he or she makes sure that one person speaks at a time by recognizing people before they can speak. A good moderator also insists that people speak to the question that is before the meeting; individual speakers must adhere to common norms by keeping their speech relevant. The moderator may even deny the floor—or attendance at the meeting—to someone who persistently violates these norms. The town meeting does not guarantee that all persons can speak whenever and however they choose, but it organizes speech fairly in order to accomplish the public business. Meiklejohn wrote, "What is essential is not that everyone shall speak, but that everything worth saying shall be said."[18] Free speech in a democracy, he insisted, derives not from a law of nature but from a political and constitutional agreement that public matters are to be decided on the basis of universal suffrage. The term "moderator" has, of course, been revived in the digital age. Various online forums and wikis must decide if, and how, to moderate comments. Forums that try to operate without a moderator sometimes discover that moderation is necessary to keep a few individuals, through their incivility, from sabotaging the value of the discussion space for the vast majority of others.

If protecting the autonomy of an individual or an enterprise (like a newspaper) to exercise free speech enhances public debate, then that autonomy is to be devoutly protected—but not for its own sake. If that autonomy itself interferes with rich public debate, then the state should have legitimate means to intervene and to protect robust debate from individuals or enterprises that might hijack it. By this argument, Pat Tornillo should have won his case. The protection of the individual autonomy of media institutions against the state is a means, not an end, even if it is a favored means.

This doctrine, unfortunately, opens up a vast array of subtle and difficult decisions. It is a far cry from Supreme Court justice Hugo Black's blunt insistence that when the First Amendment declares "Congress shall make no law abridging freedom of speech, or of the press," then "no law means no law."[19] It does suggest that Americans might have something to learn from foreign models that may serve democracy as well as or better than the liberal-libertarian First Amendment tradition in the United States.

This leads to what might be for Americans a heretical question: is freedom of expression greater in the United States or in other democracies? How could we answer such a question? By what measures could one judge that there is greater or lesser freedom? In the broadest terms, some measures are clear. For instance, do journalists get shot or imprisoned or deported or lose their jobs for reporting things the government wants to keep confidential? Is there state censorship? Were publications bombed, burned, raided, or occupied? Were their employees charged, sentenced, fined, beaten, or tortured? In 2009, according to the well-respected Freedom House annual global review, the state of freedom of the press in the world deteriorated from recent years. The study's overall measure of press freedom evaluated legal restrictions on content, political pressures on content, economic influence on content, and direct repression of journalists or their news organizations. Overall, Freedom House judged sixty-nine countries to have a free press, sixty-three a partly free press, and sixty-four a press that is not free. Africa, Asia, eastern Europe and the former Soviet Union, and the Middle East fared worst, with fewer than 20 percent of countries in those regions having a free press. Western Europe was judged to have twenty-three countries with a free press, two partly free (Italy and Turkey), and none not free. The United States fared very well, with a total rating of 18 (a rating of 0 would be perfect). Finland, Iceland, Norway, and Sweden were at the top of the list (with a rating of 10 each).[20]

It is more difficult to put a number on internal practices that enhance or repress free expression. What about the everyday practices of journalism we have discussed already? Do they serve democracy or get in its way? Sociologist Herbert Gans has argued that the routines of daily journalism actually undermine democracy. If supporting democracy means encouraging citizens to be active, informed, and critical, then the standard operating procedure of mainstream journalism subverts its own best intentions. For instance, Gans observed that most news is "top down," favoring high-level government officials over lower-level government officials, favoring government officials over unofficial groups and opposition groups, and favoring groups of any sort over unorganized citizens.[21]

Moreover, in the relentless drive toward simple stories, simple prose, and conveniently routine coverage of the materials that are most reliably available daily, journalists develop a kind of "proxy" system that endangers civic engagement. The press tends to cover politics rather than the more difficult to grasp field of society and the difficult to uncover topics of economics.

Politics, Gans asserted, becomes a proxy for the forces that shape our lives in general. A presidential election, then, becomes a proxy for politics; the "horse race" becomes a proxy for the election. Voters are covered and nonvoters are not, so voters becomes the proxy for the citizenry at large.[22] Journalists may well believe that their job is to inform citizens, that informed citizens will participate in their democracy, and that the more this happens the better off our democratic system will be. But, Gans argued, the kind of information journalists in fact provide is not the kind of information that people can use to form political judgments, nor will it motivate them to get involved.

Is Gans too harsh? He seems to be examining only one side of the news media balance sheet. His critique ignores the ways in which the media give voice to all major parties (if not small dissident groups) and provide the common informational currency that alerts organized groups (if not unorganized and disaffected citizens) of political decisions that will affect their interests. He does not take into account that the media regularly undertake a certain amount of investigative work that startles, subverts, and amazes. His analysis acknowledges but gives the media no credit for affording political news a central, almost sacred, character in the print and national television news of Western democracies. The lead story on national television or the newspapers' front page is invariably a political story. Even for local and regional dailies, the top story of the day is normally a national or international story, presented in terms of its political implications and consequences.

When in 2001 Republican senator Jim Jeffords of Vermont defected from his party, declared himself an independent, and so made the Democrats the majority party in the U.S. Senate, the press pounced on the story. The explanations about what had happened and what its impact would be were all about politics. But the story wasn't all political, as was indicated in a business-page article in *USA Today*. Reporter Adam Shell observed, "The Nasdaq's six-session winning streak was snapped amid a wave of profit taking, caused in part by news that Sen. Jim Jeffords, R-Vt., apparently is defecting from the party to become an independent."[23] Wall Street insiders worried about the uncertainty this would cause, although Shell cited others who thought Jeffords's move would be good for the stock market in the long run. "The stock market loves gridlock," one said. "Now that the Republicans no longer have the majority in both houses, gridlock is back." In theory, the event in the Senate could have been generally reported in terms of its impact on the economy. In practice, no journalist gave this possibility a second's thought. Journalists and their audiences take it for granted that general news gives pride of place to politics

Journalistic deference to democratic political institutions may be weakening, however. By the mid-1990s, not a single British newspaper offered a parliamentary page or section with verbatim extracts from legislative discussions. A symbolically loaded moment came in 1991 when London's *Times* stopped publishing extracts of parliamentary speeches on a "parliamentary page" formerly set aside for this purpose. When Parliament inquired about this move, the newspaper's editor, Simon Jenkins, remarked that he could not find anyone "apart from Members of Parliament" who read those extracts. And he declared, "We are not there to provide a public service for a particular profession or, for that matter, for a particular chamber. . . . Newspapers are about providing people with news."[24]

Jenkins may well be right that few readers will miss the parliamentary news. Still, British media scholar Ralph Negrine observed that the parliamentary page was "a symbol of the pre-eminence of the parliamentary institution and the fact that, being pre-eminent, it deserved to be covered differently. The parliamentary page also confirmed the subservience of the press. Once the press abandoned the parliamentary page, it symbolically denied the pre-eminence of parliament."[25]

Oddly enough, it can be argued that this type of development is a good thing for democracy. One concern expressed about the news media and democracy is that the media omit or marginalize voices that should be in the public space. We have already seen how critics object to the way that the media prefer "statist" to "civic" voices. Furthermore, the public discussion in the media can be entered to a large extent only on terms the media establish—and these are not necessarily neutral terms. Sociologist Nina Eliasoph carried out a provocative study of how activist political groups outside the mainstream party structure talk about politics. She observed that women who among themselves may have complex models for political analysis present themselves before television cameras or newspaper reporters as "mothers." They seek redress against chemical companies, nuclear power plants, or city councils as mothers intent on protecting their children. In other words, they depoliticize themselves in order to gain sympathetic political coverage in the general media.[26]

The news media generally—and not only elite or "quality" news media—tend to be patrons of politics and accord it a primacy in keeping with and in support of the importance of public life and the common good. At the same time, in recent years the media have traveled further afield from central political institutions in coverage of publicly significant happenings. The old-time journalist may find this threatening. Howard Simons, when he was the managing editor of the *Washington Post* in the Watergate years, took a strong interest in news that was not narrowly political, but he underlined its outsider status in the newsroom by dubbing it SMERSH—"science, medicine, education, religion, and all that shit."[27] This is exactly where news has most impressively opened up in the past several decades, enlarging what an entire society can consider together and moving ever so gently but importantly from a concept of politics as whatever is on the mind of the legislature and chief executive to a concept of politics as whatever might be shaping everyday life that should be in the public eye and available for public attention.

In a way, this returns the discussion to the models of Jurgen Habermas and Benedict Anderson, which have been so helpful in understanding the historical emergence of the news media (see chapter 4). Habermas emphasized how journalism was vital to the opening of a public sphere where private persons could freely discuss and debate public issues of the day. This is the place of news in fostering democratic politics. Anderson focused his attention on the role of news and news reading as a communal force. In promoting mass attention to a common set of stories, the new media built a sense of locale, region, and nationhood. This sense came not only from journalism's focus on politics but also from its stories, which sustained in the imagination communities that could not be experienced face-to-face. Today, journalism's global prominence may even engender a sense of world community, shared human fate, and human rights that transcend nations. Its coverage of small personal dramas of everyday life, triumphs or tragedies in science and education, and conflict or transcendence in religion and culture may create a community as much as its coverage of politics builds a public agenda. This is not to deny that the same means of global communication, which is an indispensable instrument for bringing people together, can also be used to sow hate and fear, chauvinism for one's own group and contempt for others. There is no natural law declaring that good information will triumph over bad, but nor does the opposite hold, a Gresham's law for information that bad information drives out good. There is unprecedented opportunity in the new global ecology of information to make the best we can of research and reporting in the service of humane self-government.

Chapter Twelve
THE FIRST NEWS REVOLUTION OF THE TWENTY-FIRST CENTURY

WHAT IS A JOURNALIST? Someone who gets a paycheck from a news organization for producing news stories? Or anyone with a cell phone camera or a Facebook account? What is a news story? Can a tweet, a blog post, a magazine piece, or a book based on reporting all be "news"?

What is a newsroom? Is it physically and philosophically separate from the business office, as it was long reputed to be, or is the wall between newsroom and business office only a set of movable screens? If the latter, is that a sign of the corruption of a once-proud profession, or is it a realistic adaptation of a once-arrogant guild to market realities and audience tastes?

All of the suggested answers to these questions are correct, and that is very confusing. Everything we thought we once knew about journalism needs to be rethought in the digital age. The ground journalism walks upon is shaking, and the experience for both those who work in the field and for those on the outside studying it is dizzying.

In 2011, the impact of the World Wide Web on news is still in its childhood. The first widely used web browser, Mosaic, appeared in 1993. Google did not incorporate until 1998. The *New York Times* published on the web beginning in 1996 but did not update its website round the clock until 2000.

Blogging began in the mid-1990s but did not gain a general public presence until 2002 when several bloggers led the informational campaign that forced Senator Trent Lott to resign his post as majority leader of the U.S. Senate. Online job listing sites began with Monster.com in 1994. In 1995, eBay became the first of many online sites for people to auction objects they owned, which someone, somewhere, might want to buy. Craigslist was just a local San Francisco site for classified advertising until 2000 when it began to set up city-specific sites around the country and then around the world. Individuals can place ads on Craigslist for free and reach anyone in a city or region who might want to sublet their apartment or buy a used bicycle—or they pay to place an ad in the local newspaper with its declining circulation and its negligible readership among young people, whether in print or online. Newspapers, whose income from classified advertising as a portion of their total revenues had grown from 18 percent to 40 percent between 1950 and 2000, were deeply hurt as classified advertisers flocked to the Internet.[1] The first social networking site (Friendster) began in 2002 and Facebook in 2004. YouTube launched in 2005. In 2003, when the first edition of this book appeared, the reinvention of journalism had scarcely begun because most publishers, journalists, and scholars did not then recognize just how quickly many (but not all) of the old conventions and practices were crumbling.[2]

The convulsions of the U.S. news industry in the past decade have forced new understandings of what journalism is and what it has been. There is no canonical account of this, because the changes have been multidimensional, large in some areas and small in others, faster here and slower there, and they are still in process. Looked at in global perspective, the condition of journalism is even harder to grasp because printed newspapers are gaining readers and reaping profits as never before in some countries—India is the most prominent example—whereas in some mature industrial democracies with deep Internet penetration (Finland or Sweden, for instance), the economics of the newspaper business has been far less tumultuous than in the United States. But even where economic conditions are more favorable for "legacy" media organizations, the reshuffling of what news means has been dramatic in the past decade. The boundaries of journalism, which just a few years ago seemed relatively clear, stable, and permanent, have become less distinct, and this blurring, while potentially the foundation of progress even as it is the source of risk, has given rise to a new set of journalistic principles and practices. Journalism's wavering boundaries can be broadly construed in the following six ways.

1. *The line between reader and writer has blurred.* Readers and writers have never been rigidly separated in journalism. News organizations have long invited comments from their audiences. From their beginnings, American newspapers have run letters from readers, often letters that take issue with a newspaper editorial or, later, with the way the newspaper has covered a particular topic. Beginning in the 1960s, some American papers adopted a Scandinavian system of appointing an "ombudsman" to receive comments and complaints from the public and to write an occasional column that addresses these criticisms. The ombudsman has the freedom to defend the newspaper, or to side with the readers against it, sometimes eliciting an acknowledgment of a mistake, poor judgment, or insensitivity from newspaper editors and reporters.

But not since the early nineteenth century when newspapers began to hire full-time reporters and to produce more of their content themselves have the roles of amateurs advanced so quickly as in the past decade. Most professional journalists did not welcome these changes at first. They were particularly skeptical about blogging. Bloggers were disparaged as self-absorbed, angry, extreme venters of opinion. While this may have been an accurate characterization of some blogs, many others, however, are produced by people with expert knowledge and a desire to share it or people with personal experience and a flair for writing about it. Often these bloggers develop substantial followings. In many fields or subfields of knowledge, informed members of a microcommunity find leading bloggers who write about their particular area of interest to be indispensable. This is true in a small domain we could call the "futureofjournalism" world, and it is also the case in those microcommunities focused on, for example, the economic crisis, legal issues, local sports, food and health, and so on. The *Milwaukee Journal* has spun off a subscription-only online sports blog for fans of the Green Bay Packers, the favorite American football team for the region the newspaper serves. Bloggers have a significant place in various communities of political activists. Today the quest for reliable information is addressed not only by journalists reinventing themselves but by volunteer experts. Our informational environment operates more and more according to Joy's law, an aphorism attributed to Bill Joy of Sun Microsystems: "No matter who you are, most of the smartest people work for someone else."[3] Or they work for themselves. No matter how skilled the journalists in a large newsroom or how well informed and well placed their sources, the smartest person is likely to be someone else somewhere else, and thanks to the Internet, he or she may have already started a blog or posted a comment on yours. It is Joy's law plus the intellectual curiosity—or obsessiveness—of thousands of unpaid individuals who write and correct and update entries that has made Wikipedia an invaluable online reference work and also a handy news source because it gets updated so quickly.

A milestone was passed at the end of 2008 when the *New York Times* published an obituary about Doris Dungey, an influential voice on the collapse of the mortgage market in a blog she wrote under the pseudonym "Tanta." Dungey was an Ohioan who worked in the mortgage business, knew a lot about the business, had some literary talent, and was encouraged to write for a financial website, where her posts developed a following. She analyzed what went wrong with mortgage financing, and her blog posts began to be watched closely by insiders; they were cited with approval by analysts at the Federal Reserve and by the *New York Times* columnist and Nobel Prize economist Paul Krugman.[4] The blogosphere, in some measure, rewards the loudest, but it also gives attention to the best informed and most acute. By 2008, this second face of blogging was well established and Doris Dungey's obituary showed that the conventional news media recognized it.

Readers have not only entered into producing or coproducing news content, but they have also become voluntary and selective news distribution managers, circulating news from friend to friend. As a result, news dissemination for the general public has grown more lateral and less hierarchical. That is to say, people get more of their news about the world in something like the way they have long learned news about their friends and neighbors: they pass on information or gossip to people they know. This is especially so with the growing popularity of "social media" sites like Twitter and Facebook, in which friends exchange news about the wider world as well as about one another.

2. *The distinction among tweet, blog post, newspaper story, magazine article, and book has blurred.* Scholars who study journalism invariably focus on the story and usually the front-page story. But there is a whole "curriculum" of journalism, and the front-page story, as media scholar James Carey wrote, is only the introductory course. "Journalism is a curriculum. Its first course is the breaking stories of the daily press. There one gets a bare description: the identification of the actors and the events, the scene against which the events are played out and the tools available to the protagonists. Intermediate and advanced work—the fine-grained descriptions and interpretations—await the columns of analysis and interpretation, the weekly summaries and commentaries, and the book-length exposition."[5]

In journalism studies as in journalism itself, attention centers on the front page, but reporters do not stop writing when they have left the scene of their reporting. How many journalists have written books based on their reporting on the Iraq and Afghanistan wars over the past decade? There are books by *Washington Post* reporters Rajiv Chandrasekaran (*Imperial Life in the Emerald City*), Steve Coll (*Ghost Wars*), Thomas Ricks (*The Gamble* and *Fiasco*), Anthony Shadid (*Night Draws Near*), David Finkel (*The Good Soldiers*), as well as several books by *Post* editor Bob Woodward; NBC correspondent Richard Engel (*War Journal*); *Wall Street Journal* correspondents Farnaz Fassihi (*Waiting for an Ordinary Day*) and Ron Suskind (*The One Percent Doctrine*); NPR reporter Anne Garrels (*Naked in Baghdad*); *New York Times* military reporter Michael R. Gordon (*Cobra II*); *Newsweek* reporter Michael Isikoff (*Hubris*); *New Yorker* reporter George Packer (*The Assassins' Gate*); and *U.S. News* military correspondent Linda Robinson (*Tell Me How This Ends*), to name just a few. This is journalism, too.

That the act of reporting extends from tweet to book (or, in video format, from cell phone camera shot to YouTube to TV news story to feature-length documentary) does not suggest that the story in the daily newspaper in its familiar printed form has remained just what it used to be. It is not the contained, finished product that journalists and readers once took for granted. Now when a news story is posted online or even in print, the newsroom norm and public expectation is that it will be updated regularly. As a result, there is a new pressure on reporters to stay alert to even small developments related to an already posted and printed story. The result for the writer is permanent occupational vertigo: the story is never finished, never in final form. Journalism has become a 24/7 job. News is becoming, as media scholar Mark Deuze has observed, "liquid."[6] What you see with journalists these days is a pace of work fueled not just by passion—although that is where it begins—but powered by caffeine and aggravated by the felt need to be constantly available and connected. There is no downtime. It makes one think of Charlie Chaplin on the assembly line or, as Dean Starkman envisioned it in *Columbia Journalism Review*, a hamster on a wheel.[7]

3. *The line between professional and amateur has blurred, and a variety of "pro-am" relationships have emerged.* This is not quite the

same as the murky distinction between readers and writers. There are now ways in which amateurs participate in the journalistic process without being writers or photographers. Here the professional journalist enlists amateurs as co-workers or research assistants. The Public Insight Network at Minnesota Public Radio, which its originators have shared with other public radio stations, enables each station to maintain a database of far-flung audience members they can turn to for opinions and information. ProPublica, a New York–based online-only professional news organization dedicated to investigative reporting, enlisted volunteers across the country to send in information on the disbursement and actual use of funds in the Obama administration's economic recovery program. Here members of the general public became research assistants in an activity that has been dubbed "crowdsourcing." This is not a case of readers becoming writers. Participants are not necessarily expressing themselves but rather contributing something of importance to a larger cause or project.[8]

4. *The boundaries delineating for-profit, public, and nonprofit media have blurred, and cooperation across these models of financing has developed.* American journalism has been unusual among industrial democracies in its domination by commercial media. American journalists have traditionally been hostile to any government participation in news gathering. This remains true, but more U.S. journalists are coming to acknowledge the awkward fact that the U.S. government has subsidized commercial news operations far more than First Amendment purists recognize. Beginning with the Postal Act of 1792, the government gave newspapers preferential rates for the use of the U.S. postal

service. At a time when the population was dispersed rather than highly concentrated in central cities and when newspapers themselves had no mechanism for delivering papers to customers, the availability of postal delivery at subsidized rates greatly enhanced news distribution. At a time when so many newspapers filled their pages with stories reprinted from other papers, the Postal Act's provision that newspapers could be mailed to other newspapers without paying any postage at all was a great subsidy for news content. The U.S. government has, in effect, continually subsidized an important part of local television and print news reporting since the late nineteenth century with its establishment of the National Weather Bureau; the bureau remains today the authoritative source of national weather reporting.[9] Many commercial news organizations—particularly television news—have their own weather reporting services, but in Alaska, with its small and scattered population and vast territory, the federal government provides the only weather reporting.[10] For forty years the Public Broadcasting System and National Public Radio have been producing news reports, which only public financing made possible. The First Amendment states that Congress shall not "abridge freedom of speech or of the press." It does not say that the government shall not find ways to enhance freedom of speech or of the press.[11]

Acknowledging that government has long played a part in directly underwriting commercial news gathering begins to obscure the stark conceptual divide between government-supported and independent news gathering. The image of the self-contained, independent commercial news enterprise is compromised even further by several other developments. In the emerging news environment, news gathering is becoming both more cooperative and more competitive. Today, commercial news businesses cooperate with (1) other commercial news businesses; (2) government supported news operations like PBS and NPR; (3) nonprofit news organizations, particularly the dozens that have emerged online; and (4) nonprofit news production capabilities in journalism schools and other areas of higher education.

The old tradition of news organizations competing against one another in order to survive is giving way to a new, more collaborative tradition. Now survival depends on cooperation. The incomparable independence of the individual news organizations, once their hallmark, has weakened and is being replaced with a growing sense of a common public obligation. Commercial enterprises are making agreements with other commercial enterprises to cover aspects of the news jointly or to trade stories with one another without exchanging dollars. (The eight largest Ohio newspapers launched an arrangement in 2008 whereby they freely reprint stories from one another concerning each paper's home city; the *Washington Post* and *Baltimore Sun* started a similar arrangement in 2009 in sports coverage and with respect to some other Maryland state reporting as well.)[12] New nonprofit news organizations are working with commercial news organizations and public broadcasters to get the word out: the editors of Voice of San Diego, an online news operation in San Diego, California, appear on commercial television and on public radio to discuss their online news reports; ProPublica gives its stories away to any other news organizations, commercial or nonprofit or public, that might want them; and the university-based nonprofit Wisconsin Center for Investigative Reporting has freely provided its stories to some fifty newspapers in the region.

5. *Within commercial news organizations, the line between the newsroom and the business office has blurred.* This traditional separation has long been regarded as the sacred guarantor of the integrity of news and the symbol of the virtue of the journalist who cannot be swayed by the commercial needs of the news organization. But today, even at the most venerated news organizations, this boundary is breaking down. In academic year 2009–10, for the first time in the ninety-five-year history of the Columbia Journalism School, the required introductory course that used to teach a little media history, a little First Amendment law, and a little media ethics now also includes instruction in media economics and entrepreneurship.

The risk in this is obvious—that journalists increasingly will bow to financial priorities and the stories they produce will be trash. They will abandon boring, but valuable, municipal coverage for tales of politicians, entertainers, or sports heroes laid low by sex, drugs, or gambling. Moreover, if the roles of newsroom and business office begin to commingle, "bottom line" considerations will loom larger for the reporters, coercing them to think hard about how many eyeballs are glued to their program or pages rather than to a rival's.

Can there be an upside to this? Yes. A corps of journalists untethered to an actual audience poses its own sort of risk— irrelevance, elitism, a cliquish echo-chamber world where journalists wind up talking primarily to one another. Could it turn out that the best model for journalism is a mixed model rather than a model of pure journalistic independence? That journalism can be better if it is partly dependent on, and hence sensitive to, audience preferences than if it reflects only the insular and intramural preferences of professionals themselves?[13]

Journalists are becoming more aware of what journalism professor Jay Rosen memorably called "the people formerly known as the audience."[14] And they know with some precision what in the past could only be guessed at—what their audience liked in today's news. Market research assembled such information in the past, but it arrived slowly and in relatively abstract numbers. Today, however, there is ever-present evidence of which story on a given day was most popular, which was most frequently e-mailed to friends. Should a reporter care only about the "buzz" that her story generates? Of course not. But neither can a news organization that is struggling to survive in the marketplace ignore data on which stories are most e-mailed.

Sensitivity to audience preferences is not the same as subservience to them. In 2010, *New York Times* reporter Nina Bernstein said, in receiving an award for her work, that "the best stories" are "the stories nobody knows they want or need because they don't yet know that they exist."[15] Those stories are either hidden away or lurking in the shadows where reporters rarely venture. How do journalists recognize those stories and drag them into the daylight? How do they develop knowledge, sources, and instincts about locating such stories? By professional training, skill, and experience and by independence of mind, persistence, and vision—not by reading the latest television ratings or "most e-mailed stories" list from the day before.

6. *The line between old media and new media has blurred, practically beyond recognition.* Not only do newspapers, radio, and television news operations run their own websites, but these sites are among the most widely read of all news websites. Not only have newspapers added an online product to their print editions,

but their online journalists are increasingly well integrated into the news operation as a whole rather than set apart in a secondary newsroom of their own. In 2005, when media scholar Pablo Boczkowski studied the work habits of the journalists at Clarin.com, the web operation of Argentina's leading newspaper, Clarin.com (launched in 1996) was entirely separate from the print newsroom; today it is entirely integrated into a single newsroom.[16]

Journalistic authority has grown more individual- and less institutional-based. The work of journalism can be done—and done well—in low-overhead settings that require little more than a reporter and her laptop. *New York Times'* media reporter David Carr wrote in 2009, "Somewhere down in the Flatiron, out in Brooklyn, over in Queens or up in Harlem, cabals of bright young things are watching all the disruption with more than an academic interest. Their tiny netbooks and iPhones, which serve as portals to the cloud, contain more informational firepower than entire newsrooms possessed just two decades ago. And they are ginning content from their audiences in the form of social media or finding ways of making ambient information more useful. They are jaded in the way youth requires, but have the confidence that is a gift of their age as well."[17]

There is a lot in this emerging news ecology to worry about—the quickened pace of communication, the reduction of editing, the shift from stylistic sobriety to snarkiness in parts (not all) of journalism. But none of these concerns, singly or collectively, represents the end of the world. None presage the end of long-form and book-length reporting and analysis. There is a line between the recording and reporting of moments and the reflection about moments linked together into coherent narratives. We have more of the former, to be sure. But we have more of the latter, too. There is just more of everything.

What follows from this: this is the best of times for journalists, as long as they can survive on relatively little income; show themselves agile in gathering data, connections, ideas, and relationships online; and develop the psychological makeup to handle experimentation, innovation, and risk.

But is this not also the worst of times? In the past few years major newspapers, including the *Baltimore Sun*, *Philadelphia Inquirer*, *Cleveland Plain Dealer*, *San Francisco Chronicle*, and *Los Angeles Times*, have cut their newsroom staffs in half, letting go as many as five hundred newsroom reporters, editors, and photographers. Overall, newspaper editorial staff, which had grown from thirty-nine thousand in 1971 to sixty-seven thousand in 1992, down to fifty-nine thousand in 2002, is back now to about forty thousand.[18] The number of newspaper reporters covering state capitals full-time fell from 524 in 2003 to 355 in 2009.[19] Meanwhile, between 1998 and 2010, twenty U.S. newspapers and newspaper groups that supported foreign bureaus have closed all of them, including such distinguished papers as the *Baltimore Sun*, *Boston Globe*, *Chicago Tribune*, *Miami Herald*, and *Philadelphia Inquirer*.[20]

In early 2011, the ombudsman for the *Washington Post* acknowledged that "staggering financial losses have required unrelenting expense reductions to restore profitability. The loss of newsroom talent, through forced buyouts and voluntary departures, has been breathtaking. Some of the most respected *Post* journalists have left, along with institutional knowledge and leadership so desperately needed during a period of radical change." While he proudly noted that "The *Post* on its worst days is better than most newspapers on their best days," he concluded that "the *Post*'s journalistic quality has declined."[21]

So where is the good news?

Recall how much journalism grew from 1970 on. Journalism organizations do not have a long tradition of deeply investing in news gathering. That practice was brief, and it was fueled by monopoly profits coinciding with a change in the journalistic weather in the 1960s and '70s that made investigation a priority as it had rarely been before. Has something been lost? Yes. But the prosperous, professional, growing, aggressive, critical, active journalism, which operated in a political culture that was committed to the public availability of government information and other politically relevant information, existed for a relatively short time from about the late 1960s into the early 2000s, not longer, and the fact is that online resources make reporting more efficient than ever before.

Journalism is one of those fields—like music, art, and theater—that people enter because they love it, not because they think it will be lucrative. There is no business model for poetry or string quartets or performance art, either, and all of those pursuits endure without it. They survive with the help of philanthropic support, significant subsidies from colleges and universities, and small amounts of direct government support, too.

The opportunity for passion to fuel a career has stimulated the rise of online journalism organizations, many of which have so far shown themselves resourceful. Online magazines of opinion and commentary began as early as Salon.com (1995) and Slate.com (1996) and in 2000 journalist Josh Marshall began his blog, TalkingPointsMemo, which would later evolve into a news organization that does reporting as well as analysis and commentary. The first online news organization devoted to news reporting was probably the Voice of San Diego, launched in 2005. A score of online investigative reporting-centered news organizations came together in 2009 to form the Investigative News Network. By 2011, the group boasted fifty-one member organizations—nonprofit, nonpartisan organizations dedicated to investigative reporting.[22] For the most part, they have only modest income from advertising or reader contributions and are funded primarily by foundations and private philanthropy.

There are reasons to believe they can last. They are low cost. They do not have to invest in a printing press, in paper, or in delivery trucks. Newspapers traditionally have devoted only 11–12 percent of their expenses to news gathering, news writing, and news editing. Newsprint and ink by themselves cost more than that, and the rest goes to other production, distribution, and administrative costs—and (per 2001 data) 21 percent gross profit.[23] The Internet levels the playing field and nearly eliminates the competitive advantage of the newspaper. If you need a printing press to make your business work, then first you need substantial capital—and once you get in, your presence becomes a barrier to others entering after you. If you need only to put up a website, you can be up and running with the savings from your summer job. A newspaper, someone has said, is basically in the trucking business. Not so for a news website. While it is easier for someone to launch a news enterprise in the online world than in the printing press world, what makes it difficult to sustain is that everybody else has the same advantage—no barriers to entry.

Still, the productivity of an individual journalist is enormously increased by the Internet and the personal computer.

The increased efficiency in news reporting arises not only because the reporters have computers but because governments, nonprofits, and advocacy groups have jumped into the public information and government accountability business. They hire reporters, editors, and photographers. They prepare publicly available, downloadable, and usable databases. They make use of open-government legislation, which gained significance over the past half century beginning with the Freedom of Information Act (1966) and the campaign finance laws of 1971 and 1974, which mandated the disclosure of campaign contributions and expenses. Later legislation required environmental impact statements and toxic release disclosures and other mechanisms for making information publicly available and accessible. Databases are also compiled for public use by a wide variety of nonprofit organizations, some of which develop excellent reputations among journalists for the integrity and reliability of their information. Not the least of the virtues of digital communication for journalists is that they can sit at their desks and gather information from other news organizations' websites— news outlets from around the world. Young reporters take this access for granted; their older colleagues, especially those who cover foreign affairs, cannot help but experience it as miraculous.

Another resource not to be taken lightly is the seemingly endless supply of obsessive, gritty enthusiasm that journalists typically bring to their work. Journalists who demonstrate it today follow in the footsteps of their nonmainstream predecessors who, for example, set up alternative weeklies in the sixties, wrote for political magazines or vegetarian newsletters, or even carved out their living as freelance foreign correspondents, subsisting on a combination of passion and lowered expectations for comfort. With just about everyone I talked to at the online start-ups, whether twenty-somethings at one of their first jobs or fifty-somethings who had taken buyouts or been let go from conventional news organizations, you could hear their blood pulsing. One top editor from a major daily newspaper, now working at ProPublica, told me, "I feel I have died and gone to heaven!" She was doing more of the work that had led her to journalism in the first place than at any other time in her career.

As with culture and the arts, colleges and universities have assumed a growing role in producing journalism directly for general audiences. In 2007, Pulitzer Prize winner Walter Robinson, an investigative reporter at the *Boston Globe* for several decades, returned to his alma mater, Northeastern University, to teach an investigative reporting seminar to both graduate and undergraduate students. In the first two years, the students produced twelve front-page stories in the *Boston Globe*. Robinson proudly told me, "In all the stories so far we've not had a single correction or substantive complaint."[24]

Evaluating where journalism stands today and where it is going will require not only taking account of the multiplying number of online news organizations and learning to assess the journalistic worth of digital communications but also reexamining our understanding of news in a global perspective. Despite the decline in the number of U.S. foreign correspondents working at major news organizations, and the retreat from maintaining foreign bureaus, it is not clear that our news from abroad is of lower quality than it was. Richard Sambrook, a veteran BBC journalist and former director of global news for the BBC, sees sunshine in the future for international news. He does not think expensive foreign bureaus will survive, but nor does he judge this a tragedy. He is not convinced that these bureaus were terribly useful and quoted *Washington Post* editor Marcus Brauchli's observation that many of them were established in the days of large newspaper profits "in order to be seen as 'players'" within the industry, but their readers would have been just as well served if the newspapers ran AP stories instead. Typical foreign correspondents in the twentieth century were middle-class males who worked away from the home office but remained dependent on local staff; they tended to operate with a small network of sources, boasted few nonprofessional friends in the countries reported from, and were unlikely to speak the local language. Sambrook envisions a future in which foreign correspondents will be competent in the local language, come to the job with specialized knowledge of the country, be more diverse in gender and ethnicity, work across media platforms, connect to hundreds of sources, likely work as stringers or freelancers for many news organizations rather than one, and work from home or apartment abroad rather than from a bureau. Where, in the past, they could safely assume they would be the sole source (or one of a few sources) of information on their country for readers back home, they will increasingly recognize that "they are not the only, or even main, source of information. Their role will be as much about verification, interpretation and explanation as revelation."[25] The other sources of information the foreign correspondent will be competing with—and verifying, interpreting, and explaining—will include local and regional news sources so that the reader back in the United States or Britain or Germany will be able to access directly, as never possible in the twentieth century, journalistic reports produced by citizens of the country in question for audiences in that country. This may not be the best of all possible journalistic futures, but Sambrook makes a good case that it compares favorably with what used to be. In 2010 and 2011, many people in Europe and North America who followed news of the popular revolutions in Tunisia, Egypt, and elsewhere in the Arab world found the coverage by Al Jazeera English to be exemplary. This is just the kind of possibility that Sambrook anticipated.

CODA

In 1920, in *Liberty and the News*, Walter Lippmann complained that American journalism was failing to serve the needs of modern democracy—and that it would continue to fail without help from forces beyond itself.

Why? Lippmann cited two reasons. First, journalism was in the hands of "untrained amateurs," and though the amateur "may mean well . . . he knows not how to do well."[26] Lippmann expressed some hope for expanding "a professional training in journalism in which the ideal of objective testimony is cardinal."[27] By deepening the curricular riches of journalism schools—the few that then existed, making them intellectually more ambitious, each crop of new recruits to journalism could over time raise the standards of the news.

Second, the world had become far too complex to be adequately reported by the conventional tools of journalism. The news from which the reporter "must pick and choose has long since become too complicated even for the most highly trained reporter." The problem, then, is not simply the inadequacies of individual reporters or newspapers but rather "the intricacy and unwieldiness of the subject-matter."[28] Journalism could report the complexity of the modern world only by making use of other agencies in which "a more or less expert political intelligence" provides the journalist reliable maps of the world.[29] He referred to these agencies as "political observatories" to imply that they examine human affairs with scientific instruments, methods, and outlooks.[30] He called for independent, nonpartisan scientific organizations committed to an agenda of research about the political and social world and able to produce it in a form accessible to the competent journalist. Only then could newspapers offer citizens a more thorough, complete, objective, and reliable portrait of relevant public life.

Much as Lippmann imagined, now there are political observatories aplenty. They began in Lippmann's day. The Brookings Institution in 1921 was among the first, and the General Accounting Office (today the Government Accountability Office), also 1921, was—inside government—the sort of agency of accounting and accountability that Lippmann had in mind. And since the 1970s, the proliferation of information-generating agencies has been spectacular. While this poses a challenge to journalists—how does the reporter know which of the many agencies can be relied upon, for example?—the political observatories have enriched and improved journalism.

The problem of (U.S.) print journalism today is not the Internet alone, to be sure. Before there was Craigslist, before there was Google, before dailies were undercutting themselves with impressive websites of their own available free of charge, newspapers were faltering. Young people were not adopting the newspaper habit to the same extent as their elders. Profitable newspapers were getting gobbled up by large national chains that often had little knowledge of and little concern for the peculiarities of local communities. Distinguished news corporations like the Tribune Company and even the New York Times Company had eyes bigger than their wallets and took on debt in acquisitions and new buildings at the worst possible time, just as the Internet came into its own and just before the economic recession that began in 2008.

But the Internet is particularly important because it is not going away and will therefore continue to threaten the survival of the American newspaper. At the same time, it is also the central factor in constructing a new model of what journalism can be.

In the past century, the growth of advertising helped make possible a press independent of party and congenial to the rise of ethics- and values-infused professional reporting. Especially in the past forty years, American democracy has had the benefit of serious, critical, and credible accountability journalism. This is because, as media theorist Clay Shirky put it, Wal-Mart was willing to subsidize the Baghdad bureau.[31] That has been a very happy accident for our capacity to hold government and other powerful institutions accountable to the law and to legitimate public expectations of integrity and fair play. The United States was able to subcontract an essential building block of democratic life to commercial newspapers and commercial broadcasting.

The point Shirky makes is central, but it does not stand alone—that is, advertising did not by itself make for excellence in journalism. There are still fourteen hundred daily newspapers in the United States and only a score of them have ever had a Baghdad bureau or even sent a reporter to Baghdad, and only a few dozen have ever opened a foreign bureau anywhere. For that matter, only a minority of these papers post a reporter to their own state capital. U.S. newspapers have been stunningly prosperous for a long time, but they underinvested in serious news coverage.

Moreover, the emergence of a skeptical, critical, and aggressive accountability journalism dedicated not to partisan triumph but to a sense of public service is a product of the 1960s and after. Prosperity was its necessary but never sufficient condition. Prosperity had to be supplemented by the cultural changes that came with the 1960s and '70s, including, as we have seen, an increasingly widespread and fiercely defended professionalism. Journalism, hardly faultless today, nonetheless became more independent of government and more committed to investigation and criticism from the Vietnam War on than ever before. Quality reporting also required something else that grew from these tumultuousness decades: the broadly shared presumption in U.S. political culture that public-ness or public visibility is a central democratic value. Whether it was televised presidential debates, which began in 1960, or the Freedom of Information Act of 1966, or the National Environmental Policy Act of 1970 with its requirement that new federally funded construction projects produce environmental impact statements, or the rise in the 1970s and '80s of a wide variety of advocacy and non-partisan nongovernmental organizations whose purpose was to monitor different aspects of government activity, a demand for government transparency has grown apace.

The presumption of public visibility has had global dimensions, too. Advocacy groups like Human Rights Watch hire trained journalists as human rights reporters and take the ethical responsibilities of factual reporting seriously. Human Rights Watch also hires photographers, videographers, and radio producers to work with their researchers in the field. Amnesty International is hiring professional journalists to produce human rights–related news for the general media.[32] Some critics argue that these organizations, despite themselves, compete with one another by the rules of a conventional "media logic"—for instance, by emphasizing celebrities in order to get their work noticed in the wider media.[33] Even so, they are questioning, and perhaps redefining, the boundaries of journalism in our time.

It was not profitability alone but the combination of profits, professionalism, and the growing ideal of public visibility that enabled the best journalism in American history from the 1970s on. And, of course, the presumption of public-ness has grown by leaps and bounds in the past decade, thanks to the Internet. This clearly produces new dilemmas, especially concerning the protection of personal privacy. That an organization like WikiLeaks can threaten confidential communications long judged essential to diplomacy is also now apparent, and debate over this may be with us for some time.

We have not reached the end of newspapers, but as Paul Starr has suggested, we may well be at "the end of the age of newspapers" when the urban daily newspapers were "central to both the production of news and the life of their metro regions."[34] If the age of newspapers is one in which most people get information about public affairs from reading a newspaper, the age of newspapers ended in the United States in the 1960s when television became the primary source of news for most Americans and when public service broadcasting, particularly in northern Europe, Britain, Canada, Australia, New Zealand, and elsewhere, became the indispensable news source. If the age of newspapers, however, is one in which the lion's share of original reporting on public affairs is provided by the wire services and daily newspapers, which in 2011 continue to make most of their money from their print editions, then we remain in an age of newspapers. (No one really knows what share of news is originally reported by newspapers and the wire services, but I have not seen any estimate less than 80 percent.)[35] Most of the rest of public affairs chatter continues to live off of the investment that daily newspapers make in original reporting. Some notable online-only news organizations exist that do original reporting of their own. Some radio and television news operations also do original work; National Public Radio now maintains seventeen foreign bureaus compared to six ten years ago. American newspapers, even in the digital era, are still the engines of the U.S. news network. Relatively little original on-the-ground reporting emerges from television, radio, and online organizations (leaving aside the websites of newspapers); most news outlets embroider upon a factual base established by the news stories produced by newspaper journalists. And yet U.S. newspapers remain in serious economic straits.

Is there a way out?[36] Government may be able to devise new means to offer more financial help to newspapers, but today there is little political will for this and most U.S. journalists themselves do not want to consider federal subsidy. (The fact that this has worked without diminishing free speech or free press in Britain or Sweden seems to have no traction as an argument in favor of it in the United States.) So is there a crisis in journalism or, more precisely, a crisis in public affairs news reporting? In the United States, yes, there is. In parts of Europe, the answer is yes, too, although it is less pronounced so far. In some other parts of the world, rapid economic growth in the past few decades has fueled a considerable growth in newspapers. In India, growth has been most rapid in the country's various indigenous languages. The globalization of human experience is far from total, and variations in local economic, political, and cultural conditions have an enormous impact on the state of journalism. While new technologies of news production are in most respects the same around the world, the political, economic, and social structures that organize their adoption, their use, or their repression, differ greatly. Scholars are just beginning to find frameworks for comparing the degree to which journalism in different countries faces an emergency.[37]

This is not a moment to make predictions or to suggest that we can take the measure of public affairs reporting in the world. It is in flux. To come to a more definitive conclusion would be premature. Better simply to borrow a metaphor from the early days of radio: stay tuned.

Notes

Introduction

1. Lincoln Steffens, *The Autobiography of Lincoln Steffens* (New York: Harcourt, Brace, and World, 1936).

2. Joel Best, *Random Violence* (Berkeley: University of California Press, 1999).

3. Gaye Tuchman, "Telling Stories," *Journal of Communication* 26 (1976): 97.

4. Gaye Tuchman, *Making News: A Study in the Construction of Reality* (New York: Free Press, 1978), 179.

5. Ibid., 82–83.

6. Steven Waldman, *The Bill* (New York: Viking, 1995), 240.

7. Edward Jay Epstein's *News from Nowhere* (New York: Random House, 1973), 31, found that journalists had at least twenty-four hours' notice for more than 90 percent of stories on the NBC evening news; wholly unpredictable events made up less than 2 percent of stories.

8. Cited in John McManus, *Market-Driven Journalism* (Thousand Oaks, Calif.: Sage, 1994), 94.

Chapter 1 Defining Journalism

1. Ian Watt, *The Rise of the Novel* (London: Chatto and Windus, 1957).

2. John Hartley, *Popular Reality: Journalism, Modernity, Popular Culture* (London: Arnold, 1996), 32.

3. "Fred Snodgrass, 86, Dead; Ball Player Muffed 1912 Fly," *New York Times,* April 6, 1974, 34.

4. Jostein Gripsrud, "Tabloidization, Popular Journalism, and Democracy," in *Tabloid Tales,* ed. Colin Sparks and John Tulloch (Lanham, Md.: Rowman and Littlefield, 2000), 294.

CHAPTER 2   DOES NEWS MATTER?

1. On Washington, see Michael Schudson, *The Good Citizen* (New York: Free Press, 1998), 70; on Cooper, see James Fenimore Cooper, *The American Democrat* (Baltimore: Penguin, 1969; originally published 1838), 183; on Scripps, see *Damned Old Crank: A Self-Portrait of E. W. Scripps,* ed. Charles R. McCabe (New York: Harper and Brothers, 1951), 242 (from an essay written in 1925).

2. Michael Kelly, "David Gergen, Master of the Game," *New York Times Magazine,* October 31, 1993, 64.

3. Geoff Mulgan, *Politics in an Anti-Political Age* (Cambridge, Mass.: Polity Press, 1994), 27.

4. For instance, Neil Postman, *Amusing Ourselves To Death* (New York: Penguin, 1985).

5. Joshua Meyrowitz, "The Press Rejects a Candidate," *Columbia Journalism Review* (March–April 1992): 46–47. See also Joshua Meyrowitz, "Visible and Invisible Candidates: A Case Study in 'Competing Logics' of Campaign Coverage," *Political Communication* 11 (1994): 145–64.

6. Sheryl WuDunn, "In Summit Silences, a Truce in U.S.-Japanese Trade Wars," *New York Times,* April 18, 1996, 1.

7. Compare this article to the *Chicago Tribune*'s report on December 8, 1909, of President William Howard Taft's State of the Union message: "President Taft's first annual message . . . is more notable for what it omits than for what it says."

8. Ron Suskind, "Without a Doubt," *New York Times Magazine,* October 17, 2004.

9. See Edward Jay Epstein, *Between Fact and Fiction* (New York: Vintage Books, 1975), 19–33.

10. See Daniel C. Hallin, *The "Uncensored War": The Media and Vietnam* (New York: Oxford University Press, 1986).

11. George Moss, *Vietnam: An American Ordeal* (Englewood Cliffs, N.J.: Prentice-Hall, 1990), 274.

12. Steven Livingston and Todd Eachus, "Humanitarian Crises and U.S. Foreign Policy: Somalia and the CNN Effect Reconsidered," *Political Communication* 12 (1995): 413-429; Jonathan Mermin, "Television News and American Intervention in Somalia: The Myth of a Media-Driven Foreign Policy," *Political Science Quarterly* 112 (1997): 385–403; and Jonathan Mermin, *Debating War and Peace* (Princeton: Princeton University Press, 1999).

13. Cited in Silvio Waisbord, "Secular Politics: The Modernization of Argentine Electioneering," in *Politics, Media, and Modern Democracy*, ed. David L. Swanson and Paolo Mancini (Westport, Conn.: Praeger, 1996), 223.

14. Two of our most searching cultural commentators are scathingly critical of some prominent media critics, from Noam Chomsky to Senator Paul Simon to Catharine MacKinnon to Dan Quayle. See John Leonard, "TV and the Decline of Civilization," The *Nation*, December 27, 1993, 785, 801–4; and Todd Gitlin, "The Imagebusters," *American Prospect* 17 (Winter 1994): 42–49.

15. Nancy Gibbs, "Angels Among Us," *Time*, December 27, 1993, 61.

16. Clifford Geertz, *The Interpretation of Cultures* (New York: Basic Books, 1973), 14.

17. It should be added that news does reward or punish the people who are the subject of news reports. In fact, sometimes media coverage is the primary reward or punishment a candidate or public official routinely receives. This is extremely important, but it is another matter altogether from the direct effect of news on the general audience.

18. For a review, see David Morley, "Active Audience Theory: Pendulums and Pitfalls," *Journal of Communication* 43 (1993): 13–19.

19. Associated Press, "Three Featured on 'America's Most Wanted' Captured in One Day," *San Diego Union*, October 8, 1993, A3.

20. "The President's Case," *Newsweek*, July 29, 1985, 17.

21. Herbert J. Gans, "Reopening the Black Box: Toward a Limited Effects Theory," *Journal of Communication* 43 (1993): 32–33.

22.   Shanto Iyengar and Donald R. Kinder, *News That Matters* (Chicago: University of Chicago Press, 1987).

23.   Paddy Scannell, "Public Service Broadcasting and Modern Public Life," *Media, Culture, and Society* 11 (1989): 145.

24.   Alice Walker, *In Search of Our Mothers' Gardens* (San Diego: Harcourt Brace Jovanovich, 1983), 124.

25.   Michael Suk-Young Chwe emphasizes the importance of common knowledge—not only that many people know the same thing but also that they know everyone else knows it, and they can coordinate with one another on that basis. News is not prominent among the examples he cites, but it could have been. See Michael Suk-Young Chwe, *Rational Ritual: Culture, Coordination, and Common Knowledge* (Princeton, N.J.: Princeton University Press, 2001).

26.   In contrast, in Chinese journalism, two systems of reporting coexist: the public news printed daily in the papers and the internal memos journalists write when the news they convey, if published, might be embarrassing to the Communist Party or to its key members.

CHAPTER 3   MEDIA BIAS

1.   David Broder, *Behind the Front Page* (New York: Simon and Schuster, 1987), 14.

2.   Edward Jay Epstein, *News from Nowhere* (New York: Random House, 1973), 17.

3.   Both definitions come from Todd Gitlin's important study *The Whole World Is Watching* (Berkeley: University of California Press, 1979), 6 and 7. See also William Gamson and Andre Modigliani, who define a frame as "a central organizing idea or story line that provides meaning to an unfolding strip of events, weaving a connection among them" (p. 143) in their article "The Changing Culture of Affirmative Action," *Research in Political Sociology* 3 (1987): 137–77; Dietram Scheufele, "Framing as a Theory of Media Effects," *Journal of Communication* 49 (1999): 103–22; and Stephen Reese, Oscar Gandy, Jr., and August Grant, eds., *Framing Public Life: Perspectives on Media and Our Understanding of the Social World* (Mahwah, N.J.: Lawrence Erlbaum, 2001).

4. See Robert Entman and Andrew Rojecki, *The Black Image in the White Mind* (Chicago: University of Chicago Press, 2000), 215. I develop a point that Entman and Rojecki made somewhat differently, but I am directly inspired by their discussion.

5. John Hartley, "Communicative Democracy in a Redactional Society: The Future of Journalism Studies," *Journalism* 1 (2000): 44.

6. Noam Chomsky and Edward Herman, *Manufacturing Consent: The Political Economy of the Mass Media* (New York: Pantheon, 1988). In this work Chomsky and Herman explicitly compare American news institutions to Pravda on a half-dozen occasions, intending to provoke outrage at so sacrilegious a yoking. Nowhere do they suggest that there might be important differences, but since they provoke the question, it seems fitting to answer it directly.

7. Stephen E. Bornstein, "The Politics of Scandal," in *Developments in French Politics,* ed. Peter A. Hall, Jack Hayward, and Howard Machin (London: Macmillan, 1990), 269–81. Bornstein observed, for example, that the French media "are relatively poorly equipped to serve as detectors of, and deterrents to, scandal" (p. 277). The press in France "lacks a tradition of effective, non-partisan investigative journalism" (p. 277), and the French public seems to be characterized by a "short attention span, cynicism and moral indifference" (p. 280), which makes audiences less receptive to scandalous revelations than are the British or the Americans. But there is evidence in recent years of more aggressive investigative work, as government control of broadcasting has relaxed and as French journalism comes to participate in what Erik Neveu called the "permanent professionalization of political life" (p. 451). See Erik Neveu, "Media Politics in French Political Science," *European Journal of Political Research* 33 (1998): 439–58 (especially pp. 451–52). The Latin American press has done more investigative work as it moved into the system of influence of U.S. journalism and as French and Italian "journals of opinion" declined in influence. See Silvia R. Waisbord, *Watchdog Journalism in South America* (New York: Columbia University Press, 2000), 8–11.

8. James Houck (1989), cited in Phyllis Kaniss, *Making Local News* (Chicago: University of Chicago Press, 1991), 59. This general point is stressed by Daniel C. Hallin, "The American News Media: A Critical Theory Perspective," in *Critical Theory and Public Life,* ed. John Forester (Cambridge, Mass.: MIT Press, 1985).

9.   For the distinction between statist and civil discourse, see Robert Manoff, "Covering the Bomb: The Nuclear Story and the News," *Working Papers* (Summer 1983): 19–27. For media critic Manoff, statist discourse depends on official sources, focuses on government action, and concentrates on policy. Civil discourse, found occasionally as a competing voice in the news, is a journalism of ethics rather than politics, raising questions of consequences, not causes, and giving voice to individuals outside government policy circles.

10.   On the relative immunity to standards of objectivity in foreign correspondence, see Michael J. Robinson and Margaret A. Sheehan, *Over the Wire and on TV* (New York: Russell Sage Foundation, 1983), 63–64.

11.   W. Lance Bennett, "Toward a Theory of Press-State Relations in the United States," *Journal of Communication* 40 (1990): 103–25.

12.   Peter Viles, "Dan Rather Blasts TV News," *Broadcasting & Cable*, October 4, 1993, 12. See also a useful review of the consequences of "narrowcasting" and the Federal Communication Commission's 1987 abandonment of the fairness doctrine for the broadcast of political information in Austin Ranney, "Broadcasting, Narrowcasting, and Politics," in *The New American Political System*, 2nd ed., ed. Anthony King (Washington: AEI Press, 1990), 175–201.

13.   J. Herbert Altschull, *Agents of Power* (New York: Longman, 1984), 298.

14.   S. Robert Lichter, Stanley Rothman, and Linda Lichter, *The Media Elite* (Bethesda, Md.: Adler and Adler, 1986), 28. For a critique, see Herbert Gans, "Are U.S. Journalists Dangerously Liberal?" *Columbia Journalism Review* 24 (November–December 1985): 29–33.

15.   David H. Weaver and G. Cleveland Wilhoit, *The American Journalist*, 2nd ed. (Bloomington: Indiana University Press, 1991). Weaver and Wilhoit find, for 1982, roughly the same percentage of people identifying themselves as left of center among journalists (22 percent) as in the general population (21 percent). More people in the general population identify themselves as right of center (32 percent) than among journalists (18 percent), with more journalists seeing themselves as "middle of the road" (58 percent) than do members of the general population (37 percent).

16.   See Stephen Hess, *The Washington Reporters* (Washington: Brookings Institution Press, 1981), 115; and Herbert J. Gans, *Deciding What's News* (New York: Pantheon, 1979).

17. See "The Promise of Eliot Spitzer," editorial, *New York Times*, October 22, 2006, and "For Senator and Governor in Connecticut," editorial, *New York Times*, October 13, 2010.

18. Paul Taylor, *See How They Run* (New York: Alfred A. Knopf, 1990): 26.

19. Ibid., 27.

20. Robinson and Sheehan, *Over the Wire and on TV*.

21. William Greider, *Who Will Tell the People?* (New York: Simon and Schuster, 1992), 306.

22. Merrill Goozner, personal communication, January 8, 2002.

23. Howard Kurtz, *Media Circus* (New York: Times Books, 1993), 70, 71.

24. America Rodriguez, "Made in the USA: The Construction of Univision News" (Ph.D. dissertation, Department of Communication, University of California, San Diego, 1993). See also America Rodriguez, *Making Latino News* (Thousand Oaks, Calif.: Sage, 1999).

25. William Grimes, "Randy Shilts, Author, Dies at 42; One of First to Write about AIDS," *New York Times*, February 18, 1994, national edition, C19. See also Jeffrey Schmalz, "Covering AIDS and Living It: A Reporter's Testimony," *New York Times*, December 20, 1992, sec. 4, 1, for an account of how Schmalz, who later died of AIDS, tried to hold to his identity as a news professional while covering an issue that directly concerned his identity as a member of the gay community.

26. Among the most important of these works is Leon Sigal, *Reporters and Officials* (Lexington, Mass.: D. C. Heath, 1973); Gaye Tuchman, *Making News: A Study in the Construction of Reality* (New York: Free Press, 1978), 179; Gaye Tuchman, "Objectivity as Strategic Ritual: An Examination of Newsmen's Notions of Objectivity," *American Journal of Sociology* 77 (1972): 660–79; Epstein, *News from Nowhere;* and Gans, *Deciding What's News.*

27. Tamar Liebes, "Decoding Television News: The Political Discourse of Israeli Hawks and Doves," *Theory and Society* 21 (1992): 352–82. Liebes, examining Israeli television news, comments that "Western journalism" generally has a bias that favors conflict, simplification, events, action, personification, and drama.

28. Stephen Bates, ed., *The Media and the Congress* (Columbus: Publishing Horizons, 1987), 23.

29. Timothy Cook, "News Coverage of AIDS," in *Politics and the Press*, ed. Pippa Norris (Boulder: Lynne Rienner, 1997), 221. Event-centeredness is not a constant. There is good evidence that newspaper stories have become longer, more analytical, more sensitive to process, and less fixated on events. Journalists are more likely today than in the past to write about collective entities rather than individuals and trends rather than specific events. See Kevin Barnhurst and Diana Mutz, "American Journalism and the Decline in Event-Centered Reporting," *Journal of Communication* 47 (1997): 27–53, and Diana C. Mutz, *Impersonal Influence* (Cambridge, Eng.: Cambridge University Press, 1998), 49, 288.

30. Quoted in Paddy Scannell, *Radio, Television, and Modern Life: A Phenomenological Approach* (Oxford, Eng.: Blackwell, 1996), 89.

31. Ibid., 90.

32. The story was recalled by Harry McPherson, a close Johnson aide, in his roundtable remarks at a 1983 conference, as published in Bates, *The Media and the Congress*, 50.

33. Liebes, "Decoding Television News," 359.

34. Robinson and Sheehan, *Over the Wire and on TV*, 97, 111, 212.

35. Thomas Patterson, *Out of Order* (New York: Alfred A. Knopf, 1993), 6. It must be added that campaign reporting has grown substantially more negative over the past thirty years. See ibid., 20. This has to do with journalists' shifting ideology, their post-Vietnam, post-Watergate, post-Reagan/Deaver/Ailes efforts not to be taken in.

36. Christopher Jencks, "Is Violent Crime Increasing?" *American Prospect* 4 (1991): 99.

37. Robinson and Sheehan, *Over the Wire and on TV*, 61.

38. Ibid., 206.

39. Ibid., 41–43.

40. Janet E. Steele, "Experts and the Operational Bias of Television News: The Case of the Persian Gulf War," *Journalism and Mass Communication Quarterly* 72 (Winter 1995): 799–812.

41. Daniel C. Hallin, Robert Karl Manoff, and Judy K. Weddle, "Sourcing Patterns of National Security Reporters," *Journalism Quarterly* 70 (1993): 753–66.

42. Steven R. Weisman, "Reagan Pledges Aid to Louisiana Flood Area," *New York Times*, January 3, 1983, 7; and George Skelton, "Reagan Pitches In to Help Flood Victims," *Los Angeles Times*, January 3, 1983, 14.

43. Sigal, *Reporters and Officials*, is an early study documenting the overwhelming reliance on government officials of Washington reporting. For more on the importance of sources, see chapter 7.

44. For a convincing analysis of why the U.S. news media soft-pedaled the story of the Holocaust, See Deborah E. Lipstadt, *Beyond Belief* (New York: Free Press, 1986).

45. For that evidence, see Joseph Cappella and Kathleen Hall Jamieson, *Spiral of Cynicism* (New York: Oxford University Press, 1997).

46. Ralph Nader, "My Untold Story," *Brill's Content* (February 2001): 102.

47. Ibid., 102.

48. Ibid., 154.

49. Gans, *Deciding What's News*, 39–52.

50. Vanessa Williams, "Black and White and Red All Over," in *The Business of Journalism*, ed. William Serrin (New York: New Press, 2000), 107.

51. In 1997 the death rate by homicide was seven times higher for black men than for white men. For both sexes, homicide was a more frequent cause of death for blacks than pneumonia, liver disease, or chronic pulmonary disease; for whites, homicide was half as frequent as liver disease, one-seventh as frequent as pneumonia, and one-tenth as frequent as chronic pulmonary disease. U.S. Bureau of the Census, *Statistical Abstract of the United States: 2000* (Washington, D.C.: Government Printing Office, 2000), 47 (table 128), 92 (table 134).

52. Robert Entman, "Modern Racism and the Image of Blacks in Local Television News," *Critical Studies in Mass Communication* 7 (1990): 332–45.

CHAPTER 4   WHERE NEWS CAME FROM

1. For an advocate of this view, see Mitchell Stephens, *A History of News* (New York: Viking, 1988). See also Richard Streckfuss, "News before Newspapers," *Journalism and Mass Communication Quarterly* 75 (1998): 84–97.

2. Jürgen Habermas, *The Structural Transformation of the Public Sphere* (Cambridge, Mass.: MIT Press, 1989), 181. To some degree, growing interest in media history is a by-product of the developing "history of the book" subfield. In the United States, historian Robert Darnton's stimulating explorations of the role of various media in eighteenth-century France have been especially influential, culminating in his call for more study of "how societies made sense of events and transmitted information about them" (p. 1). See Robert Darnton, "An Early Information Society: News and the Media in Eighteenth-Century Paris," *American Historical Review* 105 (February 2000): 1–35. Darnton expresses some skepticism in this article of uses to which the concept of "the public sphere" have been put.

3. Habermas, 183 and 186.

4. Benedict Anderson, *Imagined Communities: Reflections on the Origin and Spread of Nationalism* (London: Verso, 1983), 46.

5. Ibid., 39.

6. See Silvio R. Waisbord, *Watchdog Journalism in South America* (New York: Columbia University Press, 2000); and Erik Neveu, "Media and Politics in French Political Science," *European Journal of Political Research* 33 (1998): 439–58.

7. Pippa Norris, *A Virtuous Circle* (Cambridge, Eng.: Cambridge University Press, 2000), 63–73.

8. Charles E. Clark and Charles Wetherell, "The Measure of Maturity: The Pennsylvania Gazette, 1728–1765," *William and Mary Quarterly* 46 (April 1989): 292.

9. Jackson Turner Main, *The Anti-Federalists* (Chapel Hill: University of North Carolina Press, 1961), 209, 250–51.

10. Pauline Maier, *The Old Revolutionaries* (New York: Alfred A. Knopf, 1980), 30.

11. Pennsylvania jurist Alexander Addison, quoted in Richard Buel, Jr., "Freedom of the Press in Revolutionary America: The Evolution of

Libertarianism, 1760– 1820," in *The Press and the American Revolution*, ed. Bernard Bailyn and John B. Hench (Worcester, Mass.: American Antiquarian Society, 1980), 86.

12. Thomas Jefferson, letter to John Norvell, June 11, 1807, in *The Life and Selected Writings of Thomas Jefferson*, ed. Adrienne Koch and William Peden (New York: Modern Library, 1944), 581–82.

13. On the emergence of the penny press and on nineteenth-century U.S. newspapers generally, see Michael Schudson, *Discovering the News* (New York: Basic Books, 1978).

14. Donald Ritchie, *Press Gallery* (Cambridge, Mass.: Harvard University Press, 1991), 60–63.

15. Schudson, *The Good Citizen* (New York: Free Press, 1998), 177–82; and Michael McGerr, *The Decline of Popular Politics* (New York: Oxford University Press, 1986), 107–37.

16. See Schudson, *Discovering the News*; and Michael Schudson, "The Objectivity Norm in American Journalism," *Journalism* 2 (August 2001): 149–70.

17. Quoted in Oliver Gramling, *AP: The Story of News* (New York: Farrar and Rinehart, 1940), 314.

18. Paul A. Pratte, *Gods Within the Machine: A History of the American Society of Newspaper Editors, 1923–1993* (Westport, Conn.: Praeger, 1995), 206.

19. Edward Purcell's *Crisis of Democratic Theory* (Lexington: University Press of Kentucky, 1973) discusses lucidly the general prestige of objectivist or "scientific naturalist" understandings of science and social science in the 1920s.

20. The history of public relations is not well developed. The material here comes from Schudson, *Discovering the News*, 34–44. The quotation from John Dewey is in John Dewey, *Individualism Old and New* (New York: Minton, Balch, 1930), 44.

21. Jean Chalaby, "Journalism as an Anglo-American Invention," *European Journal of Communication* 11 (1996): 303–26.

22. Katharine Graham, *Personal History* (New York: Random House, 1997), 402.

23. Daniel C. Hallin, *We Keep America on Top of the World* (London: Routledge, 1994), 172.

24.   Ibid.

25.   Daniel Bell, *The End of Ideology* (New York: Free Press, 1962).

26.   On Vietnam and the media, see Daniel C. Hallin, *The "Uncensored War": The Media and Vietnam* (New York: Oxford University Press, 1986); George Donelson Moss, "News or Nemesis: Did Television Lose the Vietnam War?" in *A Vietnam Reader*, ed., George Donelson Moss (Englewood Cliffs, N.J.: Prentice Hall, 1991), 245–300; and William M. Hammond, *Reporting Vietnam* (Lawrence: University Press of Kansas, 1998). On the Pentagon Papers, see Sandy Ungar, *The Papers and the Papers* (New York: Columbia University Press, 1989); and David Rudenstine, *The Day the Presses Stopped* (Berkeley: University of California Press, 1996). On Watergate, see Michael Schudson, *The Power of News* (Cambridge, Mass.: Harvard University Press, 1995), 142–68, as well as memoirs by *Washington Post* publisher Katharine Graham (Graham, *Personal History*) and *Washington Post* editor Benjamin Bradlee (Bradlee, *A Good Life* ([New York: Simon and Schuster, 1995]).

27.   Meg Greenfield, *Washington* (New York: Public Affairs, 2001), 191.

CHAPTER 5   IN RECENT MEMORY: NEWS FROM WATERGATE TO THE WEB

1.   Thomas E. Patterson, "Doing Well and Doing Good" (Faculty Research Working Papers Series, Joan Shorenstein Center on the Press, Politics and Public Policy, John F. Kennedy School of Government, Harvard University, Cambridge, Mass., 2000), 3.

2.   Ibid., 10.

3.   Thomas E. Patterson, *Out of Order* (New York: Alfred A. Knopf, 1993).18.

4.   Ibid., 20.

5.   Edward Jay Epstein, *News from Nowhere* (New York: Random House, 1973), 215–17.

6.   Lizette Alvarez, "Senate Passes Bill for Annual Tests in Public Schools," *New York Times*, June 15, 2001, 1. In the Associated Press version of the story, as printed in the June 15, 2001, *San Diego Union-Tribune* (David Espo, "Sweeping Education Reform Bill Wins OK"), the policy implications of the bill receive no mention at all.

7. Patterson, *Out of Order*, 11–12, 68–77.

8. Committee of Concerned Journalists, "Changing Definitions of News," 1998, available at http://www.journalism.org/node/442 (accessed May 11 2011).

9. Theodore H. White, *The Making of the President, 1960* (New York: Atheneum, 1961).

10. See Michael J. Robinson and Margaret A. Sheehan, *Over the Wire and on TV* (New York: Russell Sage Foundation, 1983), 279.

11. Timothy Crouse, *The Boys on the Bus* (New York: Ballantine, 1973), 37.

12. Larry Sabato, *Feeding Frenzy* (New York: Free Press, 1991), 9, 34–35. On Safire's career as a columnist, see Michael Schudson, *Watergate in American Memory* (New York: Basic Books, 1992), 70–82.

13. Paul Taylor, *See How They Run* (New York: Alfred A. Knopf, 1990), 50–52.

14. Ibid.

15. Ibid., 56.

16. Frank Esser, "'Tabloidization' of News: A Comparative Analysis of Anglo-American and German Press Journalism," *European Journal of Communication* 14 (1999): 292. Esser cites a content analysis of the past fifty years of the German prestige press that finds no change in the emphasis in political reporting on personality, nor any increase in the use of stories presented in an emotionalized style. The analysis does show an increase—but only in the 1990s—in scandalizing stories, the first and only sign of a tendency toward tabloidization in the German prestige press (pp. 304–5). Unlike in the United Kingdom, where many national newspapers compete with one another, there is rather little newspaper competition in Germany; most German newspapers are oriented to regional markets.

17. Cited in ibid., 312.

18. Jurgen Westerstahl and Folke Johansson, "News Ideologies as Moulders of Domestic News," *European Journal of Communication* 1 (1986), 133–49 at 148. See also Monika Djerf-Pierre, "Squaring the Circle: News in Public Service and Commercial Television in Sweden, 1956–1999," *Journalism Studies* 1 (2000): 239–60.

19. Westerstahl and Johansson, 148.

20. Paddy Scannell, "Public Service Broadcasting and Modern Life," *Media, Culture and Society* 11 (1989): 143–47.

21. Ellis Krauss, "Changing Television News in Japan," *Journal of Asian Studies* 57 (1998): 686. See also Ellis Krauss, *Broadcasting Politics in Japan: NHK and Television News* (Ithaca: Cornell University Press, 2000), 219-240.

22. Martin Eide, "A New Kind of Newspaper? Understanding a Popularization Process," *Media, Culture, and Society* 19 (1997): 179.

23. Silvio Waisbord, *Watchdog Journalism in South America* (New York: Columbia University Press), 2000.

24. Liesbet van Zoonen, "A Tyranny of Intimacy? Women, Femininity, and Television News," in *Communication and Citizenship*, ed. Peter Dahlgren and Colin Sparks (London: Routledge, 1991), 217–35.

25. Taylor, *See How They Run*, 62.

26. For a history of the changing political culture of American elections, see Michael Schudson, *The Good Citizen: A History of American Civic Life* (New York: Free Press, 1998).

27. John Thompson, *Political Scandal* (Cambridge: Polity Press, 2000), 262.

28. Ibid.

29. *What the People Want from the Press* (Washington: Center for Media and Public Affairs, 1997), 35–41.

30. Daniel C. Hallin, *We Keep America on Top of the World* (London: Routledge, 1994), 147.

31. Ibid, 145.

32. Carl Sessions Stepp, "The State of the American Newspaper: Then and Now," *American Journalism Review* (September 1999): 60–75.

33. Paul Weaver, "Newspaper News and Television News," in *Understanding Television*, ed. Richard P. Adler (New York: Praeger, 1981), 277–93 at 280.

34. Ibid., 283

35. See Michael Schudson, *The Power of News* (Cambridge, Mass.: Harvard University Press, 1995), 53–71.

36. Tom Rosenstiel, "The CNN Myth," *New Republic* (August 22 and 29, 1994), 27–33.

37. Ibid.

38. Weaver, "Newspaper News and Television News," 292.

39. On women in the newsroom, see Pippa Norris, ed., *Women, Media, and Politics* (New York: Oxford University Press, 1997). The single best discussion of the topic may well be Meg Greenfield's candid memoir, *Washington* (New York: Public Affairs, 2001), 107–58.

40. The most thoughtful and provocative argument about the dangers of media fragmentation is offered by Cass Sunstein, *Republic.com 2.0* (Princeton, N.J.: Princeton University Press, 2007).

41. See Steven Kull, "Misperceptions, the Media and the Iraq War," The PIPA/ Knowledge Networks Poll (Program on International Policy Attitudes— PIPA, University of Maryland and Knowledge Networks, Menlo Park, CA), Oct. 2, 2003.

42. Pew Research Center, "Americans Spending More Time Following the News," http://people-press.org/2010/09/12/Section-2-online-and-digital-news/ (accessed 9-8-11).

43. Greenfield, *Washington*, 89.

CHAPTER 6   NEWS IN THE MARKETPLACE

1. Daniel Machalaba, "Would Closing of *Daily* News Hurt *Times?*" *Wall Street Journal*, February 5, 1982, 29.

2. See Gilbert Cranberg, Randall Bezanson, and John Soloski, *Taking Stock: Journalism and the Publicly Traded Newspaper Company* (Ames: Iowa State University Press, 2000), 90–92.

3. David Halberstam, *The Powers That Be* (New York: Alfred A. Knopf, 1979), 251.

4. Herbert J. Gans, *Deciding What's News* (New York: Pantheon, 1979), 214.

5. David Halberstam, "A Sober Look at the Profession of Journalism," *Newslink* 10 (Spring 2000): 18.

6. Cranberg, Bezanson, and Soloski, *Taking Stock*, 43.

7. Eli M. Noam, *Media Ownership and Concentration in America* (New York: Oxford University Press, 2009), 140.

8. David Demers, "Corporate Newspaper Structure, Editorial Page Vigor, and Social Change," *Journalism and Mass Communication Quarterly* 73 (1996): 857–77.

9. C. Edwin Baker, "Ownership of Newspapers: The View from Positivist Social Science" (Research Paper R-12, Joan Shorenstein Center on the Press, Politics and Public Policy, John F. Kennedy School of Government, Harvard University, Cambridge, Mass., 1994), 19.

10. Benjamin M. Compaine and Douglas Gomery, *Who Owns the Media? Competition and Concentration in the Mass Media Industry*, 3rd ed. (Mahwah, N.J.: Lawrence Erlbaum, 2000), 20-21.

11. Noam, *Media Ownership*, 141.

12. James Risser, "Lessons from L.A.: The Wall Is Heading Back," *Columbia Journalism Review* (January–February 2000), 26.

13. David Shaw, the distinguished *Los Angeles Times* media reporter, produced an extensive report on the whole affair, published in the newspaper on December 20, 1999. See also William Prochnau, "Paradise Lost?" *American Journalism Review* (January 10, 2000); and Risser "Lessons from L.A.," 26–29.

14. From *Brill's Content*, Fall 1998, cited in Jay Harris, "What Is Missing from Your News?" in *The Business of Journalism*, ed. William Serrin (New York: New Press, 2000), 152.

15. Thanks to Carrie Sloan for her research assistance on this point.

16. Marion Just, Rosalind Levine, and Kathleen Regan, "News for Sale," *Columbia Journalism Review* 40 (November–December 2001), 68.

17. Reported in Lawrence Soley, "The Power of the Press Has a Price," *Extra!* (July–August 1997), 11–13.

18. Marty Haag, quoted in Lawrence K. Grossman, "Why Local TV News Is So Awful," *Columbia Journalism Review* 36 (November–December 1997), 21.

19. Grossman, "Why Local TV News Is So Awful," 21.

20. *Damned Old Crank: A Self-Portrait of E. W. Scripps*, ed. Charles R. McCabe (New York: Harper and Brothers, 1951), 228.

21. Ibid., 229.

22. Silvio Waisbord, "Leviathan Dreams: State and Broadcasting in South America," *Communication Review* 1 (1995): 219.

23. J. Lee, "Press Freedom and Democratization: South Korea's Experience and Some Lessons," *Gazette* 59 (1997): 135–49.

24. Myung Koo Kang, "Struggle for Press Freedom and 'Un-Elected' Media Power," in *Asian Media Studies*, ed. J. Emi and S. K. Chua (London: Blackwell, 2005), 75–90.

25. Yuzhei Zhao, *Media, Market, and Democracy in China: Between the Party Line and the Bottom Line* (Urbana: University of Illinois Press, 1998).

26. Judy Polumbaum, "Political Fetters, Commercial Freedoms: Restraint and Excess in Chinese Mass Communications," in *Regional Handbook of Economic and Political Development*, vol. 1, ed. Christopher Holmes (Chicago: Fitzroy Dearborn, 1997), 211–25.

27. Zhao, *Media, Market, and Democracy*, 161.

28. Ibid. Important recent studies of the Chinese media include Guobin Yang,. *The Power of the Internet in China* (New York: Columbia University Press, 2009); and Susan L. Shirk., ed., *Changing Media, Changing China* (New York: Oxford University Press, 2011), a fine collection of essays by China scholars from China, Hong Kong, the Netherlands, and the United States.

29. Graham Murdock, "Political Deviance: The Press Presentation of a Militant Mass Demonstration," in *The Manufacture of News*, ed. Stanley Cohen and Jock Young (Beverly Hills: Sage, 1973), 172.

30. Al Tompkins, "Total Recall," *RTDNA Communicator* 54 (October 2000): 22–25.

31. Sheila Coronel, executive director, Philippine Center for Investigative Journalism, quoted in Craig L. LaMay, *Journalism and Emerging Democracy: Lessons from Societies in Transition* (Washington, D.C.: Aspen Institute, 2001), 15.

CHAPTER 7   NEWS SOURCES

1. Leon V. Sigal, "Sources Make the News," in *Reading the News*, ed. Robert K. Manoff and Michael Schudson (New York: Pantheon, 1986), 25.

2. Richard V. Ericson, Patricia M. Baranek, and Janet B. C. Chan, *Negotiating Control: A Study of News Sources* (Toronto: University of Toronto Press, 1989), 377, 3.

3.   Silvio R.Waisbord, *Watchdog Journalism in South America* (New York: Columbia University Press, 2000), 95.

4.   Philip Schlesinger, "Rethinking the Sociology of Journalism: Source Strategies and the Limits of Media-Centrism," in *Public Communication*, ed. Marjorie Ferguson (London: Sage, 1990), 61–83.

5.   Ken Silverstein, "Good Press for Dictators," *American Prospect*, April 9, 2001, 17–19.

6.   Quoted in Charles Peters, "Why the White House Press Didn't Get the Watergate Story," *Washington Monthly* (July–August 1973).

7.   Leon V. Sigal, *Reporters and Officials* (Lexington, Mass.: D. C. Heath, 1973), 121. Sigal's research was later confirmed for television in Dan Berkowitz, "TV News Sources and News Channels: A Study in Agenda-Building," *Journalism Quarterly* 64 (1987): 508–13.

8.   Paolo Mancini, "Between Trust and Suspicion: How Political Journalists Solve the Dilemma," *European Journal of Sociology* 8 (1993): 40.

9.   Ericson, Baranek, and Chan, *Negotiating Control*, 6.

10.   Ofer Feldman, *Politics and the News Media in Japan* (Ann Arbor: University of Michigan Press, 1993); Laurie Ann Freeman, *Closing the Shop: Information Cartels and Japan's Mass Media* (Princeton, N.J.: Princeton University Press, 2000); and Ellis Krauss, *Broadcasting Politics in Japan: NHK TV News* (Ithaca, N.Y.: Cornell University Press, 2000).

11.   Bernard C. Cohen, *Democracies and Foreign Policy: Public Participation in the United States and the Netherlands* (Madison: University of Wisconsin Press, 1995), 110.

12.   Theodore H. White, *The Making of the President, 1960* (New York: Atheneum, 1961), 365–66.

13.   Waisbord, *Watchdog Journalism*, 94.

14.   Morton H. Halperin, *Bureaucratic Politics and Foreign Policy* (Washington: Brookings Institution Press, 1974), 173–95.

15.   Waisbord, *Watchdog Journalism*, 108.

16.   Philip Geyelin, "Vietnam and the Press: Limited War and an Open Society," in *The Vietnam Legacy*, ed. Anthony Lake (New York: New York University Press, 1976), 175.

17.   Joan Vennochi, "The Media Make Deals with the Devil," *San Diego Union-Tribune*, August 19, 2000, B14.

18.   James Warren, "Washington Journalism," in *The Business of Journalism*, ed. William Serrin (New York: New Press, 2000), 79.

19.   Ibid., 80.

20.   Carol Matlack, "Crossing the Line?" *National Journal*, March 25, 1989, 725. Many news organizations' codes of ethics are listed on the website of the American Society of Newspaper Editors, http://www.asne.org/key_initiatives/ethics_codes.aspx (accessed 7-30-11).

21.   James Fallows, *Breaking the News* (New York: Pantheon, 1996), 103–4; and ibid.

22.   Jim Rutenberg, "Rather Apologizes for Speaking at Democratic Fund-Raiser," *New York Times*, April 5, 2001, A17.

23.   Ibid.

24.   Yuzhei Zhao, *Media, Market, and Democracy in China: Between the Party Line and the Bottom Line* (Urbana: University of Illinois Press, 1998), 72–93.

25.   Ibid., 87.

26.   José Luis Benavides, "*Gacetilla*: A Keyword for a Revisionist Approach to the Political Economy of Mexico's Print News Media," *Media, Culture, and Society* 22 (2000): 85–104. See also William A. Orme, Jr., ed., *A Culture of Collusion: An Inside Look at the Mexican Press* (Miami: North-South Center Press, 1997).

27.   "Shamans and journalists constitute two populations that thrive on access denied others in the community," wrote Barbie Zelizer in "On Communicative Practice: The 'Other Worlds' of Journalism and Shamanism," *Southern Folklore* 49 (1992): 21.

28.   Marvin Gottlieb, "Dangerous Liaisons," *Columbia Journalism Review* 28 (July–August 1989): 23.

29.   Thomas Ferenczi, "The Media and Democracy," *CSD Bulletin* 8 (Winter 2000–2001): 1–2.

30.   This account comes from David Broder, *Behind the Front Page* (New York: Simon and Schuster, 1987), 353–56.

31.   Ibid., 356.

250 NOTES TO PAGES 139–142

32. William Safire, *Safire's New Political Dictionary* (New York: Oxford University Press, 2008), 688.

33. Robert Darnton, *Kiss of Lamourette* (New York: W. W. Norton, 1990), 75. (This essay originally appeared in 1975.)

34. Frank Esser, Carstein Reinemann, and David Fan, "Spin Doctoring in British and German Election Campaigns," *European Journal of Communication* 15 (2000): 212.

35. Ibid., .212, 214, 234.

36. Broder, *Behind the Front Page*, 195.

37. Tom Rosenstiel and Bill Kovach, *Warp Speed* (New York: Twentieth Century Fund, 2000).

38. Aeron Davis, "Public Relations, News Production, and Changing Patterns of Source Access in the British National Media," *Media, Culture, and Society* 22 (2000): 47.

39. Ibid., 51–52.

40. Herbert J. Gans, *Deciding What's News* (New York: Pantheon, 1979).116; Bernard Cohen, *The Press and Foreign Policy* (Princeton, N.J.: Princeton University Press, 1963), 267; W. Lance Bennett, "The News about Foreign Policy," in *Taken by Storm: The Media, Public Opinion, and U.S. Foreign Policy in the Gulf War*, ed. W. Lance Bennett and David L. Paletz (Chicago: University of Chicago Press, 1994), 24–29; and Philip Schlesinger and Howard Tumber, *Reporting Crime: The Media Politics of Criminal Justice* (Oxford, Eng.: Clarendon Press, 1994). For the observation that government officials at least think reporters have the upper hand, see Stephen Hess, *The Government/ Press Connection* (Washington: Brookings Institution Press, 1984), 109.

41. Richard Ericson and his colleagues have suggested that the view that sources dominate is a reporter's view and that sociologists have inadvertently adopted it by having chosen to interview reporters. If they would interview sources as well, as Ericson did in his study, they would see the matter as one of negotiated meanings rather than of source domination. See Ericson, Baranek, and Chan, *Negotiating Control*, 24.

42. Delmer Dunne, *Public Officials in the Press* (Reading, Mass.: Addison-Wesley, 1969), 41.

43. Stephen Hess, *The Washington Reporters* (Washington: Brookings Institution Press, 1981), 17–18.

44. Joseph Alsop and Stewart Alsop, *The Reporter's Trade* (New York: Reynal, 1958), 6.

45. Zvi Reich, *Sourcing the News* (Cresskill, N.J.: Hampton Press, 2009), 186.

46. Edie Goldenberg, *Making the Papers* (Lexington, Mass.: D. C. Heath, 1975).

47. Bettina Boxall, personal e-mail correspondence, September 1, 2009.

48. Jonathan Mermin, "Television News and American Intervention in Somalia: The Myth of a Media-Driven Foreign Policy," *Political Science Quarterly* 112 (1997): 385–403; and Steven Livingston and Todd Eachus, "Humanitarian Crises and U.S. Foreign Policy: Somalia and the CNN Effect Reconsidered," *Political Communication* 12 (1995): 413–429.

49. W. Lance Bennett, "Toward a Theory of Press-State Relations in the United States," *Journal of Communication* 40 (1990), 106.

50. Jonathan Zaller, "Elite Leadership of Mass Opinion: New Evidence from the Gulf War," in *Taken by Storm*, ed. Bennett and Paletz, 201–2.

CHAPTER 8   THE POLITICAL CULTURE OF NEWS

1. For a fuller statement of this point, see Erik Asard and W. Lance Bennett, *Democracy and the Marketplace of Ideas* (Cambridge, Eng.: Cambridge University Press, 1997), 35–37.

2. Gianpietro Mazzoleni and Winifred Schulz, "'Mediatization' of Politics: A Challenge for Democracy?" *Political Communication* 16 (1999): 247–61.

3. On "mediatization" as a general feature of modernity, see John B. Thompson, *The Media and Modernity* (Stanford: Stanford University Press, 1995), 308.

4. John Anthony Maltese, *The Selling of Supreme Court Nominees* (Baltimore: Johns Hopkins University Press, 1995), 52–53, 85–92.

5. Samuel Kernell, *Going Public: New Strategies of Presidential Leadership* (Washington, D.C.: Congressional Quarterly Press, 1986).

6. Ibid., 93–97.

7. Ibid., 24, 27–28.

8. Steven Kelman, *Regulating America, Regulating Sweden: A Comparative Study of Occupational Safety and Health Policy* (Cambridge, Mass.: MIT Press, 1981), 163.

9.   Ibid.

10.   Bernard C. Cohen, *Democracies and Foreign Policy: Public Participation in the United States and the Netherlands* (Madison: University of Wisconsin Press, 1995), 123.

11.   Ibid.

12.   Ibid.

13.   Gerry Braun of the *San Diego Union-Tribune*, cited in Christine Ileto Pangan, "Local Political Consultants and Reporters" (unpublished paper, University of California, San Diego, 1999), 18.

14.   Nicholas Garnham, *Capitalism and Communication* (London: Sage, 1990), 104–14.

15.   John Keane, *Liberty of the Press* (Cambridge, Mass.: Polity Press, 1991).

16.   Ellis Krauss, *Broadcasting Politics in Japan: NHK TV News* (Ithaca, N.Y.: Cornell University Press, 2000), 105.

17.   Eli Skogerbo, "The Press Subsidy System in Norway," *European Journal of Communication* 12 (1997): 99–118; and Paul Murschetz, "State Support for the Daily Press in Europe: A Critical Appraisal," *European Journal of Communication* 13 (1998): 291–313.

18.   Frank Esser, "'Tabloidization' of News: A Comparative Analysis of Anglo-American and German Press Journalism," *European Journal of Communication* 14 (1999): 313.

19.   Daniel C. Hallin and Paolo Mancini, "Speaking of the President: Political Structures and Representational Forms in U.S. and Italian Television News," *Theory and Society* 13 (1984): 829–50.

20.   Rodney Benson, "What Makes News More Multiperspectival? A Field Analysis," *Poetics* 37 (Fall, 2009): 402–418. See also Rodney Benson and Daniel C. Hallin, "How States, Markets and Globalization Shape the News: The French and U.S. National Press, 1965-1997." *European Journal of Communication* 22 (March 2007): 27–48.

21.   Tamar Liebes, *Reporting the Arab-Israeli Conflict* (London: Routledge, 1997), 34.

22.   Ibid., 48.

23. Rasmus Kleis Nielsen, *Ground Wars: Personalized Communication in Political Campaigns* (Princeton University Press, 2012).

24. Kris Kodrich, "Finding a New Way: Nicaraguan Newspapers in a Globalized World" (paper presented at annual conference of the International Communication Association, Washington, D.C., May 2001).

25. Daniel Hallin and Paolo Mancini, *Comparing Media Systems:Three Models of Media and Politics* (Cambridge, Eng.: Cambridge University Press, 2004). For a useful condensation of the book, see Daniel Hallin and Paolo Mancini, "Western Media Systems in Comparative Perspective" in James Curran, ed., *Media and Society*, 5th ed. (London: Bloomsbury Academic, 2010), 103–21.

CHAPTER 9   THE AUDIENCE FOR NEWS

1. Robert DeMaria, *Samuel Johnson and the Life of Reading* (Baltimore: Johns Hopkins University Press, 1997).

2. Bernard Berelson, "What Missing the Newspaper Means," in *Communications Research 1948–1949*, ed. Paul Lazarsfeld and Frank Stanton (New York: Harper and Brothers, 1949), 36–47.

3. The phrase "para-social interaction" was coined by Donald Horton and Richard Wohl, "Mass Communication and Para-Social Interaction: Observations on Intimacy at a Distance," *Psychiatry* 19 (1956): 215–29.

4. Berelson, "What Missing the Newspaper Means," 43.

5. Ibid., 45.

6. Theodore Glasser, "Play and the Power of News," *Journalism* 1 (2000): 26.

7. From Fanny Fern, *Fern Leaves from Fanny's Port-Folio* (1854), 178–79, cited in David M. Henkin, *City Reading* (New York: Columbia University Press, 1998), 110.

8. Thomas Kessner, *Fiorello H. La Guardia and the Making of Modern New York* (New York: McGraw-Hill, 1989), 575.

9. Kevin Barnhurst and Ellen Wartella, "Newspapers and Citizenship: Young Adults' Subjective Experience of Newspapers," *Critical Studies in Mass Communications* 8 (1991): 195–209.

10. Gina Lubrano, "A Depiction That Angered Hindus," *San Diego Union-Tribune*, July 24, 2000, B7.

11. Jack Katz, "What Makes Crime 'News'?" *Media, Culture, and Society* 9 (1981): 47–75.

    The fundamental role of the Post Office Act of 1792 is explored in Richard R. John, *Spreading the News* (Cambridge, MA: Harvard University Press, 1995) and elaborated as part of a general argument about the centrality of political decisions to the growth of American media industries in Paul Starr, *The Creation of the Media* (New York: Basic Books, 2004).

12. Herbert J. Gans, *Deciding What's News* (New York: Pantheon, 1979), 230.

13. Robert Darnton, *Kiss of Lamourette* (New York: W. W. Norton, 1990), 62.

14. Clark, Martire, and Bartolomeo, Inc., "Leveraging Media Assets," a 1998 report prepared for the American Society of Newspaper Editors, available on the ASNE website at http://www.asne.org.

15. Thomas Patterson, "Young People and News" (report, Joan Shorenstein Center on the Press, Politics and Public Policy, John F. Kennedy School of Government, Harvard University, Cambridge, Mass., July 2007), 9.

16. Project for Excellence in Journalism, Pew Research Center, *The State of the News Media 2011: An Annual Report on American Journalism*, http://stateofthemedia.org/2011/online-essay/data-page-7/ (accessed 7-30-11).

17. Colin Sparks and John Tulloch, eds., *Tabloid Tales* (Lanham, Md.: Rowman and Littlefield, 2000). *The Daily Show* and *The Colbert Report* have especially attracted scholarly attention. See Jeffrey P. Jones, *Entertaining Politics* (Lanham, MD: Rowman & Littlefield, 2005); Jeffrey P. Jones, "Believing Fictions: Redactional Culture and the Will to Truthiness," in Barbie Zelizer, ed., *The Changing Faces of Journalism* (New York: Routledge, 2009), 127–143; Geoffrey Baym, *From Cronkite to Colbert* (Boulder, CO: Paradigm, 2010).

Chapter 10   News as Literature and Narrative

1. James S. Ettema and Theodore L. Glasser, "Narrative Form and Moral Force: The Realization of Innocence and Guilt through Investigative Journalism," *Journal of Communication* 38 (Summer 1988): 24.

2. Peter Parisi, "Astonishment and Understanding: On the Problem of Explanation in Journalism," *New Jersey Journal of Communication* 7 (1999): 7.

3. Gaye Tuchman, *Making News: A Study in the Construction of Reality* (New York: Free Press, 1978), 59–63. Tuchman developed the first analysis of "what a story!" stories. Her work was taken up further by Dan Berkowitz in both "Doing Double Duty: Paradigm Repair and the Princess Diana What-a-Story," *Journalism* 1 (2000): 125–43; and "Non-Routine News and Newswork: Exploring a What-a-Story," *Journal of Communication* 42 (1992): 82–94. Woodward's advice to his staff to locate "Holy shit!" stories became a vital point at issue in an ultimately unsuccessful libel suit brought against the *Washington Post* by the chairman of Mobil Oil. See the discussion of this in Michael Schudson, *Watergate in American Memory* (New York: Basic Books, 1992), 121–23.

4. Ettema and Glasser, "Narrative Form and Moral Force."

5. Ibid., 23.

6. Hayden White, "The Narrativization of Real Events," in *On Narrative*, ed. W. J. T. Mitchell (Chicago: University of Chicago Press, 1981), 253.

7. The leading work on community-building television news is Daniel Dayan and Elihu Katz, *Media Events: The Live Broadcasting of History* (Cambridge, Mass.: Harvard University Press, 1992). The most consistently interesting commentary on this feature of newspaper news (as well as TV news) comes from James Ettema and Theodore Glasser's work. See, for instance, Theodore L. Glasser and James S. Ettema, "The Language of News and the End of Morality," *Argumentation* 8 (1994): 337–44; and especially James Ettema and Theodore Glasser, *Custodians of Conscience: Investigative Journalism and Public Virtue* (New York: Columbia University Press, 1998).

8. Paul Hartman and Charles Husband, "The Mass Media and Racial Conflict," in *The Manufacture of News: A Reader*, ed. Stanley Cohen and Jock Young (Beverly Hills: Sage, 1973), 274.

9. Frank Pearce, "How to Be Immoral and Ill, Pathetic and Dangerous, All at the Same Time: Mass Media and the Homosexual," in ibid., 293.

10. Edwin Alwood, *Straight News: Gays, Lesbians, and the News Media* (New York: Columbia University Press, 1996), 315. See also Suzanna Danuta Walters, *All the Rage: The Story of Gay Visibility in America* (Chicago: University of Chicago Press, 2001), in which the author urges gays and lesbians never to forget their oppression but instead "mark those rare and chaotic moments when all the verities come tumbling down" (p. 28). In her view, the 1990s were a moment of just this sort.

11.   Jack Katz, "What Makes Crime 'News'?" *Media, Culture, and Society* 9 (1981): 47–75. This work offers a general "moral order" explanation. See also Joel Best, *Random Violence* (Berkeley: University of California Press, 1999), in which the author offers a social-organizational explanation.

12.   Dayan and Katz, *Media Events*, 108.

13.   Daniel C. Hallin, *The "Uncensored War": The Media and Vietnam* (New York: Oxford University Press, 1986), 117.

14.   Yoram Peri, "The Rabin Myth and the Press: Reconstruction of the Israeli Collective Identity," *European Journal of Communication* 12 (1997): 435–58.

15.   Michael Schudson, "What's Unusual about Covering Politics as Usual," in *Journalism after September 11*, ed. Stuart Adam and Barbie Zelizer (London: Routledge, 2002), 36–47.

16.   Soviet journalists had one advantage over Western journalists in their day: they could cover business with the same access they had to government because business was government-owned and managed. They had access to the shop floor that a reporter in the West could gain only with difficulty. See Dean Mills, "The Soviet Journalist: A Cultural Analysis" (Ph.D. dissertation, University of Illinois, Urbana-Champaign, 1981).

17.   James Carey, "Why: The Dark Continent of American Journalism," in *Reading the News*, ed. Robert K. Manoff and Michael Schudson (New York: Pantheon, 1986), 146–96.

18.   Phyllis Kaniss, *Making Local News* (Chicago: University of Chicago Press, 1991), 65.

19.   Ibid., 68.

CHAPTER 11   LAW, DEMOCRACY, AND NEWS

1.   Amartya Sen, "Freedoms and Needs," *New Republic*, January 10–17, 1994, 34. See also Jean Dreze and Amartya Sen, *Hunger and Public Action* (Oxford, Eng.: Clarendon Press, 1989), 159, 212–15, 262–64.

2.   James Carey, "Afterword: The Culture in Question," in *James Carey: A Critical Reader*, ed. Eve Stryker Munson and Catherine A. Warren (Minneapolis: University of Minnesota Press, 1997), 332.

3.   Ibid.

4. See Joseph D. Straubhaar, "Television and Video in the Transition from Military to Civilian Rule in Brazil," *Latin American Research Review* 24 (1989): 140–54; Mauro Porto, "Media Framing and Civic Competence: Television and Audiences' Interpretations of Politics in Brazil" (Ph.D. dissertation, University of California, San Diego, 2001), 177–80, and Mauro Porto, "TV News and Political Change in Brazil." Journalism 8 (2007): 363–384.

5. Rosario de Mateo, "The Evolution of the Newspaper Industry in Spain, 1939–87," *European Journal of Communication* 4 (1989): 211–26.

6. Paddy Scannell, "Public Service Broadcasting and Modern Public Life," *Media, Culture, and Society* 11 (1989): 160.

7. Judy Polumbaum, "Professionalism in China's Press Corps," in *China's Crisis of 1989*, ed. R. V. Des Forges, L. Ning, and W. Yen-bo (Albany: State University of New York Press, 1993), 295–311.

8. Kyu Ho Youm, "The Right of Reply and Freedom of the Press: An International and Comparative Perspective," *George Washington Law Review* 76 (June 2008): 1017–64.

9. *New York Times v. Sullivan*, 376 U.S. 254 (1964), 270.

10. *Miami Herald Publishing Company v. Tornillo*, 418 U.S. 241 (1974), 260.

11. Benno C. Schmidt Jr., *Freedom of the Press vs. Public Access* (New York: Praeger, 1976), 13.

12. Cass Sunstein, *Democracy and the Problem of Free Speech* (New York: Free Press, 1993), 20–21, 107.

13. Lucas A. Powe Jr., *The Fourth Estate and the Constitution* (Berkeley: University of California Press, 1991), 279.

14. See Eli Skogerbo, "The Press Subsidy System in Norway," *European Journal of Communication* 12 (1997): 99–118.

15. Owen M. Fiss, *Liberalism Divided* (Boulder: Westview, 1996), 145.

16. See ibid., 145–46; and *New York Times v. Sullivan*, 270.

17. Alexander Meiklejohn, *Political Freedom* (New York: Harper, 1960). This is a republication of the 1948 volume by Meiklejohn, *Free Speech and Its Relation to Self-Government* (New York: Harper and Brothers), plus some additional papers.

18.   Ibid., 26.

19.   Edmond Cahn, "Dimensions of First Amendment 'Absolutes': A Public Interview," in *Justice Hugo Black and the First Amendment*, ed. Everette E. Dennis, Donald M. Gillmor, and David L. Grey (Ames: Iowa State University Press, 1978), 45.

20.   Freedom House, *Freedom of the Press 2010* (New York: Freedom House, 2010), available at http://www.freedomhouse.org. See also Committee to Protect Journalists, *Attacks on the Press in 2009* (New York: Committee to Protect Journalists, 2010).

21.   Herbert J. Gans, *Democracy and the News* (New York: Oxford University Press, 2002).

22.   Ibid, 54–55.

23.   Adam Shell, "Political Drama Snaps Nasdaq Win Streak," *USA Today*, May 24, 2001, 4B.

24.   Ralph Negrine, *Parliament and the Media: A Study of Britain, Germany, and France* (London: Royal Institute of International Affairs, 1998), 2.

25.   Ibid., 134.

26.   Nina Eliasoph, *Avoiding Politics* (Cambridge, Eng.: Cambridge University Press, 1998). See also Dafna Lemish and Inbal Barzel, "'Four Mothers': The Womb in the Public Sphere," *European Journal of Communication* 15 (2000): 167.

27.   Katharine Graham, *Personal History* (New York: Random House, 1997), 411.

CHAPTER 12   THE FIRST NEWS REVOLUTION OF THE TWENTY-FIRST CENTURY

1.   See Philip Meyer, *The Vanishing Newspaper: Saving Journalism in the Information Age* (Columbia: University of Missouri Press, 2004), 37, on the importance of classified ads to newspapers. Eli Noam has offered different estimates, but they point in the same direction: Traditionally, he wrote, classified ads accounted for 25 percent of newspaper advertising but their share increased to 37 percent by 2006. See Eli M. Noam, *Media Ownership and Concentration in America* (New York: Oxford University Press, 2009), 138.

2. See Elliot King, *Free for All: The Internet's Transformation of Journalism* (Evanston, IL: Northwestern University Press, 2010), for a comprehensive account of the technological changes that have influenced journalism.

3. See Beth Noveck, *Wiki Government* (Washington, D.C.: Brookings Institution Press, 2009), 17.

4. David Streitfeld, "Doris Dungey, Prescient Finance Blogger, Dies at 47," *New York Times*, November 30, 2008. See also Alyssa Katz, "An Irresistably Readable Mortgage Critic," *Columbia Journalism Review Online* (December 10, 2008), available at http://www.cjr.org/the_audit/tribute_to_a_blogger.php (accessed May 8 2011).

5. James W. Carey, "Why and How? The Dark Continent of American Journalism" in *Reading the News*, ed. Robert Karl Manoff and Michael Schudson (New York: Pantheon Books, 1986), 151–52.

6. Mark Deuze, "Toward a Sociology of Online News," in *Making Online News*, ed. Chris Paterson and David Domingo (New York: Peter Lang, 2008), 205–6. Deuze adopted the concept of "liquid modernity" from the social theorist Zygmunt Bauman. See Deuze, *Media Work* (Cambridge, Eng.: Polity Press, 2007).

7. Dean Starkman, "The Hamster Wheel," *Columbia Journalism Review* 49 (September–October 2010), 24–28.

8. The practice of crowdsourcing may go back to the eighteenth century. Historian David Paul Nord found several interesting cases in New England at that time—see his "'Plain and Certain Facts': Four Episodes of Public Affairs Reporting in Eighteenth-Century Boston," *Journalism History* 37 (forthcoming, 2011)—but the term is generally attributed to Jeff Howe in his article "The Rise of Crowdsourcing," *Wired*, June 2006, available at http://www.wired.com/wired/archive/14.06/crowds.html (accessed December 16, 2010).

9. Robert Henson, *Weather on the Air: A History of Broadcast Meteorology* (Boston: American Meteorological Society, 2010), 5–6.

10. Ibid., 56.

11. Geoffrey Cowan and David Westphal, "Public Policy and Funding the News" (Research Series: January 2010, University of Southern California Annenberg School for Communication and Journalism, Center on Communication Leadership & Policy, Los Angeles, 2010). Available at http://fundingthenews.usc.edu/report/ (accessed May 9, 2011). See also Geoffrey

Cowan and David Westphal, "The Washington-Madison Solution" in Robert W. McChesney and Victor Pickard, eds., *Will the Last Reporter Please Turn Out the Lights: The Collapse of Journalism and What Can Be Done to Fix It* (New York: New Press, 2011), 133–137. See also Leonard Downie Jr. and Michael Schudson, "The Reconstruction of American Journalism," 2009, available at http://www.journalism.columbia.edu/journalismreport (accessed May 8, 2011). Reprinted in McChesney and Pickard, 55–90.

12. On Ohio, see http://www.onthemedia.org/transcripts/2008/04/25/04 (accessed May 8, 2011, an interview with the then editor of the *Cleveland Plain Dealer*, Susan Goldberg. On the *Post* and *Sun*, see Michael S. Rosenwald, "*Washington Post, Baltimore Sun* to Begin Sharing Some News Content," *Washington Post*, December 23, 2008.

13. See Michael Schudson, "Autonomy from What?" in *Bourdieu and the Journalistic Field*, ed. Rodney Benson and Erik Neveu (Cambridge, Eng.: Polity Press, 2005), 214–23. On competing concepts of the audience in contemporary journalistic practice, see C. W. Anderson, "Deliberative, Agonistic, and Algorithmic Audiences: Journalism's Vision of its Public in an age of Audience Transparency," *International Journal of Communication* 5 (2011): 529–547.

14. Jay Rosen, "PressThink," June 27, 2006, available at http://archive.pressthink.org/2006/06/27/ppl_frmr.html (accessed November 23, 2010).

15. For Nina Bernstein's remarks on receiving the Paul Tobenkin Memorial Award from Columbia Journalism School on May 17, 2010, see http://www.journalism.columbia.edu/system/documents/174/original/tobenkin_award_talk.pdf (accessed May 2, 2011).

16. See Michael Schudson and Julia Sonnevend, "True to Form," *Columbia Journalism Review* 49 (March–April 2010): 63; and Pablo Boczkowski, "Rethinking Hard and Soft News Production: From Common Ground to Divergent Paths," *Journal of Communication* (March 2009). Boczkowski pioneered the ethnographic study of digital news production. Others have since followed his lead, some of them—around the world—gathered in Chris Paterson and David Domingo, eds., *Making Online News: The Ethnography of New Media Production* (New York: Peter Lang, 2008).

17. David Carr, "The Fall and Rise of Media," *New York Times*, November 29, 2009.

18. See David H. Weaver, Randal A. Beam, Bonnie J. Brownlee, Paul S. Voakes, and G. Cleveland Wilhoit, *The American Journalist in the 21st Cen-*

tury: U.S. News People at the Dawn of a New Millennium (Mahwah, N.J.: Lawrence Erlbaum, 2007), 2, for the 1971, 1992, and 2002 data. The estimate of just over forty thousand newspaper newsroom employees today (41,500 for 2009) comes from the Project for Excellence in Journalism, "The State of the News Media: An Annual Report on American Journalism 2011," available at http://stateofthemedia.org/2011/ (accessed May 8 2011).

19. Jennifer Dorroh, "Statehouse Exodus," *American Journalism Review* (April–May, 2009).

20. Jodi Enda, "Retreating from the World," *American Journalism Review* (Winter 2010): 14–31.

21. Andrew Alexander, "Can the *Post* Regain Its Legacy of Excellence?" *Washington Post*, January 23, 2011.

22. See http://investigativenewsnetwork.org/about/about-inn (accessed January 10, 2011)

23. Meyer, *Vanishing Newspaper*, 37.

24. Walter Robinson, telephone interview, October 2, 2009.

25. Richard Sambrook, *Are Foreign Correspondents Redundant? The Changing Face of International News* (Oxford, Eng.: Reuters Institute for the Study of Journalism, 2010), 98–99. On foreign news in the United States, see James T. Hamilton, The (Many) Markets for International News," *Journalism Studies* 11 (2010): 650–66.

26. Walter Lippmann, *Liberty and the News* (Princeton, N.J.: Princeton University Press, 2008; originally published 1920), 45.

27. Ibid., 48.

28. Ibid., 53.

29. Ibid., 55.

30. Ibid., 56.

31. Clay Shirky, "Newspapers and Thinking the Unthinkable," March 13, 2009, available at http://www.shirky.com/weblog/2009/03/newspapers-and-thinking-the-unthinkable/ (accessed March 6, 2011). Reprinted in McChesney and Pickard, 38–44.

32. See Carroll Bogert, "Whose News? The Changing Media Landscape and NGOs," in Human Rights Watch, *World Report: 2011 Events of 2010* (New York: Human Rights Watch, 2011), 30.

33. Simon Cottle and David Nolan, "Global Humanitarianism and the Changing Aid-Media Field: 'Everyone was dying for footage,'" *Journalism Studies* 8 (December 2007) 862–78.

34. Paul Starr, "Goodbye to the Age of Newspapers (Hello to a New Era of Corruption," *The New Republic*, March 4, 2009, 28–35. Reprinted in McChesney and Pickard, 18–37.

35. Alex Jones, *Losing the News* (New York: Oxford University Press, 2009), 4, estimated that "85 percent of professionally reported accountability news comes from newspapers" but wrote that he has heard other estimates up to 95 percent.

36. Or are there multiple ways out? See Bill Grueskin, Ava Seave, and Lucas Graves, *The Story So Far: What We Know About the Business of Digital Journalism* (New York: Tow Center for Digital Journalism at the Graduate School of Journalism, Columbia University, May 2011).

37. See David A. L. Levy and Rasmus Kleis Nielsen, eds.,*The Changing Business of Journalism and Its Implications for Democracy* (Oxford, Eng.: Reuters Institute for the Study of Journalism, 2010), with chapters on Brazil, Finland, France, Germany, India, the United Kingdom, and the United States.

Index

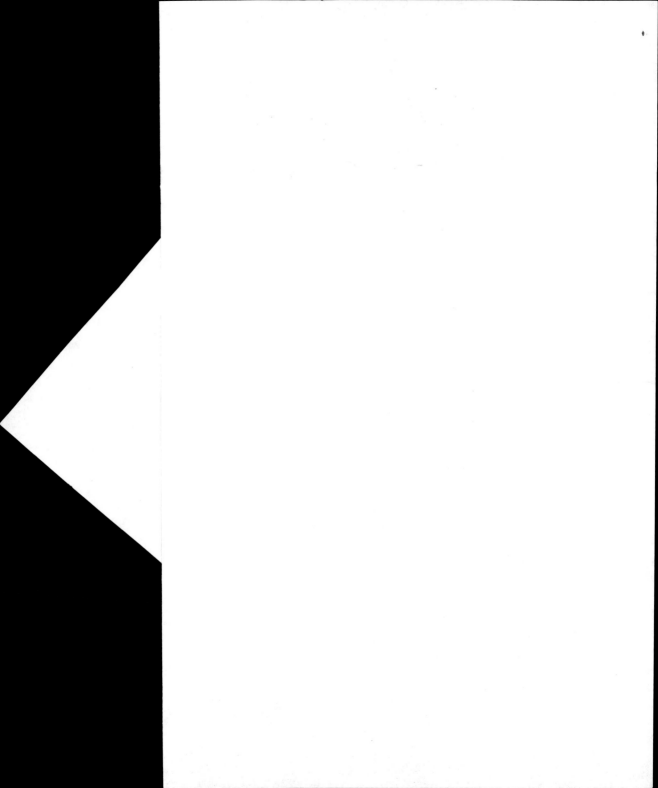

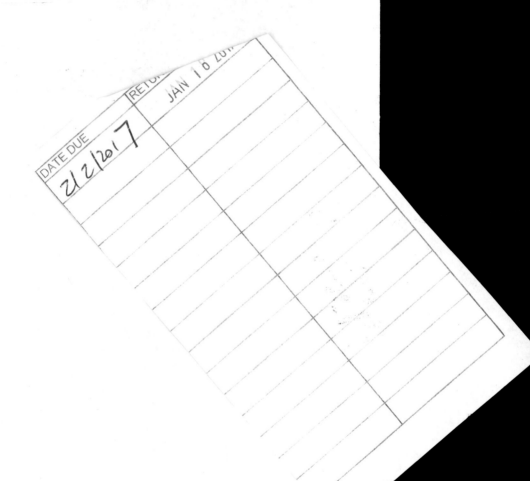